D1030871

MALENKOV: Stalin's Successor

Books by Martin Ebon:

WORLD COMMUNISM TODAY

MALENKOV: STALIN'S SUCCESSOR

The New and the Old: On October 5, 1952, Georgi M. Malenkov, then Secretary of the Central Committee, presented its report to the Nineteenth Congress of the Communist Party. Premier Stalin sits at right. (*Credit: Sovfoto.*)

MALENKOV
Stalin's Successor

by Martin Ebon

Introduction by Harry Schwartz

McGraw-Hill Book Company, Inc.

NEW YORK · TORONTO · LONDON

MALENKOV: Stalin's Successor

Copyright, 1953, by the McGraw-Hill Book Company, Inc. All rights in this book are reserved. It may not be used for dramatic, motion-, or talking-picture purposes without written authorization from the holder of these rights. Nor may the book or parts thereof be reproduced in any manner whatsoever without permission in writing, except in the case of brief quotations embodied in critical articles and reviews. For information, address the McGraw-Hill Book Company, Inc., Trade Department, 330 West 42d Street, New York 36, N.Y.

Library of Congress Catalog Card Number: 53-8672

947.085
E 16

PUBLISHED BY THE MCGRAW-HILL BOOK COMPANY, INC.

PRINTED IN THE UNITED STATES OF AMERICA

TO

the 23,000 Greek children,
abducted by Communist guerrillas
from their homeland in 1948,
whose fate behind
the Iron Curtain remains unknown

PREFACE

THE DEATH of Joseph Stalin removed a known and relatively stable factor from the world scene. The appointment of Georgi M. Malenkov as Stalin's successor awakened intense international interest in the obscure figure who had become the new Soviet Premier. This book does not pretend to be an exhaustive or definitive study of Premier Malenkov and the questions which his new eminence must necessarily arouse. Such a book, at this time, could not be written; few people in a position to speak, on either side of the Iron Curtain, have been favored by so much as a single brief conversation with the new Soviet Premier. I have, rather, sought to provide an accurate presentation of fact and a tentative analysis, designed to fill, at least partly, the gap which has existed in public knowledge of Premier Malenkov's career, personality, outlook, and relationships with other important Soviet officials.

The analysis of personalities and events in the Soviet Union offers unique problems. Over more than three decades the Soviet government has perfected a system of censorship and propaganda which has no parallel, anywhere on earth. It is especially designed to hide the realities of life in the Soviet Union and to project abroad an image of the nation and its rulers that will work to the utmost advantage of Soviet power.

The observer of the Soviet scene has two major sources: the Soviet press and radio, and reports of emigrees who, during the past few years, have reached the free world in large number. Soviet media of public opinion are subject to strict control; but the change in emphasis, the selection of subject matter, the relative prominence of personages in the news, and the character of subjects that are played down—all this provides clues to the analyst. Emigrees, for the most part, led lives of isolation. They could not, by the nature of life in the Soviet Union, obtain information from outside their immediate circle; but they *can* provide data on events within that circle. Eventually, as this disconnected information is assembled, it creates definite patterns: evidence begins to point toward certain events, to confirm them, and to provide detail.

The margin for error, in analyzing Soviet personalities and events under these conditions, is naturally wide. One can only allow for such a margin by carefully separating fact from conjecture. The facts herein are accurate; only future events can decide the validity of my hypotheses.

And future events seem already upon us. At the moment of this writing, the intensive Soviet peace offensive, with its possible repercussions on the situation in Korea, on allied cooperation, on the economic stability of America and of the world, represents a return to Communist tactics that served Moscow well in the 1930s and during World War II. Throughout the fluctuation of events one basic conviction must remain stable: that the free world in dealing with the Malenkov regime cannot for one moment relax its vigilance.

MARTIN EBON

The author is indebted to the ideas and work of Alexander Barmine, Boris I. Nicolaevsky, Lazar M. Pistrak, and Bertram D. Wolfe. He has also drawn on writings of Harry Schwartz and C. L. Sulzberger which appeared in *The New York Times*

CONTENTS

LIST OF ILLUSTRATIONS

INTRODUCTION

ANYONE WHO has ever been connected with the workings of a major power's intelligence organization—the Office
of Strategic Services during World War II, for example—
knows that its biographical division is one of its most important sections. Here are located the numerous folders which
contain every ascertainable fact—plus also many likely sound-
ing rumors—about significant personalities in every foreign
land: statesmen, diplomats, scientists, opinion molders, and
the like. It is axiomatic among those engaged in the procurement of information on which rests a nation's security that
biographical intelligence is no less important than even the
most obvious kinds of military intelligence, and that, in fact,
in time of war, it is itself a species of military intelligence.

The reasons for this situation are obvious and need not be
labored. In peace or war, the moves and countermoves of each
nation are, in the last analysis, the product of decisions by one
set of people regarding the activities, plans, and intentions of
another set of people. Therefore the policy makers of each nation must base their moves in part upon estimates of what
kinds of people they are reacting to or wish to have react. One
can only conjecture how many of this country's foreign-policy
mistakes in the closing years of World War II and immediately
thereafter were based upon the belief that Joseph Stalin was
really just "Uncle Joe," a genial bear of a man whose gruff exterior concealed a heart of gold and a moral code which guaranteed he would live up to all his commitments. A better knowledge of Joseph Stalin, of the man and his record, might have

avoided some of those illusions and therefore some of the mistakes.

That the leaders of the Soviet Union realize the strategic importance of biographical intelligence is evident from the secrecy in which they shroud themselves and their personal lives. The official biographies of most Soviet figures are merely humdrum lists of positions held and decorations won. But one looks in vain for public indication of their private lives, of the fact that they are men who love and hate, who have the joy of fatherhood and the sorrow of seeing dear ones die, who become sick and then recover. And as for the realities of Soviet rule—the realities of intrigue and counterintrigue, of jealousy and rivalry among top figures—these are not to be found in Soviet sources. Instead, their systematic effort is to present the men who rule that vast land as impersonal robots guided by a complex computer mechanism which refers each problem that arises to the classics of Marx, Engels, Lenin, and Stalin, and then automatically comes up with the answer. It goes without saying that the reality is quite different.

Against this background the importance of this present volume seems clear. Mr. Ebon has rendered a notable service in this attempt to bring together all the available concrete information regarding Georgi M. Malenkov and has supplemented this information with that reasonable speculation which is unavoidable in attempting to treat a top Soviet figure who habitually lives and prefers to live in the shadows. The parallel here with Joseph Stalin at the time of Lenin's death is almost complete. In 1924 little was known about Stalin too, and most of the outside world had never heard of him. Where Mr. Ebon is more fortunate than a would-be biographer of Stalin in 1924 is in the fact that research has already been done on Mr. Malenkov's early history—primarily by Lazar M. Pistrak of the

Voice of America staff—and this material is available to give depth and perspective to the picture. Yet no one recognizes more fully than Mr. Ebon himself that this volume cannot be a definitive biography. No such work can even be written of Stalin today, let alone of one who has lived for decades in Mr. Stalin's penumbra. Nevertheless the valuable information herein provides wise and timely guidance.

Yet even with this information in hand, gathered together here for the first time, it would be dangerous for either our policy makers or ordinary citizens like this writer to make dogmatic judgments or predictions about what Mr. Malenkov will do or about what the Soviet government will do. One obvious reason is that we do not have enough information about the subject of this biography. Another and no less important reason is that we are almost completely in the dark about the situation in which Stalin's successor as Premier finds himself as he works within the Kremlin's guarded walls.

It may be a betrayal of whatever code of ethics exist among so-called Russian "experts"—and in this connection Paul Winterton's remark that there are no experts on Russia, merely varying degrees of ignorance, should not be forgotten—but this writer must point out that no one could have predicted or did predict at the time of Stalin's death much of what actually has happened in the first five weeks since. Many of us may preen ourselves that we pointed to Malenkov as the most likely successor to Stalin's mantle, but which of us dreamed that within a month of Malenkov's assumption of what appeared to be power, the Soviet government would repudiate the infamous fabrication of the "doctor-murderers"? And which of us dreamed, even as late as March 21, that Semyon D. Ignatiev, named on that date as one of the five secretaries of the Communist Party, would be denounced for "political

blindness" barely two weeks later and dismissed from his sec-
retarial post? One may express fairly positive doubt that even
in the guarded precincts of the Central Intelligence Agency
or the British Secret Service there was sufficient prescience or
knowledge to foresee these and similar events.

The central question, of course, is: who rules Russia today?
Has Malenkov inherited all of Stalin's power or is he merely
a figurehead for others? Is it a triumvirate or a broader directorate? Are Malenkov, Beria, Molotov and the others on the
Presidium of the Central Committee of the Communist Party
working together harmoniously, or has a bitter struggle for
power already broken out? We do not know and must speculate as best we can, as Mr. Ebon has done so skillfully in this
volume.

At the risk of being proved wrong by developments even
in the short period between this writing and the time of this
volume's publication, this writer would suggest that two con-
clusions seem most probable. First, that Mr. Malenkov has
only a fraction of his predecessor's power and is, at best, one
member of a directorate making the key decisions. Second,
that the bitter power struggle which went on more or less
clandestinely among those next to Stalin while he was alive
has continued since his death, so that much that has happened
since early March, 1953, is explicable only in terms of that
power struggle and the shifting balance of strength among
the contenders.

One warning should be sounded for all contemplating the
current situation in the Soviet Union: don't sell Premier Malenkov short. At the time Stalin died there was an exaggerated
tendency in many quarters to assume that Malenkov would
automatically inherit all of Stalin's powers. Now, five weeks
later and after Malenkov's exit from the party secretariat and

other signs of weakness, there seems to be a tendency to have the pendulum swing all the way in the other direction and to assume that the Soviet Premier is on his way out. The whole course of his career, so well described in this volume, suggests that he has an amazing capacity to recover from setbacks and that few more skillful intriguers have lived in recent times.

The future will, of course, supply the answers to many questions which trouble us now. But if we are to hope to anticipate these answers and to shape our policies properly we must know with whom we are dealing. The Soviet leaders have studied well the records of our top officials. Mr. Ebon's book now offers Americans the opportunity to reciprocate that attention and to gain the advantages thereof. There can be few more important contributions that a journalist or political analyst can make today.

HARRY SCHWARTZ

April 1953

1

The Danger of Success

"THERE IS such a thing as success for the bold. Think of me what you like, but follow me."

Thus spoke Pugachov, the rebel who pretended to be Czar Peter the Third, in Alexander Pushkin's novel *The Captain's Daughter*. Pushkin's story dealt with rebellion in 1773, in the southern Urals town of Orenburg.

Another rebel from Orenburg entered the Kremlin of the Czars a hundred and eighty years later. His name was Georgi Maximilianovich Malenkov.

The state he inherited from Premier Joseph Stalin was far vaster than the czarist empire had ever been; like the thirteenth-century realm of the Mongol Emperor Genghis Khan, it reached from China into eastern Europe. Its more than 200 million people include Great Russians, Ukrainians, White Russians, Mongols, Turks, the people of the Baltic States— men and women of dozens of racial and religious origins.

Georgi M. Malenkov succeeded Stalin, who died on March 5, 1953, after twenty-nine years in power. Malenkov, the next day, became Premier, a post known formally as that of Chairman of the Council of Ministers. He was then fifty-one years old.

Throughout his career, Malenkov has lived by the tenets of Pugachov, the rebel of Orenburg. He has boldly and cun-

1

ningly striven for success; he has asked not for affection, but
for allegiance.

The Kremlin he entered is heavy with history. Peter the
Third, whom Pugachov pretended to be, was murdered at the
behest of his wife Catherine II, so she could become Empress.
The Empress Elizabeth held the child Czar Ivan VI impris-
oned until he was killed by guards. In the Kremlin itself, Ivan
the Terrible murdered his own son, and then went mad with
guilt. Here Boris Godunov, in 1591, gave the order to kill the
child Demetrius who stood between him and czardom.

Against such a background, the very excess of detail in the
Stalin death communiqués, each signed by no less than eight
physicians, could not fail to arouse questions. Stalin died less
than two months after his own medical staff had been removed, charged with causing and plotting the death of others.

Georgi Malenkov is indeed a man who can hardly inspire
either affection or trust, but who can command allegiance.
He has rewarded his friends with high posts, and he has pun-
ished his enemies. Most of his adult life Malenkov has been
the master of other people's destinies. The very structure of
his power is built of men whom he carefully placed so they
could strengthen his own position.

Malenkov was not thrust into the premiership of the Soviet
Union by the hand of fate. He had prepared his accession to
power for more than a decade; he had worked at it intensively
for more than four years. In all this time he was driven by an
inner restlessness that gave him no pause. Although he is
married and has a son and a daughter, Malenkov has had little
time for a home life. His first wife, Elena Rubatsova, whom he
married in 1939, was a secretary in Molotov's foreign ministry.
His present wife is the former actress and singer Elena Khrushchev, now director of Moscow University.

The man who succeeded Stalin is of medium height, about 5 feet 7 inches tall. Heavy eating has made him obese, and he may weigh as much as 250 pounds. Malenkov's most noticeable feature is a fleshy face, heavy-jowled and almost completely unwrinkled. It is a face behind which Georgi Malenkov has long learned to hide his feelings, as if it were a mask. Only his dark eyes, those who have met him observe, seem to glitter with a multitude of emotions.

From the few outsiders who have come face to face with Georgi Malenkov, parts of a personality mosaic emerge. There is the hesitant, soft, and spongy handshake; there is unsociable reluctance to become part of a jovial crowd, which suggests arrogance born of insecurity; there is the habit of eating very heavily, and a fondness for sweet pastries; there is the pale, waxlike skin of his face, the almost feminine long eyelashes. And there is his smile, a smile of almost contemptuous joviality.

Without too much imagination, it is easy to picture Georgi Malenkov as the plump potentate in the Near Eastern and Central Asian tradition. Indeed, he is believed to be half-Bashkir by origin. His home town, Orenburg, lies at the crossroads of Asia, Europe, and the Near East, an area where the rule of the khan is yet a vivid memory. One visitor, the former Czech diplomat Anhorst Heidrich, has said that he looks "exactly like a Turkish eunuch." Heidrich also told the columnists Joseph and Stewart Alsop that, as he sat near to Malenkov during a five-hour dinner, he saw that his eyes were "small, very black, very, very cunning, and very, very, very cruel." Another diplomat received a similarly melodramatic impression, and said: "If I knew I had to be tortured, and if I were picking people from the Politburo, the last one I would pick would be Malenkov."

During his quarter-century of work in Moscow, Malenkov has always affected the same drab party uniform; it buttons high at the neck, and its collar points are always slightly curled up. Malenkov has been awarded a number of Soviet medals, but he disdains wearing decorations and other outward signs of distinction or power. What may have begun as a habit of being inconspicuous seems to have developed into a contempt for the dandyish pretensions of Moscow's new society and its heavily bemedaled marshals and generals of the Soviet army.

Malenkov walks erect, speaks clearly and sharply. He prefers to command, rather than to converse. Although he has been known to drink heavily on occasion, he appears to avoid the danger of having alcohol loosen his tongue. The over-all impression is one of withdrawal among strangers, a desire to return to the environment of his own office and staff—to the problems which he handles with masterful precision.

Malenkov's precision shows itself in his dual personality as terrorist-technocrat. During his apprenticeship he worked closely with the Soviet secret service during the years of the Moscow trials; his tutor was the notorious secret-service chief Nikolai Yezhov. During and after the war, he achieved distinction in organizing industry and transport.

But at all times, his main concern has been people: the people in the upper echelons of the Communist Party machine, the men and women who make up the structure of power. In this, as in several other respects, he followed in Stalin's footsteps; it was Stalin's control of the party machinery which guaranteed his succession of Lenin.

When Malenkov, in turn, succeeded Stalin, he was relatively unknown outside the Soviet Union. The world at large had let itself be hypnotized by Stalin's image. It had absorbed a good deal of internal Soviet propaganda, of the Stalinist cult, of the theme that Stalin was the beginning and the end of all things Russian.

Like a top executive anywhere, however, Stalin had to rely on the ideas and the actions of those below him in rank. The fact that a proclamation, like his papers on linguistics and economics, were signed by Stalin, did not exclude the possibility that they had been drafted by others. Similarly, major policy decisions were presumably made by Stalin on the basis of suggestions by other members of the Soviet hierarchy— in late years often by Malenkov.

Malenkov's antagonist, the late Andrei A. Zhdanov, apparently instigated such an unsuccessful move as the Soviet invasion of Finland in 1939, and was at least partially responsible for the break with Marshal Tito in 1948. Malenkov, on the other hand, appears to have been responsible for stopping the Communist civil war in Greece after Zhdanov's death. He certainly instigated the important science controversy that began with genetics in 1948 and continued for years. Malenkov may also have suggested, and his supporter Eugene S. Varga possibly prepared, Stalin's 1952 thesis on *The Economic Problems of Socialism in the U.S.S.R.*

Thus Georgi Malenkov, when he became Premier, did so after he had learned how to handle many aspects of his new job as one of Stalin's understudies. He had dealt with both external and internal affairs, extensively and in detail, for years. His inner restlessness had prodded him into extending his activity more and more outside Communist Party affairs as such. His days grew crowded, as affairs of world-wide espionage, of the Cominform, scientific agriculture, and greater industrial output competed with personal matters and Kremlin intrigues.

Georgi M. Malenkov is a self-made man. He got where he is by perseverance, a fabulous memory for detail, and an apparently compulsive singleness of purpose. That purpose—power over other men.

There are dangers in success. A man who has reached the top has nowhere else to go; yet he cannot afford to stand still. He must constantly anticipate and then move to fight off dangers—dangers from the outside world, dangers within his own country, dangers even within himself. As Georgi M. Malenkov stands exposed at the top of the pyramid that is Soviet society, he must see many threats to his position; but there are some which his personality and experience prevent him from seeing, and these are the most crucial.

There is, first of all, the danger of absolute totalitarianism. Malenkov is more totalitarian than Stalin ever was. Stalin ruled through contradictions; he gave the appearance, at times, of muddling through. He let his deputies quarrel among themselves; he permitted experimental policies, even if they proved futile in the end and had to be contradicted; he was strong enough to permit himself errors.

Stalin, at all times, maintained certain pleasant fictions. There was, for instance, the fiction of legality: the Soviet Constitution, election to the Supreme Soviet, debate in pseudo-parliamentary meetings. Malenkov, within a few days of taking power, began to ignore these legal niceties. At the session of the Supreme Soviet that approved his appointment, Malenkov imposed the reduction of fifty-one ministerial portfolios to twenty-five. This move paralleled reduction of membership in the Presidium of the Communist Party from the twenty-five named at the Nineteenth Communist Party Congress, to a mere ten. Malenkov asserted that these measures had been "maturing for a long time during the life of Comrade Stalin," but he did not say in so many words that Stalin had actually approved them.

Edmund Stevens, who was Moscow correspondent of the *Christian Science Monitor* from 1943 to 1950, believes that Malenkov has shown "open disregard for the niceties of legalistic procedure and impatience with constitutional formalities." Malenkov specifically violated the Soviet Constitution and the statutes of the Communist Party on March 6, 1953. On this day, the party's Central Committee, the Council of Ministers, and the Presidium of the Supreme Soviet held combined meetings—or, at any rate, major changes were announced over their combined signatures.

Under Stalin there was considerable overlapping in the functions of leading personalities, but the legal framework was never openly violated. These interlocking directorates of party and state were supposed to show that, although the party had supreme importance, the two entities were indeed separate. Malenkov is impatient with these technicalities, which are partly rooted in Bolshevik tradition and partly represent expedient compromises made during some thirty years of Lenin-Stalin rule.

Malenkov, as electoral secretary, had in the past handpicked the very men and women who were later, with all the Soviet mumbo jumbo of balloting, "elected" by the populace. Presumably, knowing full well that this election to the Supreme Soviet was a phony façade, Malenkov has come to disdain its fake parliamentarism. But he wandered far afield, and certainly outside Stalin's footsteps, in his appointment of Marshal Klimenti E. Voroshilov as chairman of the Presidium of the Supreme Soviet.

This post is in theory the highest in the Soviet Union, somewhat like that of President of France, an honorary position above that of Premier. Malenkov seems to have railroaded Voroshilov's appointment—which meant kicking the old man upstairs—through the joint meeting of March 6, while simultaneously ousting the previous chairman, Nikolai Shvernik, from his post. At the same time, and in the same openly high-handed manner, Shvernik was put into Vasily V. Kuznetsov's post as chairman of the Soviet Trade Union Council, the all-embracing Soviet labor union which supposedly elects its own officers.

Soviet totalitarianism, under Stalin, gloried in democratic window dressing. Its supporters outside the Soviet state could thus always point to the Soviet Constitution and other statutes and procedures to prove the democratic nature of the Soviet system. At home, too, these rituals had meaning and impact. Even docile members of the Supreme Soviet may be assumed to have a certain amount of pride; they know that they are rubber stamps, but they don't want to be reminded of it. The Trade Union Council, like any other large body, probably derives a sense of precarious independence from such fictions as electing its officers; its members may easily feel offended at having their impotence so crudely exhibited to the world.

Malenkov, because of his dictatorial efficiency, lacks Stalin's finesse in dealing with human sensibilities. He also lacks his sense of humor: Stalin most likely was slightly amused by the earnest fashion in which those he commanded jumped through democratic hoops. Stalin understood, at any rate, that the bitter pill of totalitarianism goes down more easily when it has a democratic sugar-coating.

A second danger for Malenkov is his patience-turned-im-patience. It is related to the disdain with which he has ignored legalities of the Soviet Constitution. Malenkov as Premier is a volcano that has patiently rumbled for years, and is just beginning to crack open.

Since 1946, Malenkov has been pulling his punches. He tried, at that time, to push aside some of the Old Bolsheviks who talked lengthy Marxist dialectics when Malenkov felt that action was needed. But he was slapped down, hard. He made his comeback in 1948, and afterward managed to restrain impetuous impulses.

As Premier, he is likely to find it more difficult to control his pent-up hostility. He is impatient to get on with things and may be tempted to push his associates too hard. After years lost in painstaking intrigue, Malenkov must be eager to impose his personality and ideas on others. His outward bulk has created the caricaturist's image of "the fat boy," the slow, plodding schemer. This image was outmoded when he became Premier, and it was never wholly correct. His scathing criticisms, his outbursts of violent language are notorious.

But the new Soviet Premier must try, no matter how much it taxes his self-control, to cultivate some of the outward serenity which the pipe-smoking, deliberate Stalin had in full measure. Georgi Malenkov's dealings with Mao Tse-tung of China will require both discretion and continued patience. He cannot push the enormously powerful Chinese leader around, nor can he let impatience get the better of him in his dealings with Marshal Gregori K. Zhukov and the army clique. Mao is unlikely to accept peremptory orders; Malenkov may show the Supreme Soviet that he disdains its impotence, but he must observe to the letter all legal niceties in dealing with the Peiping regime. He cannot dare a conflict with Mao or the army clique while Interior Minister Lavrenti P. Beria stands ready to check Malenkov's ambitions.

Another heresy seems to stalk Malenkov. Knowing Communist hypocrisy so well from the inside, he may be tempted to push aside another Stalinist nicety—the incense of Marxist-Leninist theory which Stalin always wafted in front of the harsh realities of Soviet life. Malenkov, the terrorist-technocrat, has previously shown a marked tendency to underestimate the importance of ritual. He may tend to disregard the religio-idealistic aura which the wordy dialecticians have given even to purges and forced-labor camps.

Frederic C. Barghoorn, professor of political science at Yale University, has noted that the ideological approach gave "dignity and continuity to a regime that otherwise might have seemed one of oriental despotism rendered harsher by a measure of modern efficiency." Malenkov, a fiend for efficiency, doubtless would like to eliminate the time-wasting ritual of wordy dialectics. If he does, he will not only be a Marxist revisionist and Leninist heretic, but he will also rob himself of this handy tool of idealism.

There remained a remarkable world-wide reservoir of pro-Soviet idealism at the time of Stalin's death. It was misguided idealism, to be sure, but nonetheless sincere. A great deal of deep-rooted French and Italian radicalism, of traditional Near and Far Eastern anti-colonialism still looked upon the Soviet state as a fortress built of ideals. Malenkov the materialist runs the danger of underestimating the importance of these forces which command no divisions or well-trained cadres, and whose strength cannot be measured in output per man hour.

Malenkov also runs the danger of prejudice. He is a man of hostilities that have remained pent up for many years. One of these is anti-Semitism. Mikhail Soloviev, author of the novel *When the Gods Are Silent,* relates that he once attended a meeting of Soviet industrial leaders as a reporter for *Izvestia.*

Soloviev heard Malenkov, in a sudden burst of temper, interrupt an explanation of why nail production had fallen off, to announce that the man in charge of production was a Jew. Malenkov shouted at the man: "If these nails were for Stalin's coffin, you'd have them soon enough!"

The increasing number of Soviet expressions of anti-Semitism can be traced to a *Pravda* editorial on January 28, 1949—some six months after Malenkov's succession to Zhdanov's post in the Communist Party's secretariat. *Pravda* attacked Zionists and "cosmopolites actively serving the interests of imperialist reaction." From then on, Soviet propaganda organs used such anti-Jewish euphemisms as "passportless wanderers," "people without kith and kin," and "people without tribe."

The next target were Jewish theater critics, and Jews in other cultural fields. In late February a plenum of Ukrainian writers condemned "serious manifestations of Jewish bourgeois nationalism" in Soviet magazines. On March 14 the paper *Evening Moscow* labeled the targets of an editorial attack by publishing in brackets the Jewish names they had before adopting Russian pseudonyms, in exactly the same way in which the Nazis used to refer to Leon Trotsky as Bronstein.

It should be remembered that the Soviet Union rather unexpectedly endorsed partition of Palestine and establishment of the Republic of Israel in 1947, at a time when Malenkov had been pushed into the background and his antagonist Zhdanov was responsible for a good part of Soviet foreign policy. The anti-Israel and generally anti-Jewish line that emerged since then is apparently an expression of Malenkov's personal prejudices.

The danger of these prejudices seemed clearest during the

openly anti-Semitic purge trials in Czechoslovakia in the fall
of 1952, which puzzled and angered world opinion. But the
climax came in January, 1953, when "Jewish terrorist doctors"
were accused of a Moscow murder plot at the instigation of
"American imperialism." Beria reversed this move on April 4,
when his ministry announced that the doctors had been falsely
accused. But much damage had been done.

Remnants of idealistic illusions regarding the Soviet state
could, in the past, be maintained by pointing to Moscow's
constitutional opposition to racial or religious discrimination.
Malenkov's anti-Semitic prejudices have done much to destroy these remnants of illusion.

Malenkov, in contrast to Beria, may have underestimated
the repercussions of the Prague purges, which combined his
anti-Semitic hostilities with his desire to eliminate potentially
anti-Malenkov or too rigidly pro-Stalin elements in the
Czechoslovak Communist Party. Most likely, the two factors
were jumbled in Malenkov's mind; his anti-Semitism led him
to suspect that Jewish party officials would seek to undermine
his own power position.

In misjudging public reaction, Malenkov illustrated another danger he faces: the danger of ignorance. Compared to
him, Molotov is a "cosmopolitan"; he at least has seen much
of the world. Malenkov has merely attended brief party meetings in Warsaw, Bucharest, and Prague. He knows the world
entirely through the eyes of the Soviet espionage and diplomatic machineries.

The Old Bolsheviks who fought their way to power under
czarism knew pre-Communist Russia. Many of them, like
Lenin, lived in Switzerland, England, or other parts of Europe. Malenkov has no such background. And if he deliber-

ately continues to isolate himself from contact with foreigners, he can gain no true knowledge of the world.

This ignorance is a danger to Malenkov. It is also a danger to the Soviet Union and to the world. We cannot assume that Georgi Malenkov has the insight to sit back and sort out the facts from the loaded verbiage and twisted reports supplied by his own information and propaganda machinery. We cannot assume that Soviet officials and agents have the courage to supply the Kremlin with anything but a caricature of the world outside Soviet boundaries; they must strive to please, to provide what Moscow wants to hear.

Consequently, Malenkov is likely to find himself listening to his own voice. Thus a thorough understanding of his personality is of great importance to Western policy makers; only then will they be able to anticipate the image which is likely to form in the mind of Stalin's successor.

Malenkov has to move with caution. He cannot risk unsettling the delicate balance of power that was achieved after Stalin's death. He cannot afford to defy his opponents too openly, to crush antagonists too ruthlessly. Perhaps that is why he compromised on the fate of two old rivals: Andrei A. Andreyev was given a largely honorary position of membership in the Presidium of the Supreme Soviet, and Anastas I. Mikoyan received the title of Deputy Premier.

This raises a question absolutely central to our thinking on Russia today. Is the Soviet Union controlled by a single all-powerful dictator, Malenkov, or by a directorate of top Soviet officials? Very likely Stalin never was quite the supreme dictator he appeared to be. Two important elements tended to create the picture of Stalin as the all-knowing, all-deciding

Soviet dictator. First was the effort of the Soviet propaganda machine to have the Stalin image blot out everything else. He was presented as the superfather, actually a continuation of the "little father" symbol that served to popularize the Czars. Secondly, the world prefers to see nations as the lengthened shadow of one man: Gandhi was India to the world; Hitler was Nazi Germany; Perón is Argentina; Churchill, England. Where there is more than one important leader, such as in France, the picture becomes blurred; it doesn't suit the world's imagination. In Stalin, the world had a man who was ready-made, by courtesy of the Moscow propaganda machine, to fit the preferred pattern.

But no one man, obviously, could do all the things Stalin was supposed to have done. He had to delegate authority, to play associates and their projects against each other, to select and decide. He worked hard, but so did the men around him. Before his death, while the struggle for power among the Kremlin clique revealed itself in the satellite purges, Stalin may have been little more than a figurehead.

The Moscow regime functions in almost every field of human life, in many areas untouched by democratic governments. It controls all enterprises, from industry and agriculture to the arts and literature. Soviet state bureaucracy is enormous. Undertakings and decisions which, in a nation like the United States, are in the hands of private individuals, are in the Soviet Union the responsibility of hard-pressed officials. If the President of the United States needs large staffs of advisers, then the Premier of the Soviet Union cannot do less.

Stripped of the propaganda trimmings that made Stalin appear omniscient and ever-present, the late Soviet Premier might appear as a top executive who knew how to let others do much of his work, while he received all public credit. Thus, when Malenkov became Premier, he moved into a position of similar responsibility with the same need for sharing authority, but without Stalin's prestige and carefully built up public image. Today, Malenkov must step warily and advance his ideas with caution. *His is not a one-man dictatorship; it is a junta, a directorate, in which Malenkov stands out by virtue of drive, toughness, and the sense of inborn personal power which emanates from him—but is held in check by others.*

If Malenkov were an all-powerful dictator, he might have signed the amnesty decree of March 27, 1953, with his own name; instead, the decree was issued by the Presidium of the Supreme Soviet. If Malenkov were an all-powerful dictator, men like Andreyev and Mikoyan would probably no longer be in public life. Stalin at first shared power with Gregori Zinoviev and Leonid Kamenev. He disposed of these potential rivals and replaced them with such men as Molotov and Beria to whom he could more safely delegate authority.

Malenkov shares power with the dangerous Beria. Others of the governing junta may not necessarily be found among the first deputy premiers. Perhaps Nikita S. Khrushchev is one of the central group; others who have achieved quick prominence, such as Culture Minister Ponomarenko, may also belong to the new inner circle. Doubtless the relative importance of the men at the top will show itself more clearly in the future.

Georgi M. Malenkov cannot govern alone. Neither could Stalin. Malenkov's career shows that he has the perseverance and dynamism to hold authority and impose his will on others. But he must curb his impatience.

For Malenkov, the memory of Stalin poses still another danger. It is the image of Stalin. In one important sense, the Stalinist system made no preparations for a successor. It operated as if Stalin were immortal. The Soviet propaganda machinery, unable to prepare the nation for Stalin's death, also could not begin to build up his successor's image in the public mind. The gap between the ever-present Stalin and the relatively obscure Malenkov is therefore enormous.

It took Stalin himself at least four years before he began to overtake the image of Lenin. Stalin's task in 1924 was perhaps easier than Malenkov's is today, as there had been little calculated effort in Lenin's lifetime to popularize him as the fount of all wisdom and the "great teacher and father" of the state. Malenkov's task of dulling the memory of his predecessor is compounded because of the length of time, nearly three full decades, that the Communist propaganda organs have been blowing up the Soviet Premier into superhuman proportions. That any man should even pretend to replace Stalin —this proposition may well seem arrogant and near-sacrilege to many Russians. It must certainly seem so to Malenkov's associates, the men who know his beginnings, career, and qualifications. To them, the memory-image of Stalin provides a temporarily safe shield for sly digs at Malenkov's pretension and crudities. Any immediate or ultimate revolt against Malenkov's authority might well come in the name and guise of Stalinism.

One fascinating question which stands unanswered, and will perhaps always remain so, is the part Stalin played in Malenkov's succession to power. No testament signed by Stalin, to decide this vital issue, was published at the time of his death. No indication that Stalin had chosen his own successor could be found in funeral addresses or official public statements. One can only consider Malenkov's position of power before Stalin's death, his prestige, and the honors heaped upon him; certainly Stalin must have at least approved Malenkov's prominence in the battle for power and he may have had a hand in it himself.

On January 7, 1952, for instance, Malenkov's prominence was dramatized when the Supreme Soviet awarded him the Order of Lenin for his "outstanding services to the Communist Party and the Soviet people." At the same time, the party's Central Committee and the Council of Ministers joined in long and effusive tribute in which Malenkov was called "a loyal disciple of Lenin and a colleague of Comrade Stalin" and a man whose "entire conscious life had been devoted to the great cause of the Lenin-Stalin Party, to the struggle for the triumph of Communism." In October, 1952, there were further clear signs that Malenkov was first in line as heir to Stalin's power. During the Nineteenth Communist Party Congress, his mammoth report on nearly all phases of the Soviet Union's internal and external policies took five hours to deliver and dwarfed the performances of other officials.

The new Soviet Premier, whether or not he has Stalin's official sanction, will try, I feel certain, to turn the memory-image of his erstwhile master into a remote and cloudy Stalin myth. Malenkov probably realizes the menace which the Stalin image represents to his ambitions. He will undoubtedly be on the lookout for those around him who seem to overpraise Stalin but pay only perfunctory homage to his successor.

When he appeared before the Supreme Soviet, less than ten days after Stalin died, Malenkov mentioned the dead ruler only in passing. This, he was saying in effect, is a new era—"Stalin is dead; long live Malenkov!" It will be interesting to watch the future relative positions of Stalin's and Malenkov's portraits in Soviet parades and at public functions.

But in trying to obscure the memory of Stalin, Malenkov

may once again be tempted to underestimate the religio-ideological elements of Soviet society. To replace Stalin will take many years, and Malenkov is an aggressive and impatient man. On his power to exercise restraint, now that he has reached the top, may depend Malenkov's success or failure. Never during his violent career did he face greater dangers to his position and his very life.

Pugachov, Pushkin's bandit from Orenburg, told his followers to "think of me what you like." Yet, although he asked for allegiance and not affection, he forced the people to pretend that he was the Czar and to kiss his hand. In the end, Pugachov the Orenburg rebel impatiently overextended his power. He was beheaded, and his head was held up for all the people to see.

2

Halfway to Power

WHAT IS Malenkov? Is he a professional revolutionary, a new type of Communist statesman, an energetic industrial executive, a skilled organizer of men? Is Malenkov the possessor of a card-index mind, is he a meticulous administrator, or just a party official and palace intriguer?

Georgi Malenkov is all these things, in a measure. But mainly, as his career shows, he is a trained terrorist who traveled the road to power as a cunning, ruthless conspirator.

That is not said lightly but on the basis of evidence that illuminates the life of this man who has sought to hide behind a fog of obscurity. It is said because Malenkov chose and followed a career that is itself a character portrait. The past lives of men, at various points in their careers, reflect their personalities as much as do their acquired habits of dress, of speech, of thought and self-expression.

Premier Malenkov learned to use the tool of terror during the early part of his career, and it has served him well as he carved a way to power through the jungle of Soviet Communist society.

Malenkov has hidden his ancestry. No one knows who his parents were. Had his father been a worker or poor peasant, the biographers of the *Soviet Encyclopedia* would surely tell us so, and proudly; in the upside-down snobbery of Communist society, proletarian origin is thought essential for membership in the exclusive Soviet elite. Malenkov, an upside-down upstart, very likely is the son and grandson of a provincial official or a member of the despised "bourgeois" middle class.

When he was younger and more impetuous, Georgi Malenkov once gave public vent to his feelings about the inverted snobbery of Communist society. In a rambunctious speech on February 15, 1941, he ranted against officials who hire only people who have the proper ancestors, officials "who busy themselves with researches into a man's genealogy, with searches of who was his grandfather and grandmother," not with studying his "qualities and his abilities." Malenkov did not empower Soviet biographers to tell us who his grandfather or grandmother were, much less his father and mother —who may have had the bad judgment to belong to the wrong class for a son engaged in perfecting a classless society.

Georgi Maximilianovich Malenkov was born on January 8, 1902, south of the Ural Mountains, in the town of Orenburg; the town was later renamed Chkalov, after the Soviet flyer who crossed the North Pole on a flight to the United States in 1937. What kind of people lived in Orenburg when Malenkov was born? Census figures show that five years before he was born Orenburg had a population of 72,740. According to the *Russian Encyclopedic Dictionary* of 1897, 43 per cent of the population belonged to the lower middle class; 30 per cent to the military—which means that they were mostly Cossacks and subalterns, and only 10,570 were of peasant stock. The number of people who were workers in Orenburg cannot, on the basis of a census taken four years earlier, have been much more than 1,000 when Malenkov was born. According to Lazar M. Pistrak, the painstaking research specialist of the Voice of America, "the majority of the Orenburg 'peasants' were actually engaged in trade activities, which were flourishing in this city at the time Malenkov was born; it is very improbable that Malenkov's parents belonged to the working class."

Pistrak also noted that Malenkov's father's name, Maximilian, was rather high-brow for the time and place. The common Russian name is Maxim. Malenkov's own name, Georgi, is also rather literary, its common form being Yuri. All this evidence suggests that Georgi Malenkov has excellent reasons, in Soviet society, not to want people to dig back and "busy themselves with researches into a man's genealogy."

When the Bolshevik Revolution took place in St. Petersburg (now Leningrad) in October, 1917, Malenkov was not yet sixteen years old. It must be remembered that the Bolshevik Revolution did not immediately set up Soviet rule the length and breadth of the former czarist empire. Rather, the Red Army had to subdue the country bit by bit, in a long and bitter civil war that did not end until 1921. Was Georgi Malenkov, prevented by youth from being a pre-Revolution Bolshevik, an early fighter in the Red Army? Did he quickly ally himself with the forces which, more than three decades later, were to place him at the head of the nation? The official Soviet biographers say so, but careful analysis of the evidence contradicts this official version. We are told that Georgi Malenkov was a Red Army volunteer at eighteen, late in 1919 or early in 1920. That would indeed have made him a daring young rebel, choosing sides while the great battle was still undecided, when it wasn't yet a certainty that the Bolsheviks would conquer the country.

Malenkov, however, does not appear to have chosen sides until it was easy to spot the winner. Living in his parents' home at Orenburg, he saw the city change hands three times.

His home town was then being defended against the Red
Army by troops under the Cossack commander Ataman
(Chief) Alexander Dutov. The Cossacks held Orenburg until
January 18, 1918, when the Red Army occupied the town.
But about six months later, on July 2, Dutov's troops returned
and forced the Red Army to quit Orenburg. (The town had
been bitterly fought over in earlier wars as well. Cossacks and
peasants of the Orenburg area had risen against the Czarina
Catherine the Great in the eighteenth century.)

Shortly after Malenkov's seventeenth birthday, the Red
Army once again occupied Orenburg, on January 22, 1919.
Even though the town seemed securely in Bolshevik hands
for three months, Georgi Malenkov was not a zealous enough
revolutionary to join the Red forces just then. His caution was
justified when, on April 27, the Cossacks made another attack
on Orenburg, advancing from the east and south, and then
firing on the railroad station and the town itself. One Soviet
historian, F. Popov, in his book *The Dutov Movement,* published at Moscow in 1934, wrote that "the Orenburg proletariat, under Bolshevik guidance, grasped arms against and
made every effort to repulse the Cossack troops. . . . Workers went to the front; almost the entire [Communist] Party
organization took a stand in the trenches; and even the city
police was sent to the front line." But young Malenkov does
not seem to have felt sufficiently sympathetic with the "Orenburg proletariat," the workers in the trenches, and the Communist Party's defenders, to join the fight. Not in the spring
and summer of 1919, at any rate, although Popov reports that
"during the entire months of June and July the situation near
Orenburg remained tense."

Meanwhile the Red Army was gaining the upper hand in
its effort to extend Bolshevik rule throughout the empire.

Anti-Bolshevik resistance forces in Siberia, as well as in the southern region, were in retreat. In mid-1919, the Southern Command of the Red Army was organized separately, as the Turkestan Command, and led by Mikhail V. Frunze. The Turkestan Command, from then on, had to deal only with a native guerrilla movement. Commander Frunze himself admitted that these guerrillas, known as the "Basmach" movement, were a force of "hundreds and thousands of those whom the [Communist] authorities had hurt and offended." Frunze admitted that the Red Army had outraged the local population by lawlessness, looting, and violence. He said that the Reds, instead of acting as "defenders of the working people and the revolution," had acted as "an instrument of violence against them." The Bolshevik commander recognized that the Basmach guerrillas were "far from being simply brigands," but people who had looked in vain for a defense of their rights and who had decided to take justice and self-protection into their own hands.

These people, acting in self-defense against Red Army excesses, became the first target in Malenkov's revolutionary career—but even then not on the battlefield. According to the *Political Dictionary* published in Moscow in 1940, when Malenkov at last entered the Bolshevik Party in April, 1920, after the Bolshevik victory had become a certainty, and two and a half years after the Bolshevik Revolution, he became "engaged as a political worker" successively in "a squadron, regiment, brigade, and the Political Administration of the Turkestan Front."

Young Malenkov thus was never a front-line fighter in the Red Army, even though he joined the Communists belatedly and might have been supposed to be eager to make up for lost time. Instead, he was engaged in making sure that the local population did not try to take vengeance against the Bolsheviks. A recent historical parallel to this type of activity can be found in the role of a Gestapo agent operating during World War II in a Nazi-occupied country, ferreting out patriotic resistance fighters. As Lazar Pistrak observed in *The New Leader* on March 16, 1953, Malenkov was "the first leader in modern times to make his political debut as a policeman and an executioner."

Another parallel from World War II illustrates the functions of a Red Army "political worker" during the period of Malenkov's initiation into Bolshevik tactics. Notably in Norway, Czechoslovakia, and France, the Nazis wiped out whole sections of the population, whole towns, in order to terrorize the people into submission. The French town of Oradour is one example. The Red Army in Turkestan in 1920, surrounded by a hostile population, was in a similarly insecure position.

The very month that Malenkov entered the party, the Revolutionary Military Council of the Turkestan Front sent a significant message to the All-Russian Executive Committee of the Soviets. The message revealed two facts: first, there was practically no sympathy for the Bolsheviks in Turkestan; second, in order to enforce their rule, the Bolsheviks were ready to undertake mass killings, a "pogrom." The message, dated April 16 and signed by Shalva Eliava, stated: "Here, as far as Soviet power is concerned, there is absolutely a blank space, and as far as communism is concerned, it is a negative quantity. As it seems, it will be necessary to organize a Soviet and Party pogrom." The organization of such a "pogrom" was the task of Red Army "political workers," and it was with such a group that Malenkov received his earliest training.

In the atmosphere of violence and chaos prevailing in

Turkestan, Red Army troops, as we have seen from Frunze's admission, were wild and undisciplined bands. It was the task of "political workers" to instill a measure of discipline through terror and purges. A historical account, published in Moscow in 1924, appraised this situation candidly. Writing on *The Fergan Basmach Movement in* 1918–1922, D. D. Zuyev quoted the Turkestan Central Executive Committee of the Soviets as reporting: "The First Cavalry Regiment represents an armed gang, a complete chaos, in which criminal elements and anti-Bolshevik Whiteguardists feel like fish in water, and develop their activity to the utmost. And this is not even the worst regiment." Soviet sources do not state whether Malenkov was a political worker in the First Regiment or not. However, similar conditions seem to have prevailed throughout the Turkestan Red Army. The report observed that the whole army was in chaos, saying that "properly speaking, until now there is no Army in Turkestan, and there will be none as long as the organizational principles of the military units remains unchanged."

A political worker like Georgi Malenkov was therefore kept busy crushing the local resistance movement behind the lines, while liquidating unsuitable elements within Red Army regiments. But he also had an economic-political task, particularly in the grain-rich Fergana region whose peasants had proven stubborn in resisting the Bolsheviks and who needed to be taught a lesson in rather primitive politico-economic cooperation. The political worker engaged in seizing the farmers' grain stocks—documentation, in this case, coming from a report submitted to the Eighth Congress of Soviets, as reported in the *Great Soviet Encyclopedia* (Moscow, 1935): "The front in Fergana was of a purely internal nature, its main

significance was an economical one, because, in case of liquidation of the front, we would be able to realize the Ferganian
grain reserves, which are certainly very large."

Those were the functions of men like Malenkov, "political
workers" in the Red Army, as it imposed Bolshevik rule upon
the former czarist empire. These tasks were later amplified,
expanded on a national scale: ferreting out any effort toward
nonconformity among the civilian population; acting as a
"political commissar" within the Bolshevik apparatus; squeez-
ing as much out of the economy as terroristic pressure methods could accomplish. During his Turkestan period, Malenkov went through tough and valuable schooling.

This element of caution showed itself for a second time
during Malenkov's student years in Moscow. It was the Communist Party itself which, after the civil war, selected the politically most promising young men for study in the capital's
institutes of higher learning. According to the *Political Dictionary* reports, Georgi Malenkov, having made good as a
"political worker" in Turkestan, "after the end of the civil war
studied at the MVTU"—initials which stand for the Moscow
Higher Technical School. Whether he was serious about becoming an engineer or not, student Malenkov certainly remained politically active, because he was "secretary of the
Russian Communist Party cell for the entire school."

Malenkov's cautiousness in choosing sides revealed itself
during the controversy between Stalin and Leon Trotsky,
which eventually led to Trotsky's exile and to his assassination in Mexico. The Stalin-Trotsky controversy was a fight for
the post of successor to V. I. Lenin, a struggle which began
considerably before Lenin's death in 1924. Trotsky's brilliance
as a writer and orator made him popular among the intellec-
tually minded Moscow students. About seventy per cent of

the students favored Trotsky, which prompted him to claim that "youth is the most correct barometer of the party" and "especially students react sharply against bureaucracy." Quite a few students who had helped the Bolsheviks take over the country were disillusioned with the revolution's aftermath. They felt the Communist Party owed them more than the drab life of post-revolutionary Moscow. Where were the fruits of rebellion, where was the Marxist-Leninist utopia?

Like young people elsewhere in the world, particularly in Near and Far Eastern countries today, the Moscow students of the post-civil-war era formed an important part of Communist Party strength. In 1923, one quarter of the Moscow party organization was made up of students. They argued among themselves, they orated, they wrote flaming resolutions. The trend at the universities was clearly pro-Trotsky and anti-Stalin. Pravda reported early in 1924 that 6,594 students favored Trotsky; only 2,790 students were neutral or in favor of Stalin.

What was happening at the Moscow Higher Technical School, where Malenkov was secretary of the party cell "for the entire school"? On January 4, *Pravda* reported that the Workers Department of the school had come out for Trotsky. But Malenkov, if he was pro-Stalin, soon had a chance to state his allegiance without leaving a shadow of a doubt.

The Stalin partisans drew up an anti-Trotsky letter, a long document signed by students, which appeared in two installments in *Pravda,* on January 9 and 11. The letter carried 404 signatures, but the name of G. M. Malenkov was not on the list. Lazar Pistrak, in his Voice of America research report on Malenkov, notes that "the total number of cell secretaries in the Moscow higher schools was at that time 72," considerably less than the number of signatures. Therefore, Pistrak says, "if Malenkov, one of these secretaries, had been at that time a supporter of Stalin's line, he would have signed the anti-Trotsky letter as one of the 404."

Nevertheless, shortly after Lenin's death on January 21, 1924, Malenkov found himself in the good graces of the Stalin-led party machine. Official Soviet sources are close-mouthed about this period. The *Political Dictionary* restricts itself to the reference that Malenkov joined the "apparatus of the Central Committee of the All-Union Communist Party," where he served as a "responsible worker from 1925 to 1930." There is no word of how he came to be selected, or who did the selecting.

Close students of Kremlin operations agree that the biographical reference to the party's "apparatus" in reality refers to Stalin's personal secretariat. According to Robert Dall, a student in Moscow at the time, Malenkov was recommended for a party position by Besso Lominadze,* at that time leader of the Communist Youth League, the Komsomol. With this recommendation, Malenkov was hired by Ivan Tovstyukha, who was then looking for promising young men to staff the party secretariat. The job paid 250 rubles per month, considerably more than the five rubles students received as an allowance. Tovstyukha, Malenkov's first boss, was a cultivated, soft-spoken man who died of tuberculosis in 1927. He was succeeded by his deputy, Alexander Proskrebyshev, who remained Stalin's personal secretary for a quarter of a century.

Thus between the ages of twenty-three and twenty-five,

---

* Lominadze was one of the Comintern agents who, on December 11, 1927, organized the bloody Chinese Communist uprising that became known as the "Canton Commune." During the factional fight within the United States Communist Party in 1928, he threw Comintern support behind William Z. Foster. Lominadze was shot during the purges of 1937.

Malenkov appears to have made his mark as an up-and-coming "apparatus" man—and a man capable of serving and utilizing the machinery of the Communist Party. Without ties of senti-ment to "Old Bolsheviks," already experienced in the tactics of party terror, Malenkov was learning the practice of con-spiracy from the Master himself.

3

In Stalin's Shadow

CHILDREN in Russian schools used to chant a song with the words, "I want to be like Stalin." Malenkov, who seems to have shared this desire, saw his wish come true. Working in Stalin's shadow, he had ample opportunity to observe his idol at close hand. Above all, he saw the workings of intra-party conspiracy, the operations in which men were maneuvered to the advantage of Lenin's ruthless successor.

The years from 1925 to 1930 were decisive for the U.S.S.R. Trotsky was exiled, and Stalin prepared the downfall of his remaining opponents: Nikolai Bukharin, who had helped him to defeat Trotsky; Gregori Zinoviev, the first chief of the Communist International; Leonid Kamenev, who had a lingering affection for Trotsky. All these men had supporters within the Communist Party. First this support had to be weakened. Then each in his turn had to be isolated, surrounded by antagonists, and finally destroyed.

During these years, Malenkov learned one fundamental technique: how to use a campaign in favor of supposed ideological purity to crush an opponent. During the Stalin-Trotsky controversy and the purges that followed, Stalin created vast smoke screens of theoretical verbiage. In speeches, overloaded with Marx and Lenin quotations, these men hurled charges of obscure ideological sins at each other. Trotsky favored "permanent revolution" on an international scale;

Stalin preferred to consolidate the gains of "Socialism in one country," the Soviet Union, first of all.

It did not matter that, at heart, Stalin had no quarrel with the idea of a world-wide revolution. In fact, after ridding himself of Trotsky, he ultimately put Trotsky's theories into practice. But the main thing had been to find a talking point, a propaganda theme, a supposed heresy of which his opponent could be found guilty. No ideological concept seemed too remote and fanciful to serve in ruining an antagonist's standing. Some twenty years later, Malenkov was to use a similar tactic in dealing with supporters of his antagonist, Andrei A. Zhdanov.

When his five years with Stalin's secretariat ended in 1930, Malenkov was made a divisional director within the party's Central Committee. He participated in the party's Sixteenth Congress, representing the central party "apparatus" with a deliberative vote. That same year, Malenkov became chief of the Organizing Department in the Moscow Party Committee. His superior was Lazar M. Kaganovich—who, in 1953, was to become a First Deputy Premier under Malenkov.

Perhaps this early relationship helps to explain why Kaganovich received such a high post following Stalin's death. True, he had long been a Politburo member, and he had never been mentioned as a man harboring dangerous aspirations. But why so prominent a position—on the same level as Lavrenti Beria, Molotov, and Bulganin? Also, his appointment came at a time when anti-Semitism seemed to have become official policy in the Soviet Union and its satellites; Kaganovich is the only Jew in the top Kremlin hierarchy. Because the answer to these contradictions may be found in the early relationship between Malenkov and Kaganovich, it may be justified to digress

briefly in order to examine the career of the man who was
Malenkov's superior in the Moscow Party Committee back in
the early thirties.

Lazar Kaganovich's big square-looking head and full Stalin-
type mustache have looked, unsmiling and forbidding, at the
Western world for years. His life, not unlike that of Molotov,
is that of an Old Bolshevik and an early idealist who long ago
made his compromise with tyranny, terror, and deceit. Kaganovich and Malenkov together were at least partially responsible for the ruthless removal of Stalin's potential enemies
from the Moscow party. (Premier Stalin's third wife was a
sister of Kaganovich.)

Both men, as their careers and utterances show, are shrewd
and practical—coldly determined to get results, regardless of
price. They are meticulous organizers, capable of cutting
through mountains of bureaucratic red tape. Malenkov, in
World War II, was in charge of industrial and transportation
problems—in other words, it was his task to speed up war production. Kaganovich had dealt with similar problems in the
late 1930s. In particular, he is credited with straightening out
the chaotic Soviet railroad system.

Immediately following World War II, Kaganovich was sent
on a trouble-shooting mission to the Ukraine, charged with
suppressing anti-Soviet guerrillas and resurgent Ukrainian
nationalism. Later, he was once more placed in charge of
heavy industry and transport, and of war-production centers
in Central Asia.

Operating in the same fields, with the same kind of ma-
chinelike efficiency (whether it meant party purges or industrial production figures), may have created a measure of
mutual respect between Malenkov and Kaganovich. Possibly,
too, the relatively unambitious Kaganovich today occupies a

With and without Zhdanov: The unidentified portrait of Soviet leaders (above), taken before World War II, shows Andrei Zhdanov on Stalin's right and the young-looking Malenkov in the center of the third row. . . . Ten years later, at Zhdanov's funeral in 1948 (below), Malenkov occupies Zhdanov's former place of prominence directly beside Stalin. (*Credit: Sovfoto.*)

Kalinin's Pallbearers: Among President Kalinin's pallbearers, in June of 1946, were, left to right, Molotov, Stalin, and Malenkov. . . . An informal photograph of Soviet leaders on the reviewing stand of the Dynamo Stadium (below) on July 20, 1947. Stalin is at the extreme left, Molotov is third from left. The three to their right are Mikoyan, Beria, and Malenkov. (*Credit: Sovfoto.*)

position in the Malenkov scheme of things similar to his own trouble-shooter role under Stalin.

At any rate, the two men served Stalin well in the early 1930s. They crushed Moscow party opposition even before the great purges of the mid-thirties. Malenkov's service was rewarded with an appointment to the Moscow Provincial Party Committee on January 30, 1932. At the same time he was made a delegate to the Seventeenth All-Union Party Conference with a deliberative vote. Two years later, in January 1934, Malenkov participated in the Seventeenth All-Union Party Congress, this time with a decisive vote.

We now come to a complex set of initials, and to a madman. Both are of great importance in the life of the new Soviet Premier. The initials are ORPO and they stand for Otdel Rukovodiashchikh Partiinikh Organov, which means Department of Leading Party Organizations. The madman's name was Nikolai Yezhov.

The ORPO was set up in 1934 by the Seventeenth Party Congress, and Malenkov became its operating director. ORPO took the place of the Communist Party's personnel section, the Registration and Distribution Department. The magazine *Party Construction,* in its issue of October 15, 1935, defined the main functions of ORPO, within the party's Central Committee; it had the job of supervising the work of leading party organizations throughout the Soviet Union, that is, in the various Soviet Republics, and on provincial and regional levels. This particular phase of the task was undertaken through special territorial groups of instructors, or inspectors.

Furthermore, ORPO had the job of making and keeping a record on every prominent party member—people in the party itself, as well as in the government administration, industry, transport, agriculture, trade, education, and science. In other words, Malenkov's bureau was the Communist Party's internal secret service, Stalin's own intelligence service within the party. To this must be added, although the official Soviet biographies do not mention it, that Malenkov also headed a super hush-hush "Special Section" which reported to Stalin only.

As for the madman, Nikolai Yezhov, he was Malenkov's superior in ORPO and later became the head of the Soviet Secret Police, called NKVD at that time. During the final phase of the great purge he went too far, even by Kremlin standards, and in 1938 was done away with. This man Yezhov for a time was Malenkov's esteemed superior.

Because Yezhov eventually went wild and embarrassed Stalin, official Soviet biographers now avoid linking Malenkov with Yezhov. In fact, however, Malenkov was Yezhov's pupil. Although he may, in witnessing Yezhov's demise, have learned to avoid obvious excesses, the teacher-student relationship definitely did exist. Nowhere could a man study terror tactics more intimately than under Yezhov. Nowhere could the mechanics of conspiracy be examined more closely.

The infamous Moscow trials of 1936–1937 had to be prepared well in advance, with painstaking attention to detail. Dossiers about the accused men had to be compiled, actual facts had to be cleverly integrated with wild and fantastic accusations. Early in 1935 Yezhov became one of the party secretaries, and replaced Kaganovich as chairman of the party's Control Commission. There is no question that at this time Yezhov became Malenkov's immediate superior. The source for this information is the magazine *Party Construction* (Moscow, February, 1935). As chief of ORPO, Yezhov replaced Kaganovich.

In September of that year Yezhov was the main speaker at an ORPO meeting. Malenkov, too, spoke to the audience, but he was merely identified as an ORPO "representative." It was during this period that Yezhov and Malenkov worked closely with the NKVD, compiling incriminating dossiers on party people who were to be purged. Malenkov's speech at this particular conference was concerned with efforts to safeguard membership-card authenticity, an undertaking, in the words of *Party Construction,* designed to accomplish the "unmasking and banishing from our ranks of swindlers, rogues, Trotskyites, Zinovievites, and other kinds of rascals." Malenkov, in this speech, was most complimentary toward his superior, repeating such phrases as "Comrade Yezhov was absolutely right . . ." and "Comrade Yezhov has fully elucidated all questions. . . ."

In March, 1936, we find Malenkov as editor of *Party Construction,* replacing Yezhov. Two months later the magazine was editorially extolling Yezhov's teaching abilities, saying: "Comrade Yezhov taught us how to reorganize the party's work, how to raise organizational work to a higher level, and how to make this work more effective. . . . We strive to carry out these instructions." As Lazar Pistrak puts it: "The relations between Yezhov and Malenkov were those of a chief and a subordinate, of a teacher and pupil. They continued to be such even when Yezhov was replaced by Malenkov as chief of ORPO," in mid-1936.

Malenkov, in December, 1937, editorially hailed Yezhov for making the bloody purges possible. *Party Construction* said that "under the leadership of the Stalinist People's Commissar, Comrade Yezhov, the Soviet intelligence service inflicted merciless and striking blows at the fascist bandits," adding in a somewhat inappropriate tone of adulation: "The

Soviet people love their intelligence service, because it defends the vital interests of the people and it is their flesh and
blood. . . . The faithful guardians of Socialism—the NKVD
men—under the leadership of their Stalinist People's Commissar, Comrade Yezhov, will continue in the future to crush
and to root out, the enemies of the people—the vile Trotskyite, Bukharinite, bourgeois-nationalist and other agents of
fascism. Let the spies and traitors tremble! The punishing
hand of the Soviet people—the NKVD—will annihilate them!
Our ardent Bolshevik greetings to the Stalinist People's Commissar of Internal Affairs, Nikolai Ivanovich Yezhov."

To view this extravagant praise in historical context, we
must recall that the conveyer belt of the Moscow purges had
then reached full speed. Andrei Vishinsky, later famous for
his vitriolic diatribes at the United Nations, was the prosecutor
at the big show trials, goading his victims into confessions of
guilt. Yezhov's secret-police machinery, after wearing them
down with threat and torture, fed victim upon victim into the
trials' meat grinder, arranging for quick execution or banishment of hundreds and thousands of the accused. Behind
Yezhov stood Malenkov, compiling and supplying dossiers—
and naming the men who would take over positions vacated
by the dead and deported.

The trials and purges, in the self-generated hysteria of
NKVD persecution, reached their highest pitch in mid-1938.
Yezhov's accusations lost all link with reality, became inco-
herent, knew no bounds. He is believed to have gone so far
as to accuse Lavrenti Beria of conspiring against Stalin. In
December, 1938, Yezhov was removed as secret-police chief,
and nothing was ever again heard from Malenkov's esteemed
teacher.

But, by then, Malenkov was no longer in need of teachers.

He had already spent thirteen years at the nerve centers of Soviet power. He had observed Stalin himself, had been instructed by the cold Kaganovich, and the hysterical Yezhov. During the purge period, he had begun himself to eliminate men whom, for one reason or another, he personally wanted out of the way. He had also managed to staff the party organization to a large degree with personnel who would, from that time on, be deeply indebted to Georgi M. Malenkov. He had begun to assemble the parts of his own political machine, a party within the party.

During these years, Malenkov had little chance or cause to deal with Marxist-Leninist theory. He knew the uses of ideological arguments in a struggle for power. He knew how ideological failings could be amplified into charges of anti-party activity, of conspiracy against the Kremlin; how they could prompt a party member to fall from grace. But, as he knew the use of theoretical arguments from the inside, Malenkov clearly developed a cynical attitude toward theories and theoreticians—a cynicism which showed itself, in public utterances, during various parts of his career.

Nevertheless, Malenkov had developed a working knowledge of Marxist vernacular, although he preferred to quote Stalin rather than Marx, Engels, Lenin, or the other old-timers. He learned to dress his speeches with the proper veneer of Marxism-Leninism, but he knew that reality lay deeper. Reality meant people in their relation to each other; it meant careers broken or made, in lives crushed or fulfilled; it meant powerful men sitting in judgment on high rostra, helpless men standing beneath them—looking upward, cringing—and confessing to deeds of which they knew nothing.

Until the end of the purges, Georgi Malenkov had been satisfied to operate in the shadows. Now, slowly, he stepped into the limelight of Soviet affairs. Under the Soviet Constitution of 1937, a document that provided democratic camouflage for Stalinist tyranny, pseudo-elections were instituted in the Soviet Union. So-called delegates were to be "elected" to the Supreme Soviet—the same hand-picked group which on March 15, 1953, gave a post-facto stamp of spurious legality to Malenkov's succession to Stalin.

On October 11, 1937, Malenkov was made secretary of the Central Electoral Commission. Here the giant card index of the Communist Party came in handy. All members of the Supreme Soviet had to be, of course, completely reliable in Kremlin terms. Malenkov knew intimate details of the lives of everyone who might be considered as a candidate. As he looked down, sixteen years later, upon the men and women who legalized his power, Malenkov could know the deepest secrets behind the faces that looked up to him. As electoral secretary, he had passed judgment on each one of them before their names were submitted to the powerless voters.

There was one man whom Malenkov, as electoral secretary, could safely suggest to the Soviet voters in 1938. That man was Georgi M. Malenkov. And so he was promptly elected to the Supreme Soviet, serving in this capacity of parliamentary delegate until 1946. Membership in the Supreme Soviet was, however, so much window dressing. Quite another matter was membership in the Presidium of the Eighteenth Party Congress of 1939. That Congress named Malenkov to the party's Central Committee. The Committee, in turn, appointed him a member of its Organization Bureau (Orgbureau). He also became one of the Central Committee's secretaries.

Malenkov was moving up the ladder of command and authority quickly. The year of 1939 was crucial in his life, just as it was in the life of his later antagonist Andrei Zhdanov. Until

then, Zhdanov was well ahead in public prestige, Stalin's es-
teem, and party power. But Malenkov was gaining rapidly,
and eventually the two men were to meet violently in a col-
lision that was to shake all strata of Soviet life.

Zhdanov made the key report to the Eighteenth Party Congress—the last such Congress until the meeting of October,
1952, which gave Malenkov such overwhelming prominence.
Zhdanov in 1939 outlined important changes in the Communist Party program and statutes. Malenkov was a member
of the committee actually in charge of proposing the changes,
but he was one of twenty-seven committee members, well
below Zhdanov in importance.

Above all, however, it should be remembered that Georgi
Malenkov remained in charge of the huge dossier files, the
streamlined card-index machinery. He was made director of
the office that succeeded ORPO, the Administration of Cadres.

What are cadres? The word appears constantly in Communist Party exhortations, in the Soviet Union as well as in
parties outside the Soviet orbit. Cadres, like "cells" or "party
nuclei," are the tightly knit groups of trained, reliable Communists who operate within a larger organization, control it,
lead it, swing it into line with party aims. Even in the United
States, as in other countries outside the Iron Curtain, such
cadres have been and can be found in labor unions, at schools,
in the arts, sciences, and professions, in industrial plants, in
nonparty organizations. By parliamentary skill and pressure
methods, small cadres can swing large but lethargic groups.

Cadres, in the Soviet Union, are the hard core of Kremlin
supporters: men and women who can be relied upon to push
execution of policies, and to report back to the Administration
of Cadres anyone suspected of insufficient zeal. Upon the

performance of cadre members depends their advance or demotion within party ranks, their admittance to or exclusion
from the privileged top stratum of Soviet society—these are
the "intellectuals," who, together with workers and peasants,
now make up the three classes in a nation supposedly on its
way to a "classless society."

As we have seen, the ORPO concerned itself with keeping
close control only over leading party members. When the
Eighteenth Congress established the cadre administration,
under Malenkov, it widened his authority by extending it to
the cells, or virtually to the entire party membership. When
this step was taken, in 1939, the party had 1,588,852 members
and 888,814 candidates for party membership. Details on
every one of these men and women were on file in Malenkov's
office, staffed by hundreds of carefully selected researchers
and statisticians, equipped with up-to-date cataloguing facilities.

By this time the war in Europe had started. Stalin had made
the Nazi-Soviet Pact. Finland had resisted Soviet invasion.
The Stalin-Hitler deal gave the Kremlin a brief breathing spell
in which Stalin decided to expand party control over all fields
of Soviet life essential in war production and internal wartime
discipline. On February 15, 1941, four months before Hitler's
armies invaded the Soviet Union, Malenkov made the key
address at the Eighteenth Party Conference. His speech was
devoted to organization of industry and transport. His criticism of Soviet administrators in this field was scathing to the
point of arrogance and showed no trace of caution. He spoke
of "flaws, shortcomings, and errors" in the direction of industry and transport; he castigated Soviet bureaucrats, saying
that "some of them like to sit in swivel chairs and run things
by correspondence."

The day after this speech, Georgi M. Malenkov was named an alternate member of the all-powerful Politburo. At thirty-seven, he was thus already a power in a circle of Old Bolsheviks. In the wholesale shake-up in the upper echelons of Soviet industry that followed Malenkov's attack, Vyacheslav Molotov's wife, Polina Zhemchuzhina—who had earlier failed as Cosmetics Trust director—was ousted as People's Commissar of the Fish Industry, and had to withdraw from public life.

Victor Kravchenko, in his book *I Chose Freedom,* reports that Molotov took his wife's failure as a personal disgrace, and said: "The fault, comrades, is one which I must share myself. I have failed to give sufficient attention to the matter." To which Stalin is said to have replied, with characteristic sarcasm: "That's beside the point, Vyacheslav. The crux of the matter is that too many fish are swimming in the sea when they ought to be on citizens' tables." Whether Molotov related his wife's demotion to the tongue-lashing Malenkov gave the bureaucrats is a moot point. There can be little doubt today there is scant love lost between the two.

During the war years Malenkov's star rose. His result-getting ruthlessness was now directed against Soviet labor engaged in war production. His extraordinary organizational ability was utilized to the hilt. Shortly after the German invasion Malenkov became a member of the State Defense Committee, together with Stalin, Molotov, Voroshilov, and Beria. Malenkov, swamped with work, named an energetic young man from Leningrad to join the Committee. The Malenkov protégé was Nikolai A. Voznesensky; it is a name to remember, the name of one who tried to double-cross the man who today is Soviet Premier.

On the State Defense Committee, Malenkov's job was to break bottlenecks in war production, particularly in the tank and aircraft industries. As the Nazi armies overran the most crucial Soviet industrial areas, this became an extremely difficult task. It called for quick action, the dismantling and eastward transfer of whole plants, and for the enforcement of labor discipline at a time when chaos threatened the enforcement of Kremlin rule.

Malenkov was the enforcer of that rule. He reduced war production to essentials, cutting out civilian items almost entirely, limiting tank and airplane models to a few standard items, and enforcing mass production of these standard models. Soviet sources claim that airplane production at that time rose to 40,000 per year. Malenkov also had a hand in assuring essential steel and oil output. During the battle of Stalingrad he exhorted the defenders. Later he moved into territories vacated by the retreating Germans and whipped the population into quick rebuilding of devastated industries. He received the Order of Lenin and a Gold Medal with Hammer and Sickle in 1943, and was also made a Hero of Socialist Labor. In 1945 he received a second Order of Lenin.

In March, 1946, Malenkov became a full Politburo member. It seemed as if nothing could stop his rise now. But it appears that, at about this time, he became careless. Perhaps his antipathy against Bolshevik old-timers, men with a past rather than a present, got the better of his usually cautious judgment. In 1946, speaking in favor of new party principles, Malenkov actually called for a revision of Marxist tenets. A worshiper at the altar of his own accomplishments, he spoke out in favor of the doers, and against the theorists and the talkers.

He urged, heretically, that "we who follow the Marxists teachings, must study our contemporary experience." Communists, he said, must "incorporate it into day-by-day practical leadership. . . . The war has forged new people, new personnel capable of pushing the work ahead."

Who were these new people? Why Malenkov, of course, and the men he had appointed to wartime jobs. And who were the old people, those—according to Malenkov—ready for the trash can of history? The theorizing old-timers! Speaking of them, Malenkov said scathingly: "We have people, rightly called bookworms, who have quotations from Marx and Engels ready for every occasion and every pretext. Instead of laboring to think up something new or studying experience, they have one answer: 'No, that was not said by Marx,' or 'Engels said something else.' If Marx could rise from the grave and see such a follower—if this term is permissible—he undoubtedly would immediately disown him."

Georgi Malenkov, the upstart and post-revolutionary party member, the New Bolshevik, had committed heresy. His inside knowledge of the Marx-Engels camouflage in the Kremlin power struggle, his well-justified cynicism on matters of theoretical argument, had prompted him to excessive candor. Also, his own ambitions were showing a bit too clearly between the lines of this impatient and arrogant statement. There were those who knew that Malenkov himself had made mistakes, some of them causing international repercussions. For instance, one night in September, 1945, the cipher clerk at the Soviet Embassy in Ottawa took a number of documents from his files and turned them over to Canadian authorities. The documents testified to the extent and methods of Soviet espionage in Canada. And the name of Malenkov was contained in one of them.

Colonel Nikolai Zabotin, center of Moscow's espionage network in Ottawa, had been careless enough to submit copies of secret reports to the Soviet ambassador himself. Under Soviet espionage rules, the ambassador was not to know the extent or methods of the spy apparatus. For this, Zabotin was reprimanded by the espionage "director" from Moscow. In the spy code, the Embassy itself was called "metro"; the ambassador, "head of metro." In his apology, cabled back to Moscow on August 11, 1945, Zabotin states that he fully understood instructions about dealing with the "head of metro," as he had followed instructions given him "by the chief director and by Comrade Malenkov."

Thus Comrade Malenkov had been guilty of permitting leaks about the supersecret espionage system, with his own name undisguised in a radio message. Together with his Marxist-Leninist heresies and indiscreet manifestations of his ambition, this carelessness weighed heavily against him. There were men just waiting for ways and means of stopping the cocky, overly ambitious Georgi Malenkov in his tracks. One of these was Andrei Alexandrovich Zhdanov.

4

Death of a Rival

"WHEN THE whales fight, the shrimps are killed." This old Korean proverb neatly summarizes the upheavals that disrupted Soviet society from the end of World War II until Georgi Malenkov's emergence as Soviet Premier. Two whales were fighting. Their battle created waves and ripples throughout the Soviet Union even after it was over; it shook the Communist Party, Soviet economics, art, literature, and science.

One of the giant whales was Malenkov. The other was his rival Andrei A. Zhdanov. The two men struggled for control of the party's apparatus, for Stalin's support, and for the allegiance of people in all strata of Soviet society. Through the war years, and into 1948, Zhdanov's position and prestige was considerably greater than that of Malenkov. He was prominently mentioned as Molotov's and Beria's rival for Stalin's succession. But then, on August 31, 1948, Moscow abruptly announced that Zhdanov had died. His death was sudden; only two months earlier he had attended a Cominform meeting in Romania. Zhdanov's death cleared the way for Malenkov.

Evidence of the Malenkov-Zhdanov conflict did not, of course, appear openly in the Soviet press and was not otherwise publicized in the Soviet Union. However, reports from recent Soviet refugees who reached Western Germany, as well as the chronology of the events and changing fortunes

45

of key Soviet personalities, strongly indicate that such a conflict did take place and played an important part in Malenkov's career.

Like Malenkov, Zhdanov came from what Marxists call "bourgeois" parents. He was born in 1898 in the city of Tver, now called Kalinin, some 100 miles northwest of Moscow. Some biographies say that his father was a school inspector, others maintain his father was a parish priest. Zhdanov attended the gymnasium, where he studied French and German. After his graduation, he seems to have been under pressure from his father to enter the priesthood and attend a theological seminary.

World War I prevented Zhdanov from attending the seminary or from taking any other step toward a career. He was drafted into the army. He joined the Bolsheviks at the time of the October Revolution in 1917 and participated in the fighting in and around Leningrad. From then on, his future was tied up with that city. The first step from regional prominence as Leningrad Communist Party chairman to the national prominence of the Moscow regime took place in 1934 when Zhdanov was a principal speaker at the All-Russian Congress of Soviet writers.

Zhdanov submitted a report to the Eighteenth Party Congress in 1939 designed to help in revision of party rules. Coming as an aftermath to the great purges, this report was remarkable for the admission that such purges were "attended by many mistakes, primarily by the infringement of the Leninist principle of an individual approach to people." The report admitted that: "there were numerous cases of unwarranted expulsion from the party, and of hostile elements who had wormed their way into the party, taking advantage of the purges to persecute and ruin honest people."

The Zhdanov report marked the end of the period of internal purges. It was made in an apparent effort to patch up wounds created by the purge, and to conciliate resentment against Yezhov's purge excesses, resentment to be found both inside and outside the Communist Party. The very fact that Zhdanov was able to make a speech of such frankness points to his prominence at the time of the Eighteenth Party Congress. He had become a member of the Communist International's Executive Committee at its Seventh Congress, in 1935; he received the Order of Lenin the same year and became a candidate to the Politburo. In 1939, at forty-one, Zhdanov became a full Politburo member. He was way ahead of Malenkov.

In fact, 1939 was a high point in Zhdanov's career. It was on his advice that Premier Stalin decided upon the Soviet attack on Finland; later, when the Finns put up heroic resistance, Zhdanov's advice was revealed as unsound. His star temporarily faded, just as Malenkov entered the Politburo. However, when Nazi Germany attacked the Soviet Union in 1941, Zhdanov received new prominence as commander of the Leningrad area. Among other accomplishments, he established a supply route across frozen Lake Ladoga, which enabled the hard-pressed citizens of Leningrad to survive the Nazi siege.

Zhdanov reached his zenith of importance in international affairs with a supposedly "personal" article in *Pravda* in mid-1939. His article proved to be a trial balloon heralding the coming Soviet-Nazi Pact. It expressed doubts as to the sincerity of the Western powers, saying: "I will permit myself to voice on this subject my personal opinion, though my friends do not agree. They still believe that when the British and French Governments began to negotiate with the U.S.S.R.

a pact of reciprocal help, they had in view the creation of a powerful and strong barrier against aggression in Europe."

The Zhdanov argument became the official Soviet alibi for the Soviet-Nazi Pact which was concluded just about two months after his *Pravda* article. The official Moscow view, from then until 1941, was that the Western powers had not been sincere in their negotiations with the Soviet Union and had instead hoped to set Hitler against the Soviets.

During the war Zhdanov successively received the military ranks of lieutenant-general and colonel-general. He was placed in charge of the occupied Baltic nations, Latvia, Lithuania, and Estonia. As chairman of the Allied Control Commission in Finland after the war, Zhdanov was in effect master of Finland's postwar fate.

The war had kept Malenkov and Zhdanov apart. Malenkov had risen as production chief on the home front, Zhdanov at the war front and in the field of foreign affairs. Now the two men met, and sparks began to fly. They had one thing in common—ambition. But they differed in their methods, their background, their personalities, their likes and dislikes.

By comparison to the bulky, slow-but-sure Malenkov, Zhdanov was brilliant and erratic. When Malenkov was cautious, Zhdanov was dynamic. Where Malenkov preferred the conservative chesslike maneuver of pawns against each other, Zhdanov chose open combat. The difference in their outward appearance was striking enough. The nonmilitary Malenkov at all times wore the drab uniform of the Communist Party, unadorned, designed to hide him rather than dress him up. Zhdanov, on the other hand, with his neatly clipped mustache and carefully tightened tie, seemed almost dapper.

On a speaker's platform, Zhdanov's dynamic qualities stood out. For all his wild notions about the arts and literature, he had emotional roots in Russian culture. Zhdanov was a pseudo-intellectual, who found in his second home, Leningrad, a cultural tradition he admired and envied. Since czarist days, Leningrad (the former Petrograd) has been Russia's window to the West. When the city was the czarist capital, it drew to itself English technicians, French *couturiers,* and German physicians. It was, of course, the center of Russian literature.

Of these traditions Zhdanov was aware—in his own distorted, Bolshevik fashion. Looking back, there must have been in Andrei Zhdanov a strongly ambivalent, contradictory relation to things Western. He must have felt attracted to the forbidden ferment of the West, to the free give-and-take in politics and art—where a brilliant man could make his way on his gifts and accomplishments alone, without constantly mouthing Marxist platitudes. Malenkov, on the other hand, shared none of Zhdanov's cultural pretensions. He was faced with the eminently practical problem of keeping his political footing.

Malenkov's slighting remarks about Old Bolsheviks cost him support at the full meeting of the party's Central Committee in February, 1946. The Committee sided with Zhdanov, against Malenkov. The struggle for power continued through the summer. One striking external clue exists of the degree to which Zhdanov was able to beat down his rival. On May Day, 1946, Malenkov stood right next to Stalin on the reviewing stand overlooking the Red Square parade. One year later, he had dropped down to sixth place among the Soviet leaders on the rostrum. During the same period, Zhdanov climbed from fourth place in the line, to the position at Stalin's side on the anniversary of the Bolshevik Revolution, November 7, 1946.

Thus, in mid-1946, Malenkov suddenly and definitely fell

from favor, while Zhdanov advanced to the coveted Number
Two position on the rostrum. There was a second definite
clue: the electoral lists of Politburo members submitted to
the public. During the January, 1946, elections, Malenkov's
name was third on the list; he dropped to ninth place in November, 1947. From late in 1946 to mid-1948, Malenkov's
name never appeared as that of a member of the Communist
Party secretariat.

Zhdanov's cultural dilettantism was largely responsible for
the wild and harsh things he did from 1946 to 1947. It was a
period when he had to assert his Bolshevik will, when he had
to crush all that could be suspected of being Western in postwar Soviet society. During the war, a measure of tolerance
had been permitted Soviet economists, scientists, writers, and
artists in their treatment of Western subjects and sources.
It was Zhdanov who spearheaded the drive against things
"alien" in Soviet society. On August 21, 1946, he said in Leningrad that "if feudalism and later on, the bourgeoisie in the
period of its flourishing, could create art and literature as-
serting the new systems," then certainly "our new socialist
system, embodying all that is best in the history of human
civilization and culture, is capable of creating the most advanced literature, which will leave far behind the best crea-
tions of olden times."

The Zhdanov line on Soviet culture, as it developed from
late 1946 until early 1948, was threefold: cultural products
had to serve politico-economic ends, propagandizing such
things as the Five-Year Plan and hydroelectric power; Western "bourgeois tendencies" had to be crushed at all cost; Russian traditions and Russian themes were to be encouraged.

Armed with a resolution from the Central Committee of
the party, Zhdanov proceeded to remodel Soviet culture. Lit-

erature was first. The arts followed, one by one: painting, the theater, music, motion pictures. The Leningrad Writers Union was forced to urge its members to use such themes as "the majesty of our victory, the pathos of rehabilitation and socialist reconstruction, and the heroic deeds of the Soviet people in fulfilling and overfulfilling the new Stalin Five-Year Plan."

The composers, too, fared badly. After all, Zhdanov played the piano. At a meeting on February 10, 1948, Zhdanov said composers should write their music more "like Glinka and Tchaikovsky." One pro-Zhdanov composer said the composers ought to know more folk songs to inspire them—the way Zhdanov himself knew folk songs. "When Comrade Zhdanov was asked whether he really knew six hundred songs by heart, he replied, 'I hesitate to say I know six hundred, but I know about three hundred songs.' And how well he knows them! When he visited our choir, we presented him with an album of songs. On the following day, he returned the album with variants of texts of several of the compositions written in his own hand. Comrade Zhdanov is not a professional musician, but if our composers followed his example, we would say that they really knew our folk songs."

A day after this meeting, *Pravda* published a Central Committee resolution which criticized the opera *Great Friendship* by Vano Muradeli. The resolution had the Zhdanov touch. It criticized Muradeli because the opera had "not one melody or aria that remains in the memory." It noted that the composer "did not utilize the wealth of folk melodies, song tunes, and dance motifs in which the creative art of the peoples of the U.S.S.R. is so rich." The party resolution then went from the specific to the general:

"The Central Committee of the Communist Party of the Soviet Union considers that the failure of Muradeli's opera is a result of the formalist path taken by Muradeli, false and ruinous to the creative production of the Soviet composer. . . . The failure of Muradeli's opera is not an isolated incident, but is closely tied up with the unfortunate situation in contemporary Soviet music, with the prevalence of the formalist trend among Soviet composers."

Among the composers who suffered from the musical notions of the piano-playing Zhdanov, was one of the great figures in modern music, Dmitri Shostakovich. The composer was forced to admit that "the instructions of the Central Committee of the Communist Party open a new page in the history of Soviet art; they direct and inspire us."

The Central Committee's resolution announced that it had found the "fullest manifestation" of a "formalist trend in music" in the works of such composers as Comrades Dmitri Shostakovich, Sergei Prokofiev, Aram Khachaturian, Vissarion Y. Shebalin, Gabriel Popov, Nikolai Miaskovsy, and others. The resolution accused these composers of "formalist distortions, antidemocratic tendencies in music alien to the Soviet people and its artistic taste." The composers were further accused:

"Characteristics of such music is the negation of the basic principles of classical music; a sermon for atonality, dissonance, and disharmony, as if this were an expression of 'progress' and 'innovation' in the growth of musical form; a rejection of such important fundamentals of musical composition as melody; a passion for confused, neuropathic combinations which transform music into cacophony, into a chaotic piling up of sounds."

It was clear, at least, that Zhdanov didn't like their music. But the final indictment was obviously political: "This music reeks strongly of the spirit of contemporary modernist bour-

geois music of Europe and America, which reflects the de-
cadence of bourgeois culture, the full denial of musical art."

Zhdanov and Malenkov briefly joined forces at the meeting
that set up the Cominform, which eventually received the full
name of Information Bureau of the Communist and Workers
Parties. The Cominform, created in Warsaw in September,
1947, was the successor, to a degree, of the old Communist
International. Zhdanov had been one of the men who signed
the resolution which dissolved the Comintern, back in 1943.
Now, at Warsaw, it was his task to guide the organization and
lay down the policies of the Cominform.

Andrei Zhdanov appeared in Warsaw as the originator and
spokesman of a new Soviet foreign policy. His address on "The
International Situation," was more important than that of
a Soviet diplomat would have been. In contrast, Malenkov's
role was that of a mere technician, delivering an address on
"The Activities of the Central Committee of the Communist
Party of the Soviet Union (Bolsheviks)."

Zhdanov laid down the line of solid Soviet opposition to
the Marshall Plan. He asserted that "the new, openly expansionist orientation of the U.S.A. has as its aim the establishment of the world domination of American imperialism. . . .
The new expansionist and reactionary course of the U.S.A.
policy is orientated for a struggle against the U.S.S.R., against
the new democratic countries, against the working class
movement in every country, against the working class movement of the U.S.A. herself, and against the liberating anti-
imperialist forces of all countries throughout the world."

This speech was made, it must be remembered, only two
years after the end of the war in the Pacific. Zhdanov discarded the wartime alliance with the United States com-

pletely. Never before had a Soviet official quite so bluntly described a former ally as a vicious enemy. Zhdanov called the Marshall Plan a tool "in the realization of one of the most important tasks of the general American program: that of restoring the power of imperialism in the countries of the new democracy [the Soviet satellite nations] and to force them to renounce close economic and political cooperation with the Soviet Union."

Zhdanov also claimed that dissolution of the Comintern had forever put an end to the slanderous accusation that Communist parties "act not in the interests of their own peoples but on orders from abroad." However, Zhdanov observed with pride that in the four years since the dissolution of the Comintern a "considerable strengthening" of Communist parties had taken place in Europe and Asia.

Zhdanov, perhaps Moscow's leading "Europe First" protagonist, never once mentioned China at the Cominform meeting. He concluded with a call for defiance of the United States, saying: "Just as the Munich policy in the past gave free hand to Hitlerite aggression, so concessions to the new course of policy in the U.S.A. and to the Imperialist camp can make its inspirers only more insolent and aggressive. Therefore, the Communist parties must head the resistance to the plans of the imperialist expansion and aggression in all fields."

And so the Cominform was born under Zhdanov's aegis—on a solid anti-American platform.

Malenkov, dealing with Soviet party affairs, was even forced to pay lip service to Zhdanov's pet project, the literary purge; he hailed "the measures adopted by the Central Committee which aim at the triumph of a militant Soviet patriotic spirit among scientists and art workers." He said that these measures strengthened "adherence to Party principles in science, literature, and art, and at raising to new and higher levels all vehicles of Socialist culture—the press, propaganda, science, literature, and art."

Zhdanov's Europe-oriented policy in 1946–1947 favored establishment of a Balkan Communist federation. Greece, subdued by Communist guerrilla forces with aid from neighboring Communist countries, was to be included in the federation. Guerrilla war in Greece began in mid-1946. The federation scheme's foremost spokesmen were Marshal Tito of Yugoslavia and Georgi Dimitrov, Communist Premier of Bulgaria. With Yugoslavia the strongest member of any such federation, the plan would have greatly strengthened Tito.

Planning proceeded with Zhdanov's approval through 1947. Dimitrov outlined the scheme even to outsiders, such as Robert Kleinman, correspondent of *World Report*. Quoted in the magazine on June 17, 1947, Dimitrov referred to the federation plan as "music for the future." He envisaged a federation of Yugoslavia, Bulgaria, and Albania, adding that it might later be expanded to include "several other nations—Romania, Poland, Czechoslovakia, perhaps Hungary and perhaps Greece, after the present regime is changed." Dimitrov outlined the federation in detail in Bucharest on January 16, 1948, and his speech was printed in Moscow's *Pravda,* although without comment.

Meanwhile, the Yugoslav Communists and Moscow split on the delicate issue of Soviet espionage within the Yugoslav Communist hierarchy. Marshal Tito observed that a member of his party's Central Committee, Andreja Hebrang, was turning accounts of committee meetings over to the Soviet ambassador. Tito protested to Moscow, and the situation began to deteriorate rapidly.

Zhdanov, in backing the federation scheme, had thus been guilty of advancing a plan that would have given the rebellious Tito immense power. On January 28, therefore, *Pravda* carried an article heavily critical of the federation proposal. One scholar, Boris I. Nicolaevsky, believes that the *Pravda* statement was "personally prepared by Stalin with the aid of Malenkov." Nicolaevsky, writing in *The New Leader* on March 30, 1953, describes this episode as "the turning point in the struggle between Malenkov and Zhdanov."

Certainly, Zhdanov's position began to weaken early in 1948. Although he attended the Cominform meeting in Bucharest in June of that year, Malenkov appears to have begun to overshadow him even then. It was Malenkov, for instance, who made the decision of how to deal with General Markos (Markos Vafiades), the Greek Communist guerrilla leader, who had worked closely with Tito. Malenkov suggested that Markos be lured from Greek territory and arrested. The actual arrest was arranged by General Vsevolod N. Merkulov, now Soviet Minister of State Control. Merkulov advised Markos that he was to attend a political-military meeting at Stelnik, Bulgaria. When he arrived on Bulgarian soil, Markos was arrested on August 3, 1948; but his name continued to appear on Greek guerrilla proclamations until February, 1949, when he was officially replaced.

Yugoslav Communist leaders maintain that Dimitrov initially sided with Tito in his conflict with Moscow. The Yugoslav newspaper *Borba* said on September 29, 1949, that while "passing through Belgrade immediately after the first letter was sent by the Bolshevik party" attacking Tito, "Dimitrov told us, 'stand your ground.'" Georgi Dimitrov died in Moscow in July, 1949. A purge of his followers accused of Tito-ism rocked Bulgaria for more than a year afterward.

Tito's break with Moscow contributed directly to Zhdanov's decline and fall. As the chief Soviet spokesman in the Cominform, Zhdanov had the decisive word in advising Stalin on the break between Moscow and Marshal Tito. His theory that the Yugoslav Communist Party would oust Tito and support Moscow, turned out to be a grave error. Tito solidified his position at home and challenged Soviet power. Clearly, for such faulty judgment, for such grave lowering of Moscow's prestige, someone had to pay. Malenkov was doubtless ready to point out that his antagonist Andrei Zhdanov was deeply responsible for the disaster.

Tito's defiance became public knowledge during the early days of July, 1948. On July 20, Malenkov was back at the Communist Party's secretariat; he signed a party message to the Japanese Communist Party, congratulating Kyuichi Tokuda on surviving an assassination attempt. Four days earlier, shortly after the Tito incident, Stalin himself signed a corresponding message to Italian Communist leader Palmiro Togliatti, who had been similarly wounded.

Malenkov replaced Zhdanov almost immediately following Tito's defiance of Moscow's ill-fated provocation of the independent-minded Yugoslavs. Ana Pauker, Romanian Communist Foreign Minister at the time, advised friends at the Danube Conference in Belgrade in mid-August that Stalin told her of his annoyance with Zhdanov's handling of the Tito affair. She quoted Stalin as saying that the matter would have been handled quite differently had he realized the extent of the support that Tito had within the Yugoslav Communist Party.

The chronology seems clear. Malenkov quickly used the

Yugoslav leader's defection to replace his rival Zhdanov from
his position of power in the Soviet Communist Party. Little
more than a month later, the news came from Moscow:
Zhdanov was dead.

At Zhdanov's funeral, Malenkov once again stood next to
Stalin.

After Zhdanov's death, the star of Malenkov rose without
hindrance. Certainly the man who became Soviet Premier in
1953 benefited immensely from his rival's death. In the Moscow atmosphere of suspicion and terror, the question was
natural: had someone killed Andrei Zhdanov? Had Malenkov
been a party to such an act? As if to forestall these questions,
late though they might be in rising to the surface, a startling
announcement made on January 13, 1953, four years after
Zhdanov died, alleged that a group of "terrorist Jewish doctors" had confessed to killing Zhdanov: "The criminals confessed they made an incorrect diagnosis of his disease and,
concealing the miocardial infraction from which he suffered,
prescribed a regime which was contra-indicated for this serious illness and thereby killed Comrade A. A. Zhdanov."

The accusation named nine doctors, although only four
doctors had signed the Zhdanov death certificate in 1948,
which had said: "For many years Zhdanov suffered high blood
pressure, which was complicated by severe arterio-sclerosis,
especially in vessels supplying the heart. During the last few
years he had frequent attacks of angina pectoris, followed by
cardiac asthma. Death followed from paralysis of the heart,
accompanied by acute emphysema (swelling)."

The nine accused doctors, only six of whom were actually
Jewish, were named as Professors M. S. Vovsi, V. N. Vinogra-

dov, M. B. Kogan, B. B. Kogan, P. I. Yegorov, A. I. Feldman, I. G. Etinger, A. M. Grinstein, and B. I. Mairov. The announcement charged that the death of Zhdanov had been hastened under orders from the United States government, using as its channel to the doctors "the international Jewish bourgeois nationalist organization 'Joint,' set up by the American Intelligence Service. This reference was to the American Jewish Joint Distribution Committee, a charitable organization, whose spokesmen classed the accusation as "too ridiculous for comment."

The announcement accused the nine doctors of having planned the deaths of several other leading Soviet military figures, and added: "Investigation has established that members of this terrorist group, by taking advantage of their position as doctors and by violating the trust of ill people with premeditation, criminally undermined their health and deliberately made incorrect diagnoses and they, by incorrect healing methods, destroyed them."

This charge, coming more than four years after Zhdanov's death but shortly before Malenkov's ascension to power, seemed oddly timed. It became even more significant when its validity was denied by Beria in April, the accused doctors set free, and their accusers arrested.

These events now tend to sharpen interest in the long and deep feud between Malenkov and Zhdanov, and in the repercussions which the struggle between these two men had in all fields of Soviet society. As late as 1952, a footnote to the history of this conflict was written in Czechoslovakia when a group of high Communist Party officials was found guilty of treason and its members condemned to death or imprisonment. This group was headed by Rudolf Slansky, the party's secretary-general. It was the Slansky wing of the party which, in March, 1948, followed Zhdanov's instructions in taking power by coup d'état in Prague. One possible interpretation of these purges of 1952 is that they accomplished the elimination of the Zhdanov group within the Czechoslovak Communist Party. The Czechoslovak Zhdanovites were eliminated by Malenkov's Prague supporter, the then Premier Klement Gottwald. The anti-Semitic note of the trials indicated the Malenkov touch. Slansky's Zhdanovite group was destroyed just after the October congress in Moscow, when Malenkov was at the zenith of his rise, and Beria had temporarily been forced into the background.

Beria set out to redeem this balance at the time of Stalin's death. He wrested the Soviet Ministry of State Security from the hands of Malenkov's protégé Semyon D. Ignatiev, who had handled the satellite purges. That is why the death of Premier Gottwald, only a few days after Stalin's funeral, seemed like a warning signal of Beria's return from the shadows—to restore the balance which Malenkov had upset by his purges of men who owed their political positions to the dead Zhdanov.

5

Years of Crisis

DURING THE YEARS of the Malenkov-Zhdanov feud, some 300,000 members were dropped from the rolls of the Communist Party of the Soviet Union. The seesaw struggle affected the lives of hundreds of Soviet officials, economists, scientists, writers, and artists. Their names are many, but as an illustration, none is more significant than that of Eugene S. Varga, the Hungarian-born economist and veteran of the abortive Communist regime that ruled Hungary for 133 bloody days in 1919.

Varga is a Malenkov man. He suffered volleys of violent abuse when Zhdanov enjoyed full power. He was denounced as a quack, a traitor to the Bolshevik cause, a fool and a charlatan. His economic research institute was dissolved; his name all but disappeared from the Soviet press.

Under Malenkov, Varga has made a full comeback. He is the kind of hard-working, skilled technician Malenkov professes to like. During the 1920s and 1930s, Varga was top economist of the Communist International. His Marxist-Leninist analyses of world economic affairs were published by Communist organs throughout the world. At the end of World War II, he laid down the economic party line in a magnum opus entitled *Changes in the Capitalist Economy as a Result of the Second World War*. This book was completed in 1946 and circulated confidentially among Soviet officials.

It was published in 1947 by the Institute of World Economics and World Politics in Moscow, of which Varga was director.

Nothing in Mr. Varga's book seemed to vary greatly from what might have been expected from a Moscow economist at that time. He forecast a serious crisis in the "capitalist" countries, although he cited factors likely to delay such a crisis for several years after the war. On October 7, 1947, while Zhdanov was at the height of his influence, *Pravda* reported that Varga's Institute of World Economics had been merged with the Institute of Economics of the Soviet Academy of Sciences. Dr. Konstantin V. Ostrovityanov was named director of the new body; he was a Zhdanov man.

The anti-Varga campaign gathered momentum. It involved scores of Soviet economists; articles and reviews in the Moscow magazine *Planned Economy* echoed the controversy. Varga was denounced from all sides. The debate soon grew abstruse, exceedingly technical, and at times lost all contact with economic reality. Communist theoreticians outside the Soviet Union were hard put to interpret the controversy.

Together with that of Varga, another name should be remembered in connection with the Zhdanov-Malenkov power struggle—Nikolai A. Voznesensky, who was originally an associate of Zhdanov in Leningrad. After his transfer to Moscow he became a protégé of Malenkov, who arranged Voznesensky's appointment to the strategic State Defense Committee in 1942. However, Voznesensky appears to have counted on Zhdanov's ultimate victory over Malenkov. When his former Leningrad boss returned to Moscow from his war jobs, Voznesensky allied himself with Zhdanov against Malenkov. The reward for what must have seemed pure betrayal to Malenkov, was high: Voznesensky, in Zhdanov's 1947 heyday, became a full-fledged Politburo member.

Voznesensky led the pack against Varga, the Malenkov economist. From his exalted position as chairman of the State Planning Commission, and director of the Five-Year Plan, he castigated Varga's ideas. In his book *War Economy of the U.S.S.R. during the Patriotic War*, published in 1947, Voznesensky attacked Varga, without deigning to mention his name, as a "wocbcgone economist" and a "theoretician who thinks he is a Marxist" but writes "nonsense not worthy of attention." While his backer Zhdanov was powerful and alive, Voznesensky was safe. His work as Five-Year Plan administrator seemed satisfactory. He was the youngest member of the Politburo, an up-and-coming figure in the top Soviet bureaucracy.

But less than half a year after Zhdanov's death, Voznesensky's career came to a sudden and complete end. On March 14, 1949, he was dropped from the Politburo. He was stripped of his title as Vice-chairman of the Council of Minister and was replaced as chairman of the State Planning Commission.

A number of men who were demoted following Zhdanov's death were able to make amends, and then eventually made comebacks in the Soviet hierarchy. But the double-crossing Voznesensky disappeared completely. Quite obviously, Malenkov was making an example of the Five-Year Plan boss. Voznesensky's fate was a warning to anyone who imagined that Malenkov could be trifled with.

Just as, when Zhdanov failed, Malenkov moved upward, so did Voznesensky's fall from favor bring good fortune to Eugene Varga. The day after Voznesensky was dropped from all his posts, Varga was given the opportunity of publicizing his views in a letter to *Pravda*. In this letter, published March 15, 1949, Varga repudiated charges that he was a man of Western orientation. He said that such a classification was equal to being accused of being a "counter-revolutionary, anti-Soviet traitor to the working class" and he denied these accusations vehemently. With his antagonist Voznesensky removed, Varga was able to call the accusations against him comparable to "the worst examples of Hitler and Goebbels propaganda." He also recalled that, back in 1947, he had attacked the United States foreign-aid program, the Marshall Plan, and that this proved his Soviet orthodoxy.

From then on, Varga made a quick comeback and the Zhdanov faction was forced to retreat. The man who had succeeded Varga in 1947, K. V. Ostrovityanov, now came under attack from *Culture and Life,* the organ of the party's agitation and propaganda section. Ostrovityanov was accused, among other things, of using an alleged conversation between Karl Marx and the German Communist leader Karl Liebknecht as a Communist Party document—whereas Marx had died when Liebknecht was only twelve years old. But Ostrovityanov was permitted to recant later and unlike Voznesensky, managed to make a comeback.

Meanwhile, Varga re-emerged as the Soviet Union's leading economist. In early 1950, he was commissioned by the Communist Party of the Soviet Union to prepare a major theoretical economic work. On May 10, 1950, *Pravda* published a long article by Varga entitled "The Economics of the Capitalist Countries under the Blows of the U.S. Monopolies." The ideas expressed in this article anticipated and corresponded to those expressed in Premier Stalin's *Economic Problems of Socialism in the U.S.S.R.,* published on the eve of the 1952 party congress.

After Zhdanov's death in the fall of 1948, Malenkov systematically eliminated the "Zhdanovites" from public life. Dur-

One Dead, One Vanished: On May 1, 1948, Malenkov walked between N. A. Voznesensky and Andrei Zhdanov on their way to the Lenin Mausoleum, Moscow, to celebrate May Day. Today Zhdanov is dead and Voznesensky has not been heard from since 1949. (*Credit: Sovfoto.*)

The First Deputy Premiers: Lavrenti P. Beria, Vyacheslav A. Molotov, Marshal Nikolai A. Bulganin, Lazar M. Kaganovich. (*Credit: Sovfoto.*)

ing this campaign, Voznesensky became to Malenkov what Trotsky was to Stalin. To perpetuate Voznesensky's ideas became sheer heresy. To be accused of keeping Voznesensky's theories alive, meant one thing for certain: the accused had incurred Malenkov's displeasure. Voznesensky's name was not mentioned in the Soviet press from late 1949 until December, 1952.

One man who was caught in the middle of this battle was Georgi D. Alexandrov. From 1940 to 1947 he had been Zhdanov's deputy in the Communist Party's Propaganda and Agitation Department. Zhdanov dismissed him in 1947, accusing him of being a "prisoner" of "bourgeois philosophy." Just what, in the Zhdanov-Malenkov struggle, Alexandrov's position had been, cannot be clearly determined.

At any rate, under Malenkov, Alexandrov got his old job back. But things did not work out too well. Perhaps his seven years of service under Zhdanov made Alexandrov, in Malenkov's eyes, a doubtful risk. A July, 1949, issue of the magazine *Bolshevik* was postponed suddenly. On July 13, the Communist Party's Central Committee published a secret decree concerning the party's main theoretical organ and its editorial board. Alexandrov, a fellow board member, and the editor of the magazine were removed.

The delayed issue of *Bolshevik,* when finally published, revived the attack against Alexandrov in just about the terms the Zhdanov group had used earlier, but this time with Malenkov's obvious approval. The party's decree, not made public until December, 1952, said that "the editors of the journal *Bolshevik* made a serious mistake by offering the pages of the journal for servile glorification of N. Voznesensky's book," and "publicizing it, without any ground for so doing, as a textbook and as a profound scientific investigation." The Malenkov-sponsored decree said that "editorial workers of *Bolshevik* went so far in their servility as to insert, contrary to the desire of writers, quotations from N. Voznesensky's book into articles by these writers."

In such fashion is the memory of Voznesensky invoked whenever Malenkov wants to put an opponent in his place. During the critical period between the October, 1952, party congress and Stalin's death, the Voznesensky controversy was once again revived. Some of the men who had roused Malenkov's ire back in 1949 had meanwhile made their way back to influential positions—among them Varga's old antagonist, Konstantin V. Ostrovityanov. In 1953, Ostrovityanov was chairman of a meeting, held from January 9 to 11, under the auspices of the All-Union Society for the Dissemination of Political and Scientific Knowledge. For the most part, the participants accused themselves of errors in accepting and publicizing the Voznesensky book. A day after the meeting closed, *Pravda* accused three leading economists, associated with the magazine *Economic Problems,* of having failed to "overcome fully and to the end," alien and mistaken "subjectivist distortions of the Voznesensky type."

The Varga-Voznesensky feud had started as a shadow of the fight for power between Malenkov and Zhdanov. Eventually, being accused of favoring Voznesensky became identical with blocking Malenkov's path. The whole economics feud had numerous parallels in other sections of Soviet life. Both Zhdanov and Malenkov utilized controversies in special fields to mask their maneuvering of people, the ousting of opponents, and the placing of favorites in controlling positions.

Zhdanov had used this tactic in 1946 by pouring vitriolic criticism on allegedly nonconformist writers and artists, on "cosmopolites," and so forth. During the two years that followed, scores of Soviet artists and writers saw their careers destroyed, their works violently castigated, their motives impugned. One man, however, survived the cultural holocausts of the postwar area unscathed. He is the novelist Alexander A. Fadeyev, head of the Union of Soviet Writers, and his case is an interesting one.

Fadeyev was prominent in organizing a series of so-called "peace" conferences outside the Soviet Union. In this capacity, he made the keynote speech at the Cultural and Scientific Conference for Peace, which took place in the spring of 1949 at New York's Waldorf-Astoria Hotel. Fadeyev appears to have been low enough on the administrative ladder to have the purge storms pass over his head. Or, perhaps, he just proved himself extremely adaptable during the transition from the Zhdanov to the Malenkov period.

Fadeyev became a target of Zhdanov's literary wrath in 1947. It was Fadeyev's novel *The Young Guard,* published in 1945, which aroused the wrath of the Zhdanov group. The novel described the guerrilla activities of young Communist students in the Don coal basin during the war against Germany. The critics praised it, the book achieved mass distribution, and stage and film versions were widely shown. For two years it was held up as a model for Soviet writers. Then suddenly the novel was attacked for giving insufficient prominence to Old Bolsheviks, and for being otherwise "incorrect." While the Zhdanov-Malenkov feud raged, Fadeyev revised the book, and a new version, 150 pages longer, was eventually published in 1951. The changes are revealing.

Although the corrected version is still called *The Young Guard,* the young Communists are shunted out of central roles and replaced by Communist veterans. Instead of disorganization and panic, there is now careful planning and cool generalship by the party command. In the original text of 1945, Fadeyev described the evacuation of the coal city of Krasnodar by saying: "In all the city blocks adjoining the mine, panic swirled like a tornado. . . . The whole crowd shouted, swore, wept, jabbered, clanged."

Six years later, his memory jogged by the party, Fadeyev deletes the reference to panic. His jabbering crowd had vanished and is replaced by "columns of workers, alternating with trucks, carrying the property of the enterprises and establishments of Krasnodar." Instead of shouting, they now move "silently, with somber faces." "The leaders of the columns," who did not exist in the original version, keep the traffic moving in orderly fashion.

Also, in the original edition, Fadeyev wrote that "the Soviet military people at the front still had not learned to utilize those modern machines and men trained in production that were placed at their disposal." In the revised edition this passage is deleted, and instead we read: "Our soldier is better than the enemy soldier . . . simply in the material sense. Our commanders are immeasurably more competent, not only because of their political awareness, but also on account of their military education, their ability to grasp new things quickly."

There were other substantial changes. All of them showed that Fadeyev could adapt his writing to the dictates of whoever happened to be the party's literary oracle.

Certainly, Alexander Fadeyev showed in October, 1952, that he was conscious of Malenkov as the commanding figure at the Nineteenth Communist Party Congress. Malenkov demanded that writers portray Soviet men and women of the "new type" in "all their splendor and human dignity," and to contrast them with "ulcers and vices to which capitalism gives rise." In other words, he called for pamphleteering and caricature rather than literary truth. This was Malenkov's first expression of his theory of the "typical" in art, which is discussed more fully in a later chapter. Fadeyev's speech before the same congress was truly remarkable. Although Fadeyev paid tribute to the Soviet Premier, he quoted Stalin only three times and Malenkov five. To show the thoroughness of his indoctrination he even referred back to the 1946 party resolution on culture but, of course, was careful not to mention Zhdanov's name.

In a reference which, in this context, might well have been directed against lingering opposition to Malenkov, Fadeyev said that Soviet literature has the task of "unmasking the enemies of our cause in our country, the thieves, careerists, booklickers, bureaucrats, frauds, individualists, and grabbers of all kinds. . . . Comrade Malenkov was completely right when he outlined the new struggle of Soviet literature. . . . In Comrade Malenkov's report the shortcomings of our literature have been thoroughly unmasked." And, he continued, "of paramount importance for Soviet art as a whole is the thesis, developed in Comrade Malenkov's report, of the typical features and characters of our reality and of the weakness with which these typical characteristics are brought out in our literature. . . . The need for training the cadres to which Comrade Malenkov referred, applies to a large extent also to the cadres in the Writers Union." Finally, "We consider as yet another expression of the assistance the party is rendering in the development of literature, the straightforward, true, and passionate criticism which Comrade Malenkov voiced in his report."

Reading the Fadeyev speech, one might possibly conclude that Malenkov had replaced Stalin, at least as arbiter of

Soviet literary values, as long ago as the fall of 1952. One
thing is certain: this obsequious novelist could pay homage
and sacrifice his art with equal ease to either of these bureaucratic literati.

From mid-1948 on, a science controversy raged in the
Soviet Union. It began in genetics and spread to nearly every
other field of the natural sciences, including medicine. The
genetics phase of the controversy, the first and most widely
publicized, began with a meeting of the Lenin Academy of
Agricultural Science. At this meeting, on July 31, 1948, the
Malenkov favorite, Trofim D. Lysenko, submitted a report
that had the backing of the Communist Party. From that
moment on, Lysenko was the most influential scientist of the
Soviet Union. An American authority and Nobel prize winner, Dr. H. S. Muller, professor of zoology at Indiana University has described the Lysenko doctrine as "a mystical per-
fecting-principle" based on "no properly documented, controlled, or repeatable factual evidence."

Here, once again, the chronology is important. The Academy's meeting had been planned while Zhdanov was still a
strong figure in top Soviet leadership. When Malenkov replaced him, following the Tito debacle, Malenkov may have
revamped the itinerary and content of the conference on short
notice. At any rate, the issues that arose were hardly more
than camouflage for a demonstration of Malenkov's power
in an important stratum of Soviet society. Relying on Lysenko
in a hurry, Malenkov may have been led to make decisions
he later regretted; this would account for subsequent cautiously publicized criticisms of Lysenko's theories.

In the fall of 1948 and through 1949, Lysenko's crudely
and exclusively environmental ideas on the propagation of

species were supreme. It was Lysenko's claim that he had grafted a yellow-fruited tomato stalk on a red variety, and caused the vine to grow red fruit. He denounced as a "bourgeois fraud" the science of genetics as fathered by the Austrian Gregor Mendel and advanced by Thomas Hunt Morgan, the American Nobel prize-winning biologist who developed the theory that the nature of the genes within the chromosome is a decisive factor in human heredity. According to Lysenko, citing Marxist chapter and verse, dialectical materialism indicates that environment is the prime factor determining the characteristics of an individual.

By the time Malenkov became Premier in 1953, the Lysenko theory had run its course. Perhaps Malenkov regretted that, under pressure of time and circumstance, he had permitted this quack to become the virtual dictator of Soviet science. Such disillusionment would explain the changed status of Zhdanov's son, Yuri Zhdanov. In 1948, young Zhdanov had been ousted from his position as chief of the Communist Party's Science section. Four years later, he was restored to this position.

But the Lysenko case did serve at least one purpose for which it was intended: it gave Malenkov the opportunity to reshuffle Soviet academic society from top to bottom. It is perhaps revealing that Malenkov should have fallen for Lysenko's extreme environmental approach; it is part of his personality pattern always to seek to impose his control, or the control of the society with which he is identified, even on nature.

Perhaps this is also the reason why the conditioned-reflex findings in humans and animals of the noted Soviet physiologist Ivan P. Pavlov have been extended, in Soviet science, to subjects completely outside Dr. Pavlov's field. The works of

Charles Darwin have been revised to fit the Soviet line that man can change nature to serve his needs.

Malenkov's tendency to favor such schools of thought go hand in hand with his constant, almost compulsive, emphasis on getting results by sheer force. Thus he could easily be attracted to theories that promised results by forced growth, by controlled conditions of environment. On one hand, this tendency would make him favor such relatively harmless experiments as cloud seeding and rain-making. On the other, on a dangerously ambitious level, he, like the Nazis before him, might see merit in breeding a superrace by controlled selection.

6

Beria and Molotov

GEORGI MALENKOV became Premier of the Soviet
Union after Stalin's death, by-passing men who were his
elders and who had long histories as professional revolution-
aries. Among them were the four men who became deputy
premiers: Lavrenti P. Beria, Minister of the Interior; Vyacheslav M. Molotov, Foreign Minister; Marshal Nikolai A. Bulganin, War Minister; and Lazar M. Kaganovich, to whom no
specific ministry was assigned.

On the day of Stalin's funeral service, these top officials
climbed in a single file to the top of the Lenin-Stalin tomb in
Moscow's Red Square. First came Malenkov, then Beria. Next,
the Chinese Communist representative Chou En-lai mounted
the steps. He was followed by Marshal Bulganin, and only
then Molotov. Finally came Nikita Khrushchev, a secretary of
the party's Central Committee, followed by Kaganovich.

Over and over again, as announcement followed announcement and ceremony followed ceremony, Malenkov's name
was immediately followed by that of Beria. Together, the two
men represented the strongest internal forces of the Soviet
Union: the Communist Party machinery, and the powerful
secret police. Molotov commanded no such forces. His years
spent in dealing with world affairs, his extensive trips abroad,
had prevented him from winning the allegiance of a supporting apparatus within the Soviet Union. Marshal Bulganin

represented the armed forces, and thus in theory potential strength in a possible showdown of power. More accurately, Bulganin represented the party's army within the army: the staff of political commissars.

Behind these five top Soviet officials stood a large array of newly reshuffled officials. These were men who, in some cases, had been in and out of Kremlin favor, in and out of various tough jobs in the party, the government administration, industry, and the armed forces. These were men who would play important roles in the delicate balance of power and personalities that had helped Malenkov to reach the top. They would demand constant skillful readjustment—in the manner of a tightrope walker who has to shift his weight just slightly to one side and then another, forward and backward, almost imperceptibly but nevertheless sufficiently to assure stability.

The men who walked up to the reviewing stand atop the Lenin-Stalin tomb were representative of large and shifting forces within the Soviet Union. The mute mass of the Soviet people—of Russians, Ukrainians, Byelorussians, Moslems, and many other groups—was, after all, to be considered a potential power. The vast and delicate machinery of the party, the secret police, the government bureaucracy in Moscow and the various Soviet republics, of the army and navy,— all these were channels toward the hopes and fears of millions. Even in a dictatorship, and particularly a dictatorship of delicate balance, the mood of the people—like swift currents beneath the placid surface of the sea—must be constantly gauged and responded to.

Malenkov and Beria had become the most powerful men in the Soviet Union, officially as well as in fact. They had been powerful before, but their new leadership translated this reality into the more formal trappings of power. How had they come to this point in their life histories? How had the relationships between the three men—Malenkov, Beria, Molotov—brought them to a point of power balance? What manner of men were these comrades, antagonists, rulers, and rivals?

First, Beria. The face is familiar: the passive pseudo-scholarly face with pince-nez, the thin lips, the partly bald head, the precise bearing, the measured voice of the man who is a shrewd administrator rather than an orator. Beria may well have gone through a last-minute struggle with members of an army clique that hoped to benefit during intrigues that preceded Stalin's death. But his career had prepared him well to weather such storms.

Lavrenti Pavlovich Beria is the last in a long succession of secret-police administrators. In czarist days, the Okrana (Guard) served to spy upon citizens, to arrest them, hold them incommunicado, spirit them away into oblivion. Under Lenin, Felix Dzerzhinsky headed the Cheka. He was succeeded, in 1926, by Vyacheslav R. Menzhinsky, who was assassinated in 1934. The post was then taken by Genrikh Y. Yagoda whose name to this day conjures up pictures of horror and cruelty. It was he who developed the slave-labor camps that became a central factor in successive Five-Year Plans.

Yagoda was finally crushed by the terror machine he helped to build. During the Moscow purges of the mid-thirties he was accused of trafficking with conspirators. After he was shot, the *Soviet Encyclopedia* belatedly claimed that his predecessor Menzhinsky "was treacherously slain in 1934 on the orders of the provocateur and Fascist, Yagoda, to serve the purposes of the Trotskyite bloc." Then, for two violent years, the Soviet secret police was directed by Malenkov's one-time superior, Nikolai Yezhov. In 1938, Beria was brought by Stalin from his home region, Georgia, and the long Beria regime began.

Lavrenti Beria's predecessors were all, in varying degrees, madmen. They seemed to act out paranoid drives, revenges upon society, sadistic tastes. Not so Beria. Somewhat like Stalin, he has used terror as a matter of course, coldly, thoroughly, extensively. He appears to believe that a giant police state needs a great amount of terroristic pressure simply to keep from breaking apart. And so, tortures and imprisonment and death are everyday enforcement tools under the Beria system.

He was born March 29, 1899, in the Georgian village of Merkheuli. He came from peasant stock, attended the Polytechnical Institute at Baku, and graduated as a draftsman and engineer. He joined the Bolsheviks in 1917. He was successively a Cheka operative in Soviet Azerbaijan and in his native Georgia. He rose, both in the Cheka and in the Communist Party, to become the Georgian party's first secretary in 1931.

At the Seventeenth Soviet Communist Party Congress in 1934, Beria was appointed to the party's Central Committee. Four years later he became a Politburo nominee; the same year he was made secret-police chief. From 1941 to 1946, Beria was officially Commissar General for National Security. He retained control of the Ministry of the Interior (MVD) and the Ministry of State Security (MGB) from then on.

Beria, according to the historian Mark Vishniak, is "interested in painting, music, and architecture," is married and has children. It is difficult to associate the cruel secret-police machinery with the outwardly mild-mannered Beria. His pince-nez makes him appear schoolteacherish. He seems fussy, meticulous, retiring. Unlike his Nazi counterpart Heinrich Himmler, Beria rarely favored a uniform. He wears conservative civilian clothes and a felt hat often pulled way down over his face. He is of medium height, slightly on the stout side. His manner and speech are quiet.

His career and mannerisms suggest that he prefers the reality of power to its outward trappings. He always stood just one step behind Stalin, as he now stands half a step behind Malenkov. Despite his outward demeanor, he has very likely for years been the most hated man in the Soviet Union, a country where there is much reason for hate. Beria personifies the secret police visit at dawn; wild accusations and sadistic interrogations; years of forced labor on the basis of trifling charges; camps that are a living death; and death itself. But in front of this tapestry of horror stands Lavrenti Beria— quiet, unassuming, holding the fate of millions in his hands.

Beria was personally close to Stalin, his confidante and associate. Even so, the sudden death of Andrei Zhdanov in 1948 must have eased Beria's position in the Soviet hierarchy. The dynamic Zhdanov eclipsed Beria immediately after the war—perhaps more obviously than he overshadowed Malenkov. Evidence of this came whenever huge portraits of Soviet leaders decorated city squares, buildings, or parades. Molotov was consistently shown on Stalin's right; Beria and Zhdanov competed for the left-hand position. As a favorite son, Beria was given the choice spot in such old stamping grounds as the Caucasus; but he had to yield to Zhdanov in the Leningrad area.

This seriocomic dilemma was ingeniously solved during the anniversary of the Bolshevik Revolution, November 7, 1947: early in the day, some of the buildings showed Beria on Stalin's left, others featured Zhdanov. But the solution lasted for only a few hours. Later in the day workmen changed the layout, so that Molotov, Beria, and Zhdanov formed a semi-circle beneath the Premier's picture.

After Zhdanov's death, Beria achieved new prominence. On March 29, 1949, his fiftieth birthday, he was awarded the Order of Lenin. The press hailed him, *Pravda* and *Izvestia* publishing a two-column portrait on their front pages. The Central Committee of the Communist Party and the Council of Ministers sent him a congratulatory message which said: "We warmly congratulate you, a true pupil of Lenin and colleague of Comrade Stalin, on your fiftieth birthday. All your conscious life you have devoted to the revolutionary battle for the cause of the working class and to the victory of Communism."

On November 6, 1951, Beria gave the keynote speech at the Moscow Soviet's celebration of the Revolution. It was the year's most important address by any Soviet leader; it showed that Beria's star was shining brightly. At no time has there been any sign of conflict between Beria and Malenkov. Such clash of interest might have developed after Zhdanov's death, which cleared the road to power for both of them; but there is no evidence of disagreement. Zhdanov's death, on the contrary, seems to have strengthened their unity of interest.

Whether Malenkov tried to whittle down Beria after the Party Congress of October, 1952, is not clear. It cannot be ruled out that, for a period, army elements allied themselves with Malenkov to weaken or neutralize Beria's influence. When, early in 1953, the alleged murder of Zhdanov by a group of doctors was publicized, this news was coupled with attacks on security forces and with the statement that prominent army men had been slated to suffer Zhdanov's fate. At that time, it was felt that these attacks constituted a warning and were directed against Beria and his secret police. When, on April 6, Beria denounced the accusations against the doctors, he attacked the Malenkov protégé Semyon D. Ignatiev. This suggested that Beria, by gaining control of both the Ministry of Interior and the Ministry of State Security, had forced out Ignatiev, who had been Security Minister in January. Ignatiev had succeeded Victor S. Abakumov, a Beria appointee, in 1951 or 1952. It appeared that Malenkov had, before the 1952 Party Congress, weakened Beria by eliminating Abakumov; and in April, 1953, Beria redressed the power balance by striking at Malenkov through the person of Ignatiev.

There is also substantial reason for long-standing antagonism between Soviet army leaders and the security police. Beria's organization represents a powerful mixture of armed strength and commercial resources. It is both an army outside the army and a giant manufacturing and trading enterprise. In manpower, Beria commands an estimated full-time force of about 1,700,000; an increase of nearly half a million over prewar strength. Some 650,000 Beria men are believed·to be employed in border control. Others serve in regional command posts, forced-labor camps, and administrative offices. Some 350,000 are assigned to militia duties and this militia is independent of the Soviet army.

The secret-police militia is made up of crack troops that are kept ready to meet internal disturbances and are organized into divisions, battalions, and companies. The militia has infantry and light artillery, tanks, and other vehicles that assure mobility. Information on these forces comes from Soviet refugees who have made their way into West Germany;

these informants emphasize that border-control troops of the secret police are organized to meet local conditions and do not follow a nationwide pattern.

Beria's military power is supplemented by secret-police control over a vast segment of Soviet industry. The MVD supervises some 15 million forced laborers. It has built and runs vast enterprises staffed with men and women who have been condemned to forced labor after having been accused of conspiring against the Soviet regime. These helpless, hopeless human beings have been employed in such widely publicized undertakings as the Volga-Don Canal which was completed in 1952.

The Beria system has employed slave laborers in building state housing and defense projects, in highway and railway construction. A large number of forced laborers are employed in Siberian gold mines. Early in World War II, the secret-police enterprises were responsible for building nearly one-quarter of the railway system then constructed. They also mined nearly 3 per cent of the Soviet Union's coal, cut 12.5 per cent of its timber, mined more than 40 per cent of the chromite, and were responsible for three-quarters of the gold output.

In 1940 and 1941, secret-service enterprises used forced labor in finishing 14 per cent of the country's capital construction, amounting to over 2 billion rubles annually—more than any other single ministry. Since then, although he operates supposedly only to safeguard state security, Beria may have expanded his industrial activities. Aside from the obvious advantages he derives from maintaining an espionage apparatus among civilians, inside the Communist Party and the armed forces, Beria commands perhaps close to one-fifth of the Soviet Union's internal economic power.

As an antagonist, Malenkov must therefore find Lavrenti Beria a most serious obstacle. The Soviet Premier needs Beria as the man whose support, more than that of anyone else, assures the relative permanence of his position. Beria has certainly preserved the outward amenities, avoiding any open expression of hostility toward Malenkov. He "nominated" Malenkov at the Supreme Soviet's session on March 15, 1953. Beria went out of his way to appear much more kindly inclined toward Malenkov than did Foreign Minister Vyacheslav M. Molotov.

Beria's and Molotov's differing tactics toward Malenkov were vividly illustrated when the three men made their funeral orations for Stalin atop Lenin's tomb. Mr. Beria spoke of the measures which the regime had taken "toward ensuring uninterrupted and correct leadership of the whole life of the country." He added: "One of the most important decisions is the appointment to the post of the Chairman of the Council of Ministers of the U.S.S.R. of the talented pupil of Lenin and the faithful comrade in arms of Stalin, Georgi Maximilianovich Malenkov." Bolstering Malenkov further, Beria said that these decisions "adopted by the highest party and state organs of our country were a vivid expression of the complete unity and singleness of the leadership of the party and state."

Five days later, at the meeting of the Supreme Soviet that agreed to the changes in government, Molotov did not even speak. It was Beria who urged the deputies to endorse Malenkov, whom he called "a talented disciple of Lenin and loyal comrade-in-arms of Stalin." He expressed his "firm conviction" that the Soviet government, headed by G. M. Malenkov, will direct the entire work of building communism in our country, according to the teachings of Lenin and Stalin.

But while Beria officially hailed Malenkov, the speaker

who followed him as Stalin's funeral orator did not even mention the name of Malenkov. That speaker was Vyacheslav Molotov, the man who had been long regarded by many as Stalin's most logical successor. How strong this feeling had been was illustrated in an article which the former Soviet official Victor A. Kravchenko published in *The Saturday Evening Post* of March 22, 1947. Speaking of Stalin's most likely successor, Kravchenko said: "I cannot imagine his being anyone but Molotov. . . . I never once met a person of any standing who doubted for a minute that Molotov, if he lived, would succeed Stalin on the latter's death. Certainly I met no one of any importance who seriously believed that Stalin's successor would be either Andrei Zhdanov or Georgi Malenkov. . . ."

Mr. Kravchenko's estimate was representative of widely held opinion—including, no doubt, the opinion of Molotov himself. Surely Molotov must have considered himself Malenkov's senior in every conceivable respect. Malenkov became Premier when he was fifty-one, at which time Molotov was sixty-three years of age. Malenkov was, relatively speaking, an upstart in Soviet society, while at the time of Stalin's death, Molotov had been an active revolutionary for nearly half a century. He was born in 1890, and named Vyacheslav Mikhailovich Scriabin. Later, like many another revolutionary, he adopted a name considered fitting for a tough rebel: Molotov—the Hammer. He became a Bolshevik when only a sixteen-year-old student. He took part in the abortive revolution of 1905, was arrested and temporarily exiled in the spring of 1909. Living in the city of Kazan, he became one of the "Kazan Bolsheviks," a doctrinaire Communist group. Molotov was a humble and earnest boy, overwhelmed by the brilliance and learning around him.

His special friend in Kazan was the well-to-do Victor Tikhomirnov. Molotov fitted himself obediently into the revolutionary machinery which demanded both subservience and iron discipline. Tikhomirnov visited V. I. Lenin in Switzerland in 1911. A year later, the rich young man put up 100,000 rubles to found a small paper, named *Pravda*, in St. Petersburg. Molotov became editor, with Stalin guiding the paper from a hideout.

Molotov was twenty-two years old when he met Stalin for the first time. Their acquaintance was renewed in 1917. After the Bolsheviks took power, Molotov remained attached to Stalin. His first great moment came in 1922, while Lenin was feuding with Leon Trotsky. During a dispute over party leadership, Lenin proposed that Stalin be named General Secretary, with Molotov as his assistant.

From then on, Stalin and Molotov worked as a team, Molotov emerging as Number Two man par excellence. And so it remained, seemingly, until early in 1953. Molotov survived all the purges that came in between, the banishment and death of Trotsky, the elimination from power and the execution of nearly every one of the Old Bolsheviks, those Politburo and Comintern members who had originally shared the helm with Stalin.

In 1930 Molotov became, temporarily, titular head of the Soviet government. He was named chairman of the Council of People's Commissars, the title equivalent to Malenkov's as chairman of the Council of Ministers in 1953. But, back in 1930, Stalin remained unquestionably the source and center of power, being Secretary-General of the Communist Party.

In May, 1939, when the Kremlin was preparing its government machinery for the Nazi-Soviet Pact, the aggressive Molotov replaced the more conciliatory, idealistic Maxim

Litvinov as Foreign Commissar (later, Foreign Minister). In October of that year Molotov delivered perhaps his most startling speech, denouncing the Allied war effort against Nazi Germany. After years of violent anti-Nazi, anti-Fascist oratory, Molotov said:

"The British Government has announced that its aim in the war against Germany is nothing more or less than the destruction of Hitlerism. This means that the British and French have declared something in the nature of an 'ideological' war against Germany, reminiscent of the religious wars of ancient times. There is absolutely no justification for a war of this kind. One may accept or reject the ideology of Hitlerism, as well as any other ideological system—that is a matter of political views. But everyone should understand that an ideology cannot be destroyed by force, that it cannot be eliminated by war. It is therefore not only senseless, but criminal to wage war for the 'destruction of Hitlerism,' camouflaged as a 'fight for democracy.' "

One month before Hitler's armies invaded Germany, Stalin took over the premiership himself, with Molotov in charge of foreign affairs. Molotov remained Foreign Minister until the Kremlin crisis of March, 1949. During that shake-up, Molotov had to give up the Foreign Ministry, although he remained Deputy Premier. Half a year had passed since Zhdanov's death, and Malenkov had been able to consolidate his position. Molotov was not the only one who lost his Ministry post, but he was the most prominent. Quite possibly, the across-the-board reduction of power among Politburo members who were also heads of Ministries obscured the specific facts in the case of Molotov. Clearly, as the shake-up also brought Voznesensky's complete downfall, it involved Malenkov's power drive. We might also assume that Molotov sought to block

Malenkov, while Bulganin and others were more or less neutral during this period.

Stalin may simply have decided that being both Deputy Premiers and Politburo members was enough for members of his entourage. If their power was being reduced a bit, raising the relative importance of Malenkov, that might have been considered by Stalin as all to the good. He doubtless welcomed scrapes and friction within the Kremlin circle; such jealousy and competition permitted no single individual to consider himself without need of Stalin's support. As long as members of the circle feuded among themselves, Stalin could exercise the function of paternal arbiter.

The fact that Molotov ignored Malenkov completely in his funeral oration for Stalin suggests that he had not forgotten the treatment he received in 1949. Even though the Foreign Ministry was given back to him after Stalin's death, it must have been a bitter pill to rank below Malenkov. One reason for Molotov's bitterness must be the great difference in experience and training between the two men. Old Bolshevik Molotov is skilled in the use of Marxist-Leninist vernacular. He is steeped in Bolshevik theory, in dialectical materialism. Newcomer Malenkov has no such qualifications. He can cite no extensive theoretical works to his credit, no volumes of writings and speeches heavy with quotes from Marx, Engels, Lenin, or the more obscure dialecticians that litter the path of Communist history since the Communist Manifesto.

Rather pointedly, Molotov used his funeral oration for Stalin to emphasize the need for Marxist theoretics. He noted that "Stalin always knew how to combine the everyday, difficult activities of a Communist and revolutionary of the working class with a profound study of the theory of Marxism." Recalling the pre-Malenkov revolutionary days, Molotov said: "This is how he was in the early years in Tiflis and Baku. This is how he was in the stormy years of the Russian Revolution and in the difficult years of czarist reaction. . . . Comrade Stalin's exceptional ability as an incomparable organizer of our party and the Soviet state, and as the theoretician and genius of Marxism-Leninism, was fully developed in the years of the Revolution and the building of Socialism."

But Molotov's words received less than half the publicity accorded Malenkov's speech. The Soviet broadcasting network repeated Malenkov's address fifty-four times, Beria's thirty-five times, and Molotov's only twenty-two times.

When Malenkov became Premier, Molotov was sixty-three years old. To be shunted aside like this, must have been disheartening to the man who served the Kremlin patiently and competently for three decades. Behind his stolid face, his glittering pince-nez, his recurring stammer, there must now lie the disappointment of a faithful servant who tended to his master's every whim in the hope of a large inheritance—and who found himself abandoned to the arrogance of the young lord of the manor.

There are many instances illustrating Stalin's contempt for Molotov, of Stalin's utter disregard for his feelings, even before important foreigners. Eric Johnston, then president of the United States Chamber of Commerce, visited Stalin during World War II. Stalin agreed that a group of American correspondents might accompany Johnston on a trip to the Urals. Noting that the Foreign Ministry had not given its permission to the correspondents, Johnston said to Stalin: "But I don't know whether Mr. Molotov will approve." Whereupon Molotov quickly interjected: "I always approve of Marshal Stalin's decisions." Stalin then turned to Johnston and said, smiling, "Mr. Johnston, you really didn't expect Mr. Molotov to disagree with me, did you?"

In spite of these slights, Molotov always was Stalin's second in command, a position in the limelight of prestige and power. Now, after Stalin's death, he has been relegated to third place, shunted into the shadow of the prestige and power of a younger man. Beria, moved up to second place, is stronger than Molotov ever was when he stood next to Stalin. With the power of the secret-police machine at his command, with longer experience than Malenkov, Beria has the strength to be more subtle than Molotov.

Malenkov, it seems clear, cannot openly act against the Interior Minister. Beria alone would be likely to find pressure from Molotov and the army group uncomfortable. Together, Malenkov and Beria are reasonably sure to maintain their positions; divided, they might stumble. So long as Beria does not aspire to the title of Premier or to become President of the Council of Ministers, his alliance with Malenkov appears strong enough to withstand outside pressures; and Beria, who has tasted to the full the reality of power that comes with total terror, may be satisfied with keeping Malenkov in check and maintaining the power balance. Being, like Stalin, of Georgian birth, he may consider his origin a handicap to his succession to the premiership, since the various peoples of the U.S.S.R. might not welcome two consecutive Georgian leaders.

Will the Malenkov-Beria coalition last? Will internal struggles cause Malenkov's early or eventual downfall? These questions were asked, the world over, within days of Stalin's death. But those who questioned, and who then suggested wishful answers, did not consider that the Malenkov regime had been in the making for exactly four years. During that period, Malenkov, Beria, Molotov, and the army clique had taken each other's measure. They had come to realize that they could not openly bring about each other's downfall; that the existence of each group was necessary to retain the delicate balance of Kremlin power.

In addition, the joint interest of all members of the Kremlin hierarchy now lies in presenting a united front to the world. They share the need to have the Soviet "peace offensive" appear as dictated by purely tactical reasons—rather than as an expression of internal weakness and division, as an effort to buy time and win friends while the new Kremlin structure is still shaky.

Although the Soviet leadership's attention was absorbed by internal efforts to keep the Kremlin power balance, it nevertheless managed to organize a series of external "peace" maneuvers in late March and early April. The chronology of these events, beginning with Malenkov's speech before the Supreme Soviet and leading toward stopping the Korean War, suggest that they had been well planned.

The peace offensive generally followed policies of the Nineteenth Party Congress of October, 1952, designed to split the Western allies; it appeared well planned, possibly only delayed by the internal Soviet power struggle before Stalin's death. The Premier's death was the starting signal of a peace offensive, which rather successfully distracted the free world's attention from the internal conflict in the top Kremlin hierarchy.

7

The Army Clique

MARSHAL NIKOLAI A. BULGANIN, although a First Deputy Premier and Minister of War, did not rate high enough in the Malenkov regime to mourn Stalin from the top of Lenin's tomb. There was little reference to the Soviet army in the speeches of Malenkov and Beria. Malenkov merely said in his funeral oration that, "under the direct leadership of Stalin, the Soviet army was created and strengthened." Beria, in an even more offhand remark, simply called for "further strengthening of the economic and military might of the state."

Thus it was left to Molotov to pay glowing tribute to the army. It was Molotov who showed appreciation of the army's officer corps, men who in any future struggle for Kremlin power would make important allies or antagonists. Molotov not only paid tribute to Stalin as wartime army leader, but added: "To be faithful and worthy continuers of Stalin means always to remember and constantly to care about the strengthening of the Soviet Army and Navy, ensuring the worthy preparedness of the Soviet armed forces in the event of any move of the aggressor against our country."

Molotov, it appeared, was making a discreet appeal to the army's officer corps. If so, he was appealing to the army clique over the head of Marshal Bulganin—a man who is much less an army representative in the Kremlin, as a Kremlin representative within the army. The professional officer is more accurately personified in Gregori K. Zhukov who, together with Marshal A. Vassilevsky, is Deputy War Minister under Bulganin.

No one outside the top Soviet leadership circle can pretend to fully understand the relationship between Marshal Zhukov and Georgi Malenkov. They worked side by side during World War II as members of the inner cabinet known as the State Defense Committee. Malenkov was at that time largely responsible for assuring the production of armaments. Zhukov acted as Stalin's deputy, at a time when Stalin had assumed the position of Supreme Commander of all Soviet armed forces.

Former Soviet officers, now living as refugees in West Germany, assert that Zhukov was at one time at odds with Malenkov over the quality and design of certain aircraft models. Malenkov, in his effort to maintain maximum production, had frozen aircraft design. Zhukov is represented as charging that these planes were obsolete when they left the plants.

The chronology of Malenkov's and Zhukov's respective periods of disgrace suggests at least one thing: both had antagonized powerful elements and were demoted when Andrei Zhdanov had reached the peak of his influence. The temporary victory of Zhdanov over Malenkov took place in the early spring and was consolidated in the fall of 1946. Zhukov's demotion from the post of Commander in Chief of all Soviet ground forces took place in April or early May of that year.

Zhukov made a slow comeback after Zhdanov's death. In July, 1951, he was a prominent participant in state ceremonies at Warsaw, Poland. When Malenkov achieved the premiership in March, 1953, Zhukov emerged into the bright Moscow limelight as perhaps the strongest figure in the Soviet War Ministry.

The two Marshals, Zhukov and Bulganin, personify entirely different schools of tradition and purpose within the Soviet army. Bulganin is not at all a professional soldier. He has had no real military career, despite his heavily bemedaled uniform. Bulganin, rather, represents the corps of "political commissars" within the armed forces—and resentment of these commissars is probably the greatest unresolved conflict inside the Soviet military machine.

Nothing illustrates the conflict between the soldiery and the Communist Party's secret services more clearly than the institution, abandonment, reinstitution, reabandonment, and eventual re-reinstitution of the system of political commissars inside the army. This seesawing between the army on the one hand, and the party and the secret police on the other, began during the Bolshevik Revolution—while Malenkov was serving as political commissar in Turkestan—and extended through World War II.

The personalities of Marshals Zhukov and Bulganin reflect their differing careers and viewpoints. Zhukov, although a veteran Communist Party man, holds little brief for hairsplitting theorists. He is a high-tempered, dynamic, egocentric man of action with the face of a bulldog. He became fairly well acquainted with American commanders at the close of World War II. General Eisenhower, who praised Zhukov's military qualities during his presidential campaign in 1952, has observed that he had "a longer experience as a responsible leader in great battles than any other man of our time." General Walter Bedell Smith, now Undersecretary of State in the Eisenhower Administration, has written that he was impressed not only with Zhukov's soldierly ability, but also his "frank and straightforward attitude." He added that, at the end of the war, there was nevertheless "still an arm's length between us in our dealings." Eisenhower never doubted that Zhukov was a "firm believer in the Communist system."

Like Malenkov, Zhukov has a reputation for being exceedingly rough and tough with underlings. He is opinionated and outspoken and, again like Malenkov, quite impatient with bungling and professional ineptitude. Throughout his career he has antagonized a good part of the army's top officers, but the very ebullience of his personality has made him popular in the ranks and among the civilian population.

By comparison, Marshal Bulganin, though quite personable, is a colorless figure. While Zhukov is an experienced and highly successful field commander, Bulganin is mainly an efficient administrator. These administrative abilities were originally those of a state banker and utilities executive. Only during World War II did Bulganin get into uniform, and then as the Kremlin's chief missionary to the political heathens of the armed forces.

The anti-Communist underground radio station, Free Russia, addressing Soviet troops in East Germany and the Soviet Union on March 8, 1953, capitalized on this obvious contrast between Zhukov and Bulganin. The Russian language commentary noted that "Marshal Zhukov, the hero of the Fatherland War, a fighting general before whom the banners of Hitler's army were lowered, has been made a Deputy War Minister" under Bulganin, "who never was a military man and never participated in a single battle."

It is a justifiable guess that Zhukov must view Bulganin with a double dose of contempt: first, because the man whose deputy Zhukov has become never once commanded troops in

a successful battle; and second, because Bulganin represents the deeply disliked army-within-the-army of political
commissars—thought by many regular officers to be spy-
ing, scheming parasites on the body of the Soviet armed
forces.

Zhukov, again somewhat like Malenkov, seems to have a
dark spot in his early life: he was commissioned a junior cavalry officer in the czarist Imperial Army. In the Bolshevik
tradition, czarist officers who switched to the Red Army are
doubtful turncoats, men who bear watching. But Zhukov's
genealogy, at least, is properly proletarian. His parents were
poor peasants and he himself served his apprenticeship as a
leather dresser and furrier.

Zhukov entered the czarist army in 1914. Three years later
his fellow-soldiers elected him to the regimental Soviet. He
joined the Red Army in 1918, the Communist Party in 1919.
During the civil war he won the Order of Lenin and became
protégé of Mikhail Frunze, the Red Army commander who
was at the top of the military ladder when Malenkov was
serving as political worker in Turkestan.

At the end of the civil fighting, Zhukov attended the Frunze
Military Academy to study armored warfare. He became, successively, commander of a regiment, a brigade, a division and
a corps of cavalry. In 1929, Zhukov studied at a German military institute. While other top officers were, during the Moscow trials of the 1930s, accused of dealing with Nazis and
Trotskyists, Zhukov managed to avoid the tangled web of
accusations and purges.

During the Spanish Civil War, Zhukov was one of Moscow's military observers in Spain, testing Russian tanks and
his own theories of armored warfare in actual battle. Zhukov's
next military experience was against the Japanese in Outer

Mongolia in 1939. Undeclared but serious warfare raged between Japan and the Soviets in this strategic inner-Asian territory. Hanson W. Baldwin, writing in *Collier's* in January, 1952, observed that "the importance of these battles to the traditions and psychology of the Red Army, and to its training and growth, never have been understood in America." Zhukov's forces in Outer Mongolia virtually destroyed the Japanese Sixth Army, and he was named Hero of the Soviet Union. He had handled, Mr. Baldwin writes, "for the first time in actual war, mass Soviet armored formations, and had proved the practicability of applying the old cavalry tactics to armor."

During the Soviet attack on Finland in 1939 and 1940, Zhukov had to pull Andrei Zhdanov's chestnuts out of the fire. It was Zhdanov who had assumed that the Finns would collapse quickly, but Zhukov's forces managed to pierce the Mannerheim Line only after weeks of bitter winter fighting. After the Soviet-Finnish armistice, Zhukov took command of the Kiev military district and there made a talk pointedly critical of the political-commissar system, shortly before that system was discontinued.

As Stalin's deputy on the State Defense Committee, Zhukov served the Soviet leader from late 1941 to the fall of 1942. He organized the defense of Stalingrad while Malenkov arrived on the scene to whip up civilian fervor. Zhukov's "Hold or Die!" order carried the day; Stalingrad withstood attack in one of the great battles of history.

At Leningrad, where Zhdanov and Marshal Klimenti I. Voroshilov were at loggerheads, Zhukov sent Voroshilov home and managed to lift the German blockade of the city late in 1941. His other trouble-shooting assignments included the march into Romania. Eventually—and for this he achieved world-wide fame—Zhukov led the triumphant Red Army advance into Berlin.

Every victory added to the impressive array of medals on Zhukov's chest. During a parade in Berlin in the summer of 1945, he wore them all atop a sky-blue dress uniform. He so outshone General George Patton, himself no introvert, that Patton turned to General Lucius Clay, and exclaimed: "Damn it, Lucius! Why didn't you tell me he was going to wear all his medals? I've got just as many as he has, and I would have worn mine!"

In August, shortly after this incident, General Eisenhower visited Moscow, where he briefly met Malenkov. Zhukov accepted an invitation to come to the United States, then canceled his trip abruptly. He had done his job, and now the time had come for Zhukov and other army leaders to step into the background. Andrei Zhdanov had returned to Moscow, and presently the great war hero disappeared into the obscurity of the Odessa regional command. Not until the fall of 1948, following Zhdanov's death, did Zhukov leave Odessa; on November 7 of that year, another officer reviewed the Odessa troops.

One eminent scholar, Boris I. Nicolaevsky, has noted that Zhukov, in 1946, opposed the appointment of Zhdanov's man Colonel-General I. V. Shikin as chief of the army's Political Department, in charge of the political commissars.* Mr.

* *The New York Times* chief foreign correspondent, C. L. Sulzberger, in a dispatch from Paris published June 19, 1949, wrote that General Shikin was "reported to have disappeared during the last few months." The dispatch stated that "Shikin, although little known abroad, was one of the most important figures in the Soviet army administration," adding: "General Shikin was directly linked with Andrei Zhdanov. He went to Leningrad in 1940 as deputy chief of the Leningrad Military District when General Zhdanov was both civil and military commander of that key region. He remained there under General Zhdanov during the first years of the German siege of the city, which began in the late summer of 1941, and had daily dealings with his chief."

Nicolaevsky believes that Zhdanov effected Zhukov's banishment, and that Malenkov reappointed him to the very post
he held in 1946, hoping that "this former ally against Zhdanov
can help him in the future."

It is significant that the Zhukov-Zhdanov break occurred, in
all probability, over the issue of the political commissars. This
issue must be the key, too, in any power struggle between
the Malenkov-Beria alliance and the army clique. The Political Administration, the army-within-the-army, is beholden
to the Communist Party and the secret police; it reports to
Malenkov and Beria—through Marshal Nikolai A. Bulganin.

Born in the town of Gorki in 1895, Bulganin was fifty-eight
years old when Stalin died. He had fought in the Red Army
during the Bolshevik Revolution in Turkestan, and later became a factory director in Moscow. In 1931 he took over the
Moscow city administration as chairman of the Moscow Soviet. In 1937 he was appointed administrative head of the
Soviet State Bank, became a deputy in the Supreme Soviet,
and assistant Communist Party chairman for the Moscow
area.

At the outbreak of World War II, Bulganin was named to
coordinate the commissariats of ferrous metals, nonferrous
metals, cellulose and paper, sulfites, hydraulics, and rubber.
When Moscow was under attack by the armies of Nazi Germany, he ran the city's civilian-defense system. In 1941 Bulganin became Stalin's political trouble shooter within the
army, at a time when the Kremlin subjected the armed forces
to constant indoctrination to make sure that their loyalty to
the Communist Party did not lag. Later Bulganin was political
commissar of the Second Baltic and First White Russian
armies facing Warsaw; he also helped set up the so-called

On the Reviewing Stand: Malenkov and Stalin greet the march-
ers in the Moscow May Day Parade, May 1, 1949. . . . Three
years later, on May 1, 1952, Beria and Malenkov in almost the
same pose for the same celebration. (*Credit: Sovfoto.*)

Stalin's Mourners: On March 8, 1953, Stalin's coffin bearers were (on left) Kaganovich, Bulganin, Molotov, Lt. Gen. Vassily Stalin (Stalin's son), and Malenkov. Beria is on the right. . . . Below, Georgi Malenkov stands beside Stalin's bier in Moscow's Hall of Columns. (*Credit: Sovfoto.*)

"Polish Committee for National Liberation," which ultimately grew into Poland's Communist government. After the war, Bulganin returned to Moscow and eventually replaced Premier Stalin in the War Ministry.

At the beginning of the war, Stalin had made himself head of the Soviet armed forces. He did so on June 30, 1941, four days after Nazi troops crossed the Soviet frontier. On March 3, 1947, Stalin resigned from this post and Bulganin took his place as War Minister; at the same time, he became Deputy Premier.

Bulganin was named to full-fledged membership in the Politburo at a secret meeting of the party's Central Committee. Volume VI of the new *Great Soviet Encyclopedia* stated that he received this distinction at a meeting in February, 1948. He was removed from the War Ministry in March, 1949, shortly after Molotov was removed as head of the Foreign Ministry but both men retained their Politburo positions.

Bulganin's emergence as a "military man" in 1941 coincided with restitution of the system of political commissars which Zhukov and Marshal Semyon Timoshenko had succeeded in ending temporarily. The purges of the late 1930s had been successful in eliminating all possible anti-Stalin opposition from the army, but they had also thoroughly demoralized the army. This demoralization was revealed by the poor performance of Soviet forces in Outer Mongolia and Finland, before Zhukov stepped in. Abolition of the commissar system in 1940 was part of an effort to raise army morale and strengthen a direct line of command.

Yet the Communist Party and the secret police remained distrustful of professional officers. Within a month of the German invasion of Russia, the political commissars made their reappearance through the edict of July 16, 1941. The next two years were extremely critical for the Soviet Union. German advances eroded confidence and discipline even as the political commissars sought to assure the army's loyalty to Stalin. At the same time, behind the regular army stood Beria's own secret-service army, ready to act against mutiny among troops or rebellion among the civilian population.

The Beria army considers itself an elite group superior to the regular troops. While the Germans were attacking successfully, the Kremlin sought to heighten the regular army's vigor by reinstituting rank insignia, shoulder straps, and medals as "patriotic reforms." One secret-service militia man, after escaping from the Soviet Union, in 1947 wrote in the New York Russian-language paper, *Socialist Courier*, that Beria's group in 1942–1943 feared that these "patriotic reforms," which were, in fact, concessions to the regular army troops, would undermine its supremacy and sweep away its privileges.

According to this report, Malenkov, the wartime trouble shooter assured secret-police troops in Stalin's name that "important changes are not contemplated and will not be enacted." He is said to have dwelt on the difficulties of the war situation and stressed that this was no time to bother about trifles. The main objective at that moment was to keep the government's power unchallenged, and this required a good deal of maneuvering. The report added: "Malenkov did not explicitly say so, but the main danger to the party and Stalin was seen as coming from the Red Army, its generals and marshals. This fact was often mentioned in the political instructor's talks with the men, and was the general topic of conversation among us."

The apparent crisis of January, 1953—when deep-running intrigues showed themselves briefly and inconclusively in Moscow announcements—seems to have involved Zhukov. Despite his slow, steady, re-emergence since Zhdanov's death, Zhukov's name did not appear in a detailed listing of army generals who signed an obituary for one of their colleagues in the newspaper *Red Star*. Once again it looked as if Zhukov had tangled with a powerful opponent.

Therefore it is very difficult to determine exactly what Zhukov's relationship to the new regime is to be. Allowing the re-emergence of Zhukov may represent a calculated risk on the part of Premier Malenkov, but one he may deem worth while if the support of the army clique can thus be assured.

Also during the first weeks of 1953, the fantastic story of the plot by "terrorist Jewish doctors" was announced in Moscow. The announcement not only asserted that this group had "confessed" to killing Andrei Zhdanov, but had also been guilty of shortening the life of Alexander S. Shcherbakov, who was Zhdanov's brother-in-law. Before Shcherbakov died in 1945, he had been chief of the army's Political Administration. The truly incredible announcement also alleged that the group of doctors had a number of future victims on their list. All of these supposed targets were army men, namely:

Marshal Alexander M. Vassilevsky, then Soviet War Minister; Marshal Ivan S. Konev, commander of ground forces; Marshal Leonid A. Govorov, commander of the Leningrad army who led Soviet forces in Leningrad during World War II; Admiral G. I. Levchenko, Deputy Minister of the Navy, and General S. M. Shtemenko, who was removed as Chief of Staff of Soviet land forces.

No clarification followed this announcement. No text of

the supposed confessions was released. In fact, the whole matter dropped from the public eye until Beria denounced it two months later. Meanwhile Stalin was dying, and the struggle for power between the ambitious inheritors of Stalin's mantle must have been at its peak.

In truth, the circumstances of top-level intrigues just before Stalin's death—or while Stalin was already dead and the news withheld by the Kremlin palace guard—may never be fully known. To this day, the facts of Lenin's death are in dispute. The truth about a number of mysterious deaths, including that of Stalin's second wife Nadiezhda Alliluyeva (October 10, 1932), is still hidden. The Moscow announcement of the supposed doctors' plot deepens rather than lessens the mystery surrounding Zhdanov's death.

In view of this, speculation as to the real facts is bound to develop. This writer wishes to submit one highly tentative theory, which deals with five elements that may have played a role in Malenkov's struggle for power, and in Stalin's death:

1. Malenkov's effort to extend the allegiance he enjoyed within the machinery of the Soviet Communist Party, and an attempt to weaken Beria.

2. Malenkov's emotional anti-Semitism, and his suspicion that Jewish party officials would not be reliable in their allegiance to him.

3. Soviet army opposition to the political-commissar system, and to the emergence of Malenkov and Beria, representing the party and secret police, as top officials among Stalin's successors.

4. The possible role which Malenkov may have played in bringing about or hastening the deaths of Zhdanov and Stalin.

5. The possible assassination of Alexander Shcherbakov,

head of the hated system of political commissars within the army.

With these five elements in mind, the following supposition may be considered:

In January, 1953, preparations were crystallizing to meet the eventuality of Stalin's death. During the preceding year, Malenkov had instigated the purges that were sweeping Communist parties in the satellite nations, with Jewish officials prominent among the accused. Against this background, the January announcement was designed to achieve the following results:

1. It was to make the "Jewish terrorist doctors" scapegoats for anything that might from then on befall high Soviet officials—particularly in the army and the navy.

2. It was to warn Beria that the apparatus of his secret police was not sacrosanct, and that Malenkov—through his man Ignatiev—might even replace Beria himself, should he refuse to cooperate.

3. It was to facilitate access of other doctors, perhaps of Malenkov's own choosing, to the bedside of the ailing Stalin.

To this must be added that the circumstances of Stalin's death were certainly not without suspicion. The successive communiqués of Stalin's illness were extremely elaborate in their clinical detail; they were signed by eight doctors and went to great lengths in stating the dying man's reported pulse rate, breathing, temperature, and other symptoms. According to Soviet principles of news dissemination, such details were excessive. For years, all news on Stalin's health had been withheld, just as all other information on the personal affairs and habits of Soviet officials are completely hidden behind Moscow censorship. But suddenly all barriers were down, the world was invited to what was represented to be Stalin's deathbed.

Just as unusual was the detailed documentation of the causes of Stalin's death. Because the consequences of Stalin's passing overshadowed this announcement at the time, the full text of this autopsy report is presented here, complete with the names of the eight physicians, as it appeared in the Soviet press:

> The post mortem examination of J. V. Stalin established a large area of hemorrhage in the grey matter of the left hemisphere of the brain. This hemorrhage destroyed vital functions of the brain and resulted in fatal disturbances of respiration and blood circulation. In addition to the cerebral hemorrhage, there were established considerable hypertrophia of the left cardiac ventricle, numerous hemorrhages in the cardiac muscle, and in the mucous membrane of the stomach and intestines, and arteriosclerotic affection of the vessels, particularly pronounced in the brain arteries.
>
> These processes resulted from hypertonicity. Post mortem results fully confirm the diagnosis made by the professors and doctors attending J. V. Stalin. Data of the post mortem examination established the fatal nature of Stalin's illness from the moment the cerebral hemorrhage first occurred. Therefore, the radical measures of treatment could not yield positive results nor avert a fatal outcome.
>
> *Signed:* U.S.S.R. Minister of Health, A. F. Tretyakov; Head of the Health Sanitary Administration of the Kremlin, I. I. Kuperin; President of the U.S.S.R. Academy of Medical Sciences, Academician N. N. Qanichkov; Member of the U.S.S.R. Academy of Medical Sciences, Prof. M. A. Skvortsov; Associate Member of the U.S.S.R. Academy of Medical Sciences, A. I. Strukov; Associate Member of the U.S.S.R. Academy of Medical Sciences, Prof. S. R.

Mardashev; Head of the Pathological-Anatomical Section of the U.S.S.R. Ministry of Health, Prof. B. I. Migunov; Prof. A. V. Rusakov; Docent B. M. Uskov.

This sudden reversal, this excess of detail, where a brief and dignified announcement of the Premier's death would have been completely natural, must raise doubts.

The tentative theory that Malenkov may have taken steps to hasten Stalin's death is given a degree of credence by two authorities: Boris Nicolaevsky and Franz Borkenau.* Nicolaevsky believes that the announcement of the alleged doctors' plot helps to explain Malenkov's possible interest in Stalin's death. Borkenau, in two articles published in the weekly *Rheinischer Merkur,* of Coblenz, Germany, expressed a similar view.

Writing on January 23 and 30, 1953, Borkenau pointed out that only three of the accused doctors had ever been involved in treating top Kremlin leaders; two of these three including Dr. P. I. Yegorov, were not Jews at all. Yegorov was head of the Kremlin medical administration, and Borkenau regarded the announcement as an attack on the Kremlin medical administration as such. He pictured the Kremlin doctors as loyal to, and trusted by, Stalin. Borkenau therefore saw the attack on these doctors as an effort to dispose of them, and thus gain control of Stalin's fate. He further concluded that it was Malenkov who was most interested in gaining such control at the time.

Borkenau believes that the Nineteenth Communist Party Congress of 1952 had not resulted in a complete Malenkov

* Boris I. Nicolaevsky directed the Historico-Revolutionary Archives in Moscow from 1919 to 1921. Among his works is *Karl Marx: Man and Fighter;* he is the co-author, with David Dallin, of *Forced Labor in Soviet Russia.* Franz Borkenau is a German authority on Communist tactics, and author of *World Communism: A History of the Communist International.*

victory; that, instead, elements of the army leadership and other sections of the Soviet administration had allied themselves against Malenkov; and that, further, Stalin had given these anti-Malenkov forces just enough balance to prevent Malenkov's being proclaimed his heir while Stalin was still alive. But Malenkov, according to Borkenau, had gone too far to retreat without endangering his ultimate chances of success. Therefore, Malenkov may have decided to force the issue by "getting Stalin's person into his power" by removing Stalin's personal physicians from the scene and replacing them with his own men.

Certainly, the announcement about the alleged doctors' plot was strange enough to encourage such speculation. Beria's later denunciation of these accusations was stranger still. The relating of the deaths of Zhdanov and Shcherbakov with supposed designs on the lives of high armed-forces officials suggested involvement of the army clique.

Whatever the validity of this theory, without doubt wide and bitter struggles for power took place in Moscow between the Nineteenth Party Congress and the announcement of Stalin's death. The month of January, 1953, and the period just before and after, may well have been decisive in Malenkov's succession to Stalin. Zhukov's appointment to an influential position in the War Ministry suggests Malenkov's temporary victory over, or appeasement of, the army clique. Certainly Zhukov's importance overshadows that of First Deputy Premier Bulganin.

Together, Malenkov and Beria can probably keep the army clique in check. They must limit their own feud to strengthen still further their political commissars under Bulganin. Thus a continued power struggle is likely to be fought within the ranks of the Soviet army itself—at its headquarters and even within each regiment, battalion, and company. The more determined Malenkov is in his effort to wipe out army opposition, the louder will be warnings that the Soviet army must guard itself against spies, saboteurs, and other destructive elements. This theme was used on March 15, 1953, in a broadcast by Radio Volga, the Soviet-controlled transmitter in Berlin. This station, broadcasting in Russian to Soviet troops, urged that "high political vigilance" should be directed against "all activities of our enemies, their agents, and the imperialistic governments." The broadcast quoted Malenkov as saying: "We have to educate all Communists and workers to high political vigilance and to teach them to fight against all interior and exterior enemies." In the struggle for Kremlin power, the Soviet army is a major battleground.

8

Malenkov and Mao

GEORGI MALENKOV and Mao Tse-tung, head of China's Communist regime, met when Mao visited Moscow from December 12, 1949, to February 17, 1950, to negotiate the Sino-Soviet Treaty. It was, as far as is publicly known, Mao's first visit to the Soviet Union. Although there is no official information to suggest that Malenkov has ever visited China, some scholars believe that Malenkov may have gone to Peiping in the fall of 1950 to prepare the ground for Red China's intervention in the Korean War.

Certainly Malenkov has shown much greater interest in China than did his late antagonist Andrei A. Zhdanov. In his key Cominform address in 1947, Zhdanov restricted his comments entirely to Europe. Two years later, speaking at the anniversary of the Bolshevik Revolution shortly before Mao's arrival in Moscow, Malenkov dealt with China in detail and with exuberance.

Malenkov said that the Communist victory in China had historic significance. He recalled that Lenin regarded the outcome of the "world struggle between capitalism and communism" as depending on the fact that "Russia, India, and China comprise the overwhelming majority of the population" of the world. As for American aims in China, he said: "American imperialism counted on utilizing China as the chief base for its domination in Asia and the Pacific, as one of the decisive links in the encirclement of the Soviet Union. With this object the imperialists intended to transform China into an enormous colonial appendage to the American world empire."

Malenkov said that the Chinese Communist Party had arrived at the "height of its historic mission." He referred to the "experienced guidance of its leader, Mao Tse-tung" who had created forces that "smashed the Kuomintang hordes— hordes armed with American equipment and actually directed by American staffs." Malenkov then looked beyond China, toward "all the peoples of Asia." He said that the Chinese Communist victory had moved what he called "the national liberation struggle of the peoples of Asia, of the Pacific, of the entire colonial world," to "a new and considerably higher stage."

Although Malenkov thus early expressed his high regard for Mao Tse-tung's success, Mao did not attend Stalin's funeral in Moscow. All other Communist-governed countries were represented by their heads of state. However, in a purely technical sense, Peiping was properly represented. It sent its Premier and Foreign Minister, Chou En-lai. In reality, Chou is second to Mao in internal prestige and international standing. Was Mao's absence a slight? Was it indicative of a possible rift between Mao and Malenkov?

Certainly the Malenkov regime showed itself most cordial toward Peiping. As Malenkov approached the Lenin-Stalin tomb on Moscow's Red Square, he was flanked by Deputy Premier Lavrenti Beria and Chou En-lai. As the group walked to the rostrum, Chou immediately followed Beria, preceding even Foreign Minister Molotov. No other foreign Communist leader was given such prominence.

Premier Malenkov, in his funeral oration for Stalin, went

to considerable length to show Soviet appreciation of the
successful Chinese Communist regime. He listed it first
among the Communist-governed countries, and then said:
"We must in every way consolidate the eternal, indestructible, and fraternal friendship of the Soviet Union with the
great Chinese people and with the workers in all countries of
the People's Democracy."

Clearly, in Malenkov's world view of Communist-governed
countries, China has priority Number One. All other satellite
nations are secondary in importance, having real weight only
when viewed as a group. A curious way of illustrating Malenkov's personal desire to appear closely linked with the cause
of Red China was demonstrated in the *Pravda* issue of March
10, 1953, published the day after Stalin's funeral. The Moscow newspaper printed a photograph showing, from left to
right, Stalin, Mao, and Malenkov. The caption beneath the
picture said that this was a photograph taken February 14,
1950, at the time of the signing of the Soviet-Chinese Treaty
of Friendship, Alliance, and Mutual Aid.

And so it was, but the picture had been radically altered.
In the original photograph, Molotov, Stalin, and Mao stood
together in one group at the left side of the picture; Malenkov
and Beria were on the extreme right. The two groups were
separated by four other people, one of them being Vishinsky,
who was seated and signing the treaty. But the 1953 *Pravda*
version had dropped everyone else out of the picture, including Beria and Molotov, and moved Malenkov directly
next to Stalin and Mao.

This was a somewhat crude visual way of saying what
Malenkov emphasized throughout his first weeks in power:
that he personally regarded Mao Tse-tung and the Chinese
Communists highly, and hoped for continued Sino-Soviet

unity. In Peiping, meanwhile, the official atmosphere was no less cordial. There were no efforts at pictorial forgery, but official statements emphasized the same theme of continued "indestructible unity."

However, in his Stalin memorial essay, entitled *The Greatest Friendship,* Mao mentioned Stalin's name twenty-nine times—and Malenkov only once, when he said: "We fully believe that the Central Committee of the Communist Party of the Soviet Union and the Soviet Government, headed by Comrade Malenkov, will definitely be able to follow Comrade Stalin's behest to drive forward the great cause of Communism and carry it to further glorious fruition."

Quite obviously, the name Malenkov can hardly carry with the Chinese Communists the same weight as did that of Stalin. In fact, a minor linguistic factor may somewhat impair efforts to popularize Malenkov in China. The Chinese language is monosyllabic and lends itself exceedingly well to short, simple names. Stalin, in Chinese, became "Sze-ta-lin." Malenkov, however, becomes a four-character tongue twister: "Ma-lun-k'a-fu." This combination clearly lacks the simplicity of Stalin's name, and will prove difficult to use in propaganda slogans, or on banners for parades and rallies.

An effort to make Malenkov and his ideas familiar to the Chinese took place even before Stalin's death. His address to the Nineteenth Party Congress was translated into Chinese, and given to the 47,150 cadre members who form the core of the Chinese Communist Party.

Malenkov's, Beria's and Molotov's funeral orations for Stalin were also made obligatory reading for Chinese party members. There were, in other words, conscious efforts on both sides to underline common interests. But long-range relations between Peiping and Moscow must be viewed in terms of two factors: first, the personalities of Mao and Malenkov; second, historical and current Chinese-Soviet interests.

Physically, there is a definite similarity between the two men. Both have full round faces and tend toward double chins. Of the two, Mao is favored with the more expressive and sensitive features. Both prefer simple and severe uniforms—medals and ribbons and flashing gold stars are clearly not for them. Their uniforms have a sackcloth look of austerity. Both men are grown portly. Mao, however, is hardly the stereotype of the lax fat man, grown soft with too much civilization. He has been, at various moments of his career, a general in the field, the leader of a long and tortuous forced march, a cave dweller, a prolific writer, an energetic organizer. He has waged a long and apparently successful battle with an ordinarily wasting scourge, tuberculosis.

The year 1920 was important in the lives of both men. In Russia, Malenkov became a member of the party; in China, a group named the Society for the Study of Marxism, which a year later was to become the Chinese Communist Party, was formed in Shanghai and numbered Mao Tse-tung among its active members. Mao is perhaps the principle Marxist theoretician to survive Stalin; he assigned to the peasantry a historical role in Communist revolutionary thought. As a Communist thinker, he would definitely seem to eclipse Malenkov, but in terms of actual party experience, Mao is in no sense the Soviet Premier's senior.

When Malenkov was initiated into the Communist Party, Mao was working as a labor organizer in China. He read avidly and widely, but his feelings about the Bolshevik Revolution were almost entirely emotional. His knowledge of Marxist theory was not first hand. In China, torn by war-

lordism and strife, the men who wanted to introduce communism waited for an opening under the watchful eyes of
Comintern agent Gregori Voitinsky.

China has never had a middle class to speak of, and yet
Mao's parents, probably like those of Malenkov, were of
better than average economic substance. They owned their
house and land, they employed farm labor. Mao was able to
attend school and a university. His position as a library assistant at Peking University put him in touch with people
who read books, and over cups of jasmine tea he could listen
to fellow intellectuals dissect the West, discuss Marx, and
plan for the future.

Lenin, after the turmoil of the October Revolution, saw
that China represented a vast Communist potential, although
he believed that a land with so wide an agrarian base could
not move quickly toward communism, that a working-class
base was needed. Meanwhile he sought to capture Chinese
attention by many gestures, such as the decision to renounce
Russian extraterritorial claims in China. He also spoke constantly of liberating the oppressed peoples of the East from
colonial bondage, and the reiteration of this theme attracted
many Chinese who fiercely resented foreign intrusion.

China's revolutionary leader Sun Yat-sen welcomed assistance from the Soviet Union, and this paved the way for
large-scale Soviet aid to China during the 1920s. For a time,
Soviet army officers and advisors were treated as friendly
princes from afar. But the honeymoon ended when the Communists tried to entrench themselves and were expelled from
the Kuomintang in 1927.

Thus, at the outset of Sino-Soviet relations, both Soviet
material and ideological help was welcomed, particularly aid

designed to facilitate organization. The Chinese had for centuries failed in organizational procedures. There was no common feeling for the "state" as such, beyond resentment toward taxation and conscription, and feelings of unity and obligation were concentrated within the kinship system, the family, the village.

The tradition of Soviet aid was revived after the Communists succeeded in conquering the Chinese mainland in 1949. Since then, the Chinese Communist Party has, at every turn, officially welcomed Soviet aid. It professes not to see Soviet aid as a disguise for future exploitation, but rather as fraternal help. The open Soviet looting of Manchuria immediately following V-J Day—a systematic theft estimated to represent some 2 billion dollars—caused severe embarrassment to the Peiping regime. To combat initial Chinese sensitivity to this type of highhanded operation, the Communists brushed it aside by stating that if the Soviets had not removed it, it would have been destroyed by the Kuomintang. Then Peiping propagandists found it more advantageous to go on the offensive, emphasizing Soviet-Chinese solidarity and turning their vitriolic pens against the West and the United States in particular.

A small army of Soviet technical advisors has been in China since early 1950 and they have been in large measure responsible for overseeing construction of new railroad networks, highways, and irrigation projects. Their influence has been felt in related fields, from Stakhanovite coal-mining methods, to oil drilling and airfield development.

Some 20,000 branch offices of an organization known as the Sino-Soviet Friendship Association have sprung up all over China. Some of the branches are in factories and schools, some in former Western mission homes, some in elaborate buildings of their own. A membership running into millions is claimed. This is quite possible, because by a simple fiat, all Communist soldiers received automatic membership, and many Chinese have found that membership in the association is a reasonably good insurance policy against being branded counterrevolutionary.

Sino-Soviet joint stock companies, born out of the treaty of 1950, have expanded substantially. They are located principally in Sinkiang Province, in China's relatively unexploited but mineral-rich Northwest. There is also evidence pointing to the existence of an atomic center and proving ground in Sinkiang. Manchuria and Sinkiang are regions where the Soviet Union has established a degree of economic hegemony. Together with Outer Mongolia, these are potential danger points in relations between Malenkov and Mao, because Moscow's and Peiping's interest in them must ultimately conflict. The delicate case of Outer Mongolia was probably discussed in Moscow in 1952 when the region's head of state, Prime Minister Yumzhagil Tsedenbal of the Mongolian People's Republic, joined Sino-Soviet talks on August 28.

Outer Mongolia has long been a source of discord between Russia and China. In 1925 the government of Sun Yat-sen signed a pact with the Soviet Union which said: "The Government of the U.S.S.R. recognises that Outer Mongolia is a part of the Chinese Republic and honors the sovereign rights of China. The U.S.S.R. declares that as soon as withdrawal of Soviet troops is practical, they will be withdrawn from Outer Mongolia." But the Soviet regime never lived up to this agreement. It has kept the Outer Mongolian frontiers closed to China and the rest of the world. Again, in 1945 the Soviet Union signed an agreement with the Chinese government of Generalissimo Chiang Kai-shek, promising that a plebiscite would be held on the proposed independence of Outer Mongolia. Then the Soviets simply announced that such a plebiscite had been held—and that the vote had been unanimously for "independence." Although technically sovereign, the state is actually run as a Soviet province. Prime Minister Tsedenbal is head of the local Communist Party. As such he is subordinate to G. I. Bannikov, who has the title U.S.S.R. Ambassador to the Mongolian People's Republic.

Malenkov's dilemma is underlined by a strongly worded statement which Mao Tse-tung made in 1936: "The relationship between Outer Mongolia and the Soviet Union, now and in the past, has always been based on the principle of complete equality. When the people's revolution has been victorious in China, the Outer Mongolian Republic will automatically become a part of the Chinese Federation of its own will." Moscow's and Peiping's maps also differ on the boundary line that divides Moscow-controlled Outer Mongolia from Peiping-controlled Inner Mongolia.

Such historic territorial conflicts are not easily resolved, even though both Malenkov and Mao may consider them secondary matters, greatly overshadowed by factors that emphasize continued Moscow-Peiping cooperation. Certainly Malenkov must step gingerly in all territorial matters affecting China. Soviet highhandedness in regions under Chinese sovereignty may arouse latent chauvinism even among the Peiping Communist leadership.

Some observers divide the Peiping regime into two factions. The so-called "nationalist" faction is presumed to be headed by Mao Tse-tung and General Chu Teh. The party leaders Liu Shao-chi, Li Li-san, Kao Kang, and Po I-po are considered part of the slavishly pro-Moscow "internationalist" bloc. If these groups were ever to split on the issue of support for Malenkov, Communist unity in China would be sorely shaken. Given such an eventuality, we would probably witness a turbulent division of power in China, with the pro-Moscow faction holding sway in the north and northeast, close by the Soviet Union, and the opposing group camping in the central and southern regions. A new grouping of Chinese "war lords" might thus emerge.

Elements running counter to such a split are, however, very strong. Mao Tse-tung's debt to Moscow is clear and undeniable. Without Moscow's continued ideological guidance and moral support, without the symbol of Marxism-Leninism-Stalinism, without Moscow's financial assistance and advice on such vital matters as organization and propaganda, Mao Tse-tung, for all his independent accomplishments, might not today be exercising the most complete control of China that has been known in all of its 4,000-year history. Mao himself has asked the question, on July 1, 1949, in his *Essay on Democratic Dictatorship:* "Do you seriously think that it was possible for us to come out victorious without the Soviet Union?" And he himself answered curtly: "Decidedly not!"

From the Soviet viewpoint, Malenkov obviously realizes that China's value to the U.S.S.R. far exceeds the value to Moscow of any other single Communist-governed state. China and the Soviet Union share a long, common border, in about the manner of Canada and the United States. The Soviets have long expressed an almost obsessive need for friendly "buffer regions." A pro-Soviet China is therefore not merely in Moscow's interest; it is a necessity, dictated by real or imagined fears. A Soviet China, together with the Soviet Maritime East (provinces on the Pacific coast), provides Moscow with an ideal protective flank. From the point of view of military strategy, a friendly China is invaluable to Moscow, as the Korean War so well demonstrated. There Communist China tied down large numbers of American troops, while not one single Soviet soldier's life is endangered.

Beyond military security, China can be a vast supplier of raw materials and natural resources, of light manufactures including consumer goods, and of foodstuffs, particularly grains. By the end of 1952, Communist China's exports to the Soviet Union totaled 70 per cent of all Chinese exports, and signs that the percentage would increase were obvious. Communist China's trade with the non-Communist world was decreasing rapidly, save for items unobtainable from the Soviet Union, including certain pharmaceuticals and rare drugs, and rubber.

On January 1, 1953, the Peiping regime launched an ambitious Five-Year Plan of industrialization, but shortly afterward it cut the building plans of various ministries by 30 per cent. It seemed that Peiping was hard pressed for capital goods, of which the Soviet Union was its only source. On March 25, Moscow and Peiping signed a trade protocol that pledged Soviet assistance in the construction of power stations and in the metallurgical, mining, machine-construction, and chemical industries, as well as supplying agricultural machinery, pedigreed cattle, and seeds. In turn, China was to provide the Soviet Union with light metals, rice, vegetable oil, meat, tobacco, tea, fruits, wool, jute, raw silk, silk textiles, leather goods, and other products. New but unpublished Soviet credits to China were also said to have been granted.

This is not to imply that the Kremlin has made no allowance for any Chinese action it might interpret as unfriendly. From ten to twelve Soviet infantry divisions are stationed above China's northernmost border. They are there, ostensibly, for normal security and garrison reasons, but they could, if need be, flood down into China and be in Peiping at short notice. The China mainland itself is filled with Soviet personnel, estimated at as many as 40,000. Each Soviet representative in China, quite apart from his openly declared organization, is under Vasily V. Kuznetzov, Soviet Ambassador to China. The slightest indication of an anti-Soviet trend in China would be reported back to Moscow immediately and appropriate countermeasures would be taken.

However, in the immediate future, grounds do not exist for a Sino-Soviet rupture. As a friendly associate of the Soviet Union—not a satellite—China stands to profit greatly. The gains made thus far in Chinese production, in economic stability, in military strength, in laying the groundwork for industrialization—all these are clearly apparent and in part can be traced to Soviet assistance. Save for the possibility of Kremlin recklessness, there is nothing on the horizon to give substance to a Sino-Soviet split in the next few years. Soviet experience with Yugoslavia was bitter; Malenkov is not likely to repeat Zhdanov's Yugoslav mistake in Asia.

What, then, are the chances of a break between Mao and Malenkov, viewed in long-range terms? The intensive Marxist remolding of Chinese people goes beyond the control of the pro-Moscow Communist Party element. The present resurgence of Chinese strength may eventually channel into a stream of antiforeignism that will permit the dominance of no alien power in China, including the Soviet Union. Although Communist cultural genocide has destroyed a number of traditional Chinese concepts, intense Chinese nationalism and sensitivity to every kind of foreign imperialism has not been entirely purged. Thus far, antiforeign sentiment has in fact *served* the Communists in encouraging Chinese wrath against the Western powers.

Yet another consideration is the fact that the Chinese are an immensely practical and realistic people. Even as it is classic Chinese strategy to make strategic withdrawals, so may it also be strategy to accept gifts from questionable friends. If the gifts be industrialization, organization, material assistance, well and good—the Chinese can use such gifts. None can doubt that a strong China is a Chinese Communist aim. And independence can be asserted only when there is strength to maintain it.

The Malenkov-Mao relationship lacks the Stalin-Mao teacher-student relationship. But Malenkov, like Mao, is a high priest at the shrine of the Stalin myth. As long as this "coexistence," this seeming equality is maintained, there will be no radical change in Sino-Soviet relations. Communist China, in its relationship to Moscow, sees itself as a younger brother who is rapidly growing up.

As a disciple of Stalin, Malenkov must understand China's immense strategic and economic importance to the Soviet Union. Perhaps he will have to make concessions to China's role in Asia. Even while Stalin was alive, such Communist parties as those of Japan and India were looking to Peiping as well as to Moscow for guidance. Chinese in other lands, especially throughout southern Asia, play an important role in Communist agitation. In a manner of speaking, Peiping has, since 1950, developed into a revolutionary center that, in some ways, rivals Moscow.

This condition has not, in the past, led to open friction. If Malenkov curbs his characteristic brusqueness and impatience in dealing with Mao, the adjustment in Peiping-

Moscow relations can take place without noticeable friction. Mao has declared himself unswervingly faithful to the Communist Party of the Soviet Union, headed by Malenkov. The two men are bound together by the Stalin myth and, perhaps even more strongly, by the realization that they need each other.

Moscow and Peiping certainly acted in concert when, as soon as he had returned from Stalin's funeral, Chou En-lai opened the way for new Korean truce talks. His statement of March 30 was an important and integral part of the new Soviet peace offensive that found the Western countries emotionally and tactically unprepared, and which seemed designed to exploit the "internal contradictions" which the Nineteenth Soviet Communist Party Congress had noted among the Western allies.

Both Malenkov and Mao stood to gain from this tactical maneuver. Malenkov, engaged in a power struggle at home, could turn his attention elsewhere. Mao, his troops trained on the Korean battlefield and equipped with Soviet arms, could disengage himself from actual war while keeping and amplifying their armed strength.

9

What Does He Believe?

WHAT DOES Georgi M. Malenkov believe? These, as far as one can tell, are his professed articles of faith:

1. Peaceful "coexistence," on Soviet terms, with the West. But this is predicated on the supposition that American "billionaires" will drop their "terrorist" policy which he believes, or says he believes, is designed for American world conquest.

2. Atomic weapons should be outlawed. He believes in the use of atomic energy only for productive purposes, but he would not hesitate to use any weapon against "aggression."

3. The "imperialist camp"—meaning the West—cannot exist on a peacetime economy, and economic crises will produce further warfare. Such warfare will "dig the grave of world capitalism."

4. Peace for the Soviet Union, but not a pacifist, inactive peace. His idea of peace is "to struggle actively against warmongers."

5. The United States and other Western Powers are using spies and saboteurs to infiltrate the satellites and Russia, to poison Communist doctrine, to interrupt Communist production.

6. For Russia and the Communist world: equality between the Soviet Union and the satellites.

7. Tighter organization and purer doctrine in the Communist Party.

8. More industrial and agricultural production through greater efficiency, greater labor "enthusiasm," and modern techniques.

9. Transition from socialism to pure communism in the Soviet Union.

10. The growth of communism throughout the world.

This interpretation of Malenkov's credo is based mostly on analyses of his six major speeches between 1941 and 1953.* But one must be careful in examining these papers to translate not only from Russian into English, but also from the ingrown, private Communist vernacular into terms understood by the rest of the world. In 1947, for example, Malenkov spoke of "morality," but this had nothing to do with ethics, philosophy, or religion. He was talking about Communist Party morality, political purity acceptable to the party. In 1941 and after, he spoke of "labor enthusiasm" which might better be interpreted as "demonstrations of labor obedience to the Party." By the word "democracy," Malenkov means "people's democracy" or socialism in the Soviet sense, which has nothing to do with democracy as we know it. When he says "cooperation," or "coexistence," the non-Communist reader should immediately add, "on Soviet Communist terms." When the new Premier mentions "peace," he usually means peace for Russian Communists and on their

* The speeches were "Tasks of the Party Organization in Industry and Transport," delivered to the Eighteenth All-Union Conference of the Communist Party of the Soviet Union, February 15, 1941; "The Activities of the Central Committee of the Communist Party of the Soviet Union (Bolsheviks)," delivered to the secret meeting of the parties of nine nations which formed the Information Bureau (Cominform) in Poland, September, 1947; the speech before the Moscow Soviet delivered in November, 1949; Report to the Nineteenth Congress of the Communist Party of the Soviet Union, delivered in Moscow, October 5, 1952; Stalin Funeral Oration in Moscow, March 9, 1953; speech to the Supreme Soviet, March 15, 1953. The full text of the last three speeches appear in the Appendix.

own terms. Any act to stem the expansion of Russian communism, is, to Malenkov, "aggression," while it might merely be interpreted by a non-Communist as defense.

The Soviet attitude on peace and the coexistence of capitalism and communism has been described several times by Stalin. There is no indication in Malenkov's six major speeches that he differs. In 1947 Malenkov told the Cominform:

"We proceed from the fact that the coexistence of two systems—capitalism and socialism—is inevitable for a long period of time and we follow the line of maintaining loyal, good neighborly relations with all states manifesting a desire for friendly cooperation . . . The U.S.S.R., true to international treaties . . . pursues this policy with the utmost consistency and firmness."

This sounds like a reasonable, statesmanlike approach to international relations. But a few moments later in this talk, Malenkov spelled out Soviet policy a little more clearly: ". . . we are prepared to repel any policy hostile to the Soviet Union. The Soviet Union . . . invariably exposes all enemies of peace . . . all enemies of international cooperation on a democratic basis."

The key to Malenkov's policy lies in the last lines. His idea of coexistence does not, in the long run, mean coexistence with the antagonists of communism whom he regards as "enemies of peace"; and the peace he favors is a peace maintained by the rest of the world's giving in to communism. Malenkov's coexistence cannot benefit enemies of "cooperation on a democratic basis," by which he means a Communist basis. He never uses the word "democratic" except in conjunction with Communist states and Communist organizations.

Atomic energy, Malenkov said in his 1949 speech to the

Moscow Soviet, "must be a mighty instrument of technical progress . . . and an instrument for the further rapid development of the productive forces of our country." Although later in the 1949 oration he said flatly that the Soviet government "possesses the atomic weapon," by 1952 he was more evasive, begging the question with talk of using atomic energy for peaceful purposes: "While possessing real possibilities for producing atomic energy, the Soviet state is deeply interested in seeing this new type of energy used for peaceful purposes, for the good of the people, since such a use of atomic energy vastly extends man's dominion over the elements and opens up before humanity colossal opportunities for increasing the productive forces, for technical and cultural progress, and for multiplying the social wealth."

He did not say in 1952, as he did in 1949, that the U.S.S.R. had atomic weapons, much less give any indication of what kind of atomic tools the Soviet might have.

Malenkov has consistently expressed Moscow's official "peace" policy. In 1949 he said that the main element of foreign policy was that the U.S.S.R. "stands for peace and defends the cause of peace. . . . We do not want war and will do everything possible to prevent it." He added that "the socialist state has no need for foreign expansion." Stalin had also said something similar shortly before subduing what are now the satellites.

The official peace policy which Malenkov supports is an exercise in semantics. He demonstrated what he meant by peace when he said, in 1949, that the Soviet people were discharging their responsibility to history by their actions toward "certain successors of the fascist barbarians" who "are extending the bloody hand of a new war over the world." Presumably, "fascist barbarians" was Malenkov's description of

Americans who were then supporting the legal government of China against Communist insurrection.

If there was any doubt about what Malenkov meant by peace, he eliminated it in the same speech as follows: "The world movement of the supporters of peace is based not upon pacifist ideology . . . but upon a firm determination to struggle actively against warmongers and to block their insidious plans and schemes. . . . The people have ceased to be passive and are prepared to defend actively the cause of peace. . . ."

On March 9, 1953, in his funeral oration for Stalin, Malenkov again mentions peace, but the subject is far down the list of topics covered. On that occasion he gave far more attention to "unity" of party and state, undoubtedly because here lay a potential threat to his own position. He gave almost as much emphasis to plans for strengthening the Soviet armed forces as he did to peace. But peace he did mention:

"The foreign policy of the Soviet state, a policy of peace and friendship between peoples, forms a shattering barrier to the unleashing of a new war. . . ." The Soviet policy, he said, was "based on the Lenin-Stalin premise of the possibility of the prolonged coexistence and peaceful competition of two different systems, capitalist and socialist." And later in the oration, "the Government must serve their people faithfully, and the peoples thirst for peace and curse war."

Malenkov carried the peace theme still further in his speech to the Supreme Soviet on March 15, 1953. Some commentators interpreted the speech as a bid for a conference with President Eisenhower to eliminate causes of tension. But in the ten days preceding, Communist armed forces had shot down one American aircraft, seriously damaged another, shot down a British bomber killing seven men, and made flying passes at other British aircraft. As the victims of the plane incidents were being buried, Malenkov boldly told the Supreme Soviet and the Western diplomats in the audience:

1. The Soviet policy was based on respect for the rights of all countries . . . the norms of international law and the strict observance of all treaties.

2. In the present and future, there do not exist any troublesome and unsolved questions that cannot be resolved by peaceful means.

3. Any country, including the United States, could be assured of the firm policy for peace of the Soviet Union.

Perhaps what he did say was not as important as what he did not say, either in the funeral oration or on the Ides of March. Malenkov did not excoriate foreign "ruling circles," he did not rant about "imperialist warmongers." He spoke of the "enemy," but did not focus on any one nation or group of nations. In both speeches, the great deviation from the past was the absence of slanderous attack on the motives and leadership of the non-Communist world. Also significant was the fact that Malenkov did not permit Beria or Molotov to lash at "warmongers" either, even in reference to Korea where the North Koreans were pictured merely as fighting for their "independence."

Malenkov in early 1953 may have been sparring for time. He had stated before, in 1949, that Communist foreign policy favored five-power conferences and the reduction of armaments. But Malenkov has a Communist vocabulary. Even if new international conferences materialize, if heads of state meet to discuss the removal of tensions, Malenkov's attitudes will very probably show that coexistence and peace have a meaning for Communists entirely different from what they do for the West.

Malenkov's attitude toward the United States, toward American "billionaires" and the American "terrorist" policy, is that of a Communist who, *having spent his entire adult life within the intellectual prison of the Communist Party*, knows that black is white.

The new Soviet Premier's suspicion of the United States is not something recently acquired. In 1947 he believed that American spies and agents were trying to subvert any of the Russian intelligentsia who still had ties with Western culture or who were, as Malenkov put it, "infected with the disease of servility to everything foreign."

By 1947 Malenkov had become convinced that the world was split in two. He claimed that the United States had adopted a "new openly expansionist policy aimed at establishing American world supremacy." Two opposite trends had begun to take shape, he said. The first trend was the foreign policy of the Soviet Union "designed to undermine imperialism," while the opposite trend in world politics was headed by "American imperialists" who had taken the path of outright expansion, of "enthralling the weakened capitalist states of Europe and the colonial dependent countries. It has chosen the path of hatching new war plans against the U.S.S.R."

It was at this point that Malenkov declared his belief in the coexistence of capitalism and socialism—on a "democratic" basis—but he was not very hopeful that the West would be satisfied with the coexistence on his terms. He charged the United States and Great Britain with pursuing a "terrorist policy," of bullying, of interference in the internal affairs of the Soviet satellites, and of conducting propaganda for a third world war. And finally, in preparing the minds of his party for any eventuality, he called the Western powers "would-be aggressors" and repeated the charge that the West wants war. Malenkov gave this interpretation of affairs the stamp of party approval, saying: "Such are the foundations of the foreign policy of the Communist Party of the Soviet Union."

Two years later, in 1949, his ideas had not changed. To Malenkov, the North Atlantic Pact signified the preparation of a new imperialist war. The Marshall Plan spurred on a "debauch" of militarism. But history he believed, was on Moscow's side: the "first imperialist war" (World War I) led to the Russian revolution and the creation of a "socialist state"; the Second World War, also unleashed by "imperialists," led to the creation of "democratic" regimes in Central and Southeastern Europe and to the "victory of the Chinese people." Finally he asked: "Can there be any doubt whatever that, if the imperialists unleash a third world war, this will be the grave . . . for the whole world of capitalism?"

He speaks of the grave of capitalism. Yet during World War II, directly engaged in expediting war production as he was, Malenkov must have watched with not a little awe and amazement just under 11 billion dollars' worth of American armament and supplies pour into Russia under Lend-Lease. He must realize, unless he has been blindfolded by his own propaganda, our vast industrial potential, for war or peace. This firsthand contact with the enormous productivity of American capitalism must certainly play a part in his thinking about Russia's future relationship with the United States.

Yet by 1952 his convictions about the United States had, if

anything, hardened: "U.S. imperialism is at present not only the aggressor, it is the world gendarme seeking to strangle freedom wherever possible and to implant fascism."

The technique used by Americans to establish world domination, according to Malenkov, was to finance allies, then use them to fight aggressive wars. He called the United States the "principal aggressive power" which was whipping other capitalist countries toward war, using the territory of others for military bases, dictating policy, and forming power blocs.

The line of reasoning is an indication of Malenkov's own approach to world politics, for he here attributed to the United States methods and means which Moscow has used successfully under similar conditions. This twisted interpretation of world affairs brings to mind the wartime conversation between Churchill and Stalin in which Churchill asked if Stalin really thought the rest of the allies were joining forces against the Soviet. Stalin replied, "Yes. That's what I would do if I were you." It is quite probable that Malenkov's mind works in the same channel.

Toward the West generally, Malenkov is equally suspicious but less vitriolic, because the West, in his opinion, is not as immediate and powerful a threat to Soviet aspirations as is the United States.

In 1947 Malenkov told the Cominform that the Bolshevik Revolution liberated the Russian peoples from "economic and spiritual enslavement to foreign capital." On the relatively few occasions that he mentions Western culture, he portrays it as decadent, infected, and bourgeois. From this, it is easy for Malenkov to proceed to the theory that the economically and spiritually weak Western nations succumbed quickly to American "enslavement."

Moscow edits a Photograph: The top photo, from *Pravda*, March 10, 1953, would seem to be one of Stalin, Mao Tse-tung, and Malenkov in intimate conversation. Actually it is a severely edited version of the photograph below, taken early in 1950, at the signing of the Treaty of Friendship between the Soviet Union and the Communist Chinese People's Republic. Andrei Vishinsky (signing treaty) and three other officials have been eliminated from the *Pravda* version, and Malenkov has been moved next to Mao. (*Credit: Sovfoto.*)

Mao Tse-tung: The Chinese Communist leader reviews a parade on October 1, 1952, in Peiping. (*Credit: Eastfoto.*)

Malenkov's foreign-policy objectives in 1949 called for a five-power conference to condemn war, the outlawing of the atom bomb, and the establishment of "suitable" antimilitarism controls. He would have had the five powers conclude a pact to strengthen the peace—the same old peace, of course, based on tolerance for Communist expansion.

Twice in the 1949 talk, Malenkov charged American exploitation of Western Europeans. The Marshall Plan, he said, was a bribe to force Europeans to enter the armaments race: despite artificially stimulated industry, capitalist Europe was in a decline; industrial production had remained the same in non-Communist Europe for twenty years, while Soviet production increased ninefold. World trade had dropped, Europe's currency was inflated, living conditions had fallen, and there were 40 million unemployed and partially unemployed in the world's capitalist countries. Western European nations were losing their colonies while Americans were moving in to replace them.

Malenkov asserted that Greece, Turkey, and Yugoslavia had been turned into American colonies. The ruling circles of France, Italy, Britain, Western Germany and Japan had "harnessed themselves to the chariot of U.S. imperialism." In contrast to his virulence toward America, the language used toward Europeans is, for Malenkov, mild. His remarks were part of an effort to drive a wedge between Europe and the United States.

For it is basic Communist strategy to sow distrust between the capitalist nations, to create a split, to isolate the United States. Along this line, Malenkov said in 1952: "One can suppose that in the countries doomed to play the role of obedient pawns of the American dictators, there will be found truly peace-loving, democratic forces which will implement their own independent, peace-loving policy and which will find a way out of the dead end into which they have been chased by their American dictators. Having entered into this new path, the European and other countries will meet with complete understanding from all peace-loving countries."

Translated from party jargon, this means that Malenkov would have the Communist front organizations—the people who circulate party-line petitions and run so-called "peace and cultural conferences"—create as much friction as possible within the non-Communist world. Normal frictions, exacerbated by the Communists, might flare into war between non-Communists; at least, according to Malenkov's strategy, this should lead to the fall of old governments, and the creation of "Popular Front" governments which would break with the United States. The Communist Party could then develop the Popular Fronts into outright Communist governments and the United States would then be isolated. While Malenkov's strategy goes no further, it seems plausible that he believes that an isolated United States could not survive.

Although Premier Malenkov's beliefs about, and strategy toward, the United States and the West are of great interest to Western students, Malenkov's chief interest for many years lay in:

1. Soviet industrial production, and
2. Communist Party organization.

In these fields, Malenkov appears as a bureaucrat who despised bureaucracy, a party disciplinarian who seldom discussed ideology, and an efficiency expert who was almost a faddist about the subject of modern techniques.

Malenkov's major tasks, during and after World War II,

were to produce more goods, build more war planes, expand the railways, and build bigger factories. To these tasks he brought great faith in the direct approach, an attitude he called "Bolshevik directness." It was blunt, harsh and demanding. But it would take all those qualities and more to obtain his objective—economic independence for the Soviet Union. In 1941 Malenkov reported to a party conference:

"Stalin said that to outstrip the principal capitalist countries economically, above all requires a great and indomitable desire to forge ahead . . . In order not to become an appendage of a capitalist economy, we must have everything at our disposal. Guided by this instruction, our Party has ensured the independence of the national economy of the U.S.S.R."

In "forging ahead," Malenkov excoriated inefficient workers, shocking Old Bolsheviks by demanding that nonparty workers should be promoted on the basis of merit. He attacked bureaucrats who hired and promoted on the basis of questionnaires and family connections. Being himself probably of a bourgeois origin, he attacked the "biological approach in selecting cadres." Some nonparty workers and executives, he said, were doing better jobs than Communists with long tenure.

"Weak-willed and unfit workers . . . must be relieved of their jobs whether they are Party or non-Party people." Thus Malenkov came perilously close to heresy in 1941. "Some of them are ignoramuses who . . . pay no attention whatsoever to advice and instructions. It is necessary to unmask ignoramuses . . . and kick them out. It is inadmissable to tolerate ignoramuses at the top of enterprises. . . ."

In 1947, after supervising the restoration of war-damaged Soviet areas, Malenkov told the Cominform proudly that, contrary to the decline prevalent in capitalist countries, "the Soviet Union, thanks to its socialist system of national economy, has been spared such postwar upheavals. In the Soviet Union there are neither crises nor unemployment, but a steady development of production and improvement in the welfare of the people." (Unemployment was then being eliminated by the slave labor system.)

Here, briefly, he discussed raising the living standard of the people. But first priority went to heavy industrial output which, Malenkov said, must be raised to the prewar level by 1948. After that date, priority would go to rehabilitation of heavy industries and railways, without which further expansion would be impossible.

In contrast to specific target dates and target objectives for heavy industry, Malenkov's interest in consumer goods was vague. He said: "We have to surpass the prewar level of national income and national consumption, eliminate in the near future the rationing system; we have to devote special attention to raising the standard of living."

He did not say when these objectives could be accomplished, or how much specifically could be done for the consumer. This slighting of the consumer has been a continuing fixture in Malenkov's speeches. In 1952, he pointed out that industrial output had increased 240 per cent over prewar figures; production of consumer goods, however, was up only 43 per cent.

Malenkov believes in the future. He predicts, just around the corner of the next Five-Year Plan, millions of new hectares of wheat, millions of new "enthusiastic" workers, new factories crammed with the latest devices. In 1952 he said that new power stations would make possible the "introduction of electric plowing."

Although the Soviet Premier has visions, he does not dream. He is above all a man of action, one who insists on efficiency. The most recent and dramatic example of his faith in efficiency was the reorganization of the Soviet Government. His first act as Premier was to streamline the sprawling Soviet bureaucracy. He annihilated whole ministries and within two weeks of Stalin's death, he had cut the bureaus almost in half. He reduced the number of ministries and special committees attached to the Council of Ministers from a total of fifty to only twenty-seven.

He has a respect for efficiency which, after all, is usually associated in capitalist countries with "big business." In his 1952 speech to the party congress, for example, he attacked viciously all inefficient workers and executives, concluding, "It is the problem of profitability that gives us pain."

Another extreme example of his preoccupation with production: In 1947 Malenkov gave over a considerable part of his Cominform speech to "problems of building the Party." In his long discussion he mentioned Stalin four times, on three of which occasions Stalin's name was in the title of books being published by the party. It was significant— almost typical—that Malenkov told the audience how many copies of the book were printed, but not what was in them.

Malenkov believes it is his mission not to theorize, but to produce, to direct, to discipline.

On the subject of agriculture, Malenkov stated in 1941 that "the grain problem and the task of securing an annual harvest" have "mostly been solved." In 1952 he eliminated the word "mostly," saying that "the grain problem has been successfully solved." He skirted the delicate question of the collective farms, suggesting that "the collective-farm system had been firmly established in 1939." In reality, peasant resistance to complete collectivization has slowed up the schedule of Kremlin planning considerably, in spite of the state-induced famines of the early 1930s.

Malenkov said in his 1952 speech that "amalgamation of the small collective farms" into big collectives was making progress. He then referred to the abortive effort of "hasty, mass resettlement of villages to form big collective-farm towns," known as collective-farm cities or "agro-cities." This scheme had envisaged a rural proletariat, living in apartment houses, that would work on supercollectives in the manner of factory workers.

Malenkov accused the backers of these schemes of forgetting the principal production needs, and of advancing "amenities in the collective farms." He also accused party workers of "pilfering farm property," of taking advantage of their official positions "to occupy collective land, make collective-farm chairmen provide them with grain, meat, milk, and other commodities free of charge or at a low price." He also accused the farms of being slow in adopting new production methods, although he admitted that "agricultural science still lags behind the needs of collective-farm and state-farm production."

Malenkov's ideas on Soviet culture reflect his impatience with intellectual processes. As in the field of agriculture and industry, he wants to see results that reflect instructions from above. In 1952 he said that the ideological and artistic level of many works was not high enough. He explained that some works "distort Soviet reality," are boring and without spirit, are mediocre and dull. To improve their work, writers and motion-picture makers should "pillory the faults, shortcomings, and unhealthy phenomena to be met with in society; they must create positive artistic images of the men and women of the new type in all their splendor and human dignity." This he said, would show readers traits, habits, and customs "free from the ulcers and vices to which capitalism gives rise."

In other words, Malenkov sees literature as a tool to reshape the reading public in the image of a "new Soviet man." He also asked for scorching satire which would "burn out all that is negative, decaying, and moribund, everything that acts as a brake on our march onward." Malenkov warned writers not to think of the Soviet man as "sort of statistical average." He explained that "the typical" was not "that which is most frequently encountered," but that which "most fully and pointedly expresses the essence of the given social force." (Thus, in the new Soviet dictionary, the word "typical" has come to mean "ideal.") He went further: "Conscious hyperbole and accentuation of an image does not exclude typicalness but discloses it more fully and emphasizes it." Malenkov, in other words, wants writers to contrast the new Soviet superman imagined by the Kremlin, with the "negative, decaying" elements that may still fail to live up to the Communist Party's expectations. He wants literature to create an image after which the average Soviet man and woman can model themselves.

What does he believe is the future of the Soviet Union? Where is Malenkov going?

In his funeral oration over Stalin's bier, he declared that

the Soviet Union had "accomplished the greatest revolution in the history of mankind . . . and entered upon a new path, the path of socialism." But Malenkov, together with other Moscow spokesmen, believe that the Soviets are only half way to their goal. That goal is pure communism—that most elusive of all conditions—where peasants produce but do not sell, where laborers work only five hours a day, where all property is public property, where Stalin's slogan, "from each according to his ability, to each according to his labor," will be succeeded by Marx's original formula: "From each according to his ability, to each according to his needs."

Pure communism in the Sovet Union is only part of the goal. In his 1952 speech, Malenkov said: "The Lenin-Stalin ideas shed the bright light of revolutionary theory on the tasks and perspectives of the struggle of the masses in all lands against imperialism, for peace, democracy, and Socialism."

The task *in all lands* is the struggle against "imperialism," for "peace"—but again it must be understood that he talks of a Communist peace—and for socialism. Malenkov concluded his 1952 speech with these words:

"There are no forces in the world capable of halting the onward movement of Soviet society. Ours is an invincible cause. We must take firm hold of the helm and pursue our course, yielding neither to provocations nor to intimidation.

"Under the banner of the immortal Lenin, under the wise leadership of the great Stalin, forward to the victory of Communism!"

Malenkov's views as expressed in his public addresses do not differ greatly from the basic ideas expressed by Joseph Stalin during the last years of his life. From 1948 through

1952, the impact of Malenkov's personality and beliefs could be increasingly felt in the internal and external affairs of the Soviet Union. There is, therefore, a natural identity between the views expressed by Stalin, Malenkov, and other Soviet leaders in recent years. Malenkov's speeches do, however, reflect a shift in emphasis and approach as the younger man replaces the older—a new note of concrete challenge, an aggressive and plain-spoken tone that seems to echo the new Soviet leader's impatient nature and "practical" approach.

10

Malenkov and the World

GEORGI M. MALENKOV, viewing the world from his desk in the Kremlin, must see it in a series of circles. First there is the narrow inner circle of the Kremlin itself, of the men who are his close associates, his friends, his enemies. Then there is the wider circle of top men in Soviet society— in the Communist Party, the army, the secret police. The next circle encompasses the vast majority of the more than 200 million people within the borders of the Soviet Union: Great Russians, Ukrainians, Byelorussians, Balts, Moslems, Armenians, Mongols—diverse groups, brought together by czarist imperialism, now held together by Communist force.

There are other, and still wider circles. Within them can be found the Eastern European nations under Communist control: Poland, Romania, Czechoslovakia, Hungary, Bulgaria, and dangerously isolated Albania. Eastern Austria and Soviet-controlled Eastern Germany are important parts of this satellite circle.

As he ponders over the still wider circles outside the Soviet empire, Malenkov may want to go downstairs into Stalin's old map room to take a closer look at countries and capitals he has never seen—and which, beyond the reports he has read, must be enigmas to him. There is Peiping, capital of a Communist-governed nation twice as populous as the Soviet

138

Union; Peiping, seat of the regime of Mao Tse-tung, whose power rivals that of Georgi Malenkov himself.

The nations of Western Europe—Great Britain, France, Germany, Austria, the Lowlands and Scandinavia, Switzerland and the Iberian countries—all these are parts of a still wider circle. So, also, are the Near East and southern Asia, the far Pacific, and Latin America. And, separated by two oceans from the Eurasian mainland over which the Soviet Union stretches, there is another powerful nation, a challenger to Kremlin expansionism: the United States of America.

Joseph Stalin, in all his seventy-three years, never ventured further away from Soviet borders than Teheran, just to the south. And yet, Stalin's name was known everywhere; Stalin's power was felt and feared everywhere; Stalin's followers fought his battles from Indo-China to Guatemala, from Korea to Iran.

Georgi Malenkov, returning from the map room to his own office, has much to weigh, to hope, to fear. He is no novice in world affairs, although much of his work has been on internal Soviet matters. He knows the world through reports of the Soviet intelligence services, whose work he supervised; he knows it through the machinery of the Cominform, which he helped create in 1947. He knows it from reports submitted by Soviet diplomatic missions abroad. He knows it from card-indexed dossiers at the Foreign Ministry and at the Communist Party's Central Committee. Although subject to distortions inherent in the Soviet system, these reports are detailed and extensive.

In the nearly three decades of his Moscow career, Georgi Malenkov has succeeded by thinking mainly in terms of one factor: people. He has learned much about the ambitions, the strengths, and the failings of people, of men who are potentially both loyal and disloyal, heroic or cowardly, narrow-minded or farsighted, wise or foolish, dynamic or careful. Malenkov knows that today's friend may be tomorrow's enemy; he has also learned that a crushed enemy can be made into a frightened and therefore particularly eager supporter.

Malenkov has learned to maneuver people, to move them about like pawns on a chessboard. These living figures, on the giant chessboard that is the world, are what must count to Georgi Malenkov. They are what he knows most about.

Many of the figures on the world chessboard are new men in history. Malenkov believes firmly, and said so in 1946, that new and vigorous leaders must take the place of men by-passed by history.

With Stalin, symbol of the past, lying dead in the tomb on Red Square, others are dead—dead in actual fact, or dead in the chess game of power. Outside the circle formed by the frontiers of the Soviet Union, one man died just a day before the Supreme Soviet affirmed Malenkov's appointment as Stalin's successor. That man was Klement Gottwald, who had run the Czechoslovak Communist Party for more than a quarter-century and who had possibly become a victim of Malenkov's enemies.

Others, too, had died. In September, 1947, when the Cominform was founded in Poland, fourteen men signed the declaration in the name of nine Communist parties. Where were they now? Zhdanov, Malenkov's enemy—dead. The Bulgar Vladimir Poptomov—dead. The Czech Rudolf Slansky —executed as a traitor to communism. Edvard Kardelj and Milovan Djilas of Yugoslavia—read out of the Communist community, together with their leader Marshal Tito. Wladyslaw Gomolka of Poland—charged with treachery, behind

The Christian Science Monitor

"Long Narrow Bridge"

bars, accused of "activities hostile to the Polish state." Another Czech, Stefan Bastovansky—purged from office as one of Slansky's men. Ana Pauker of Romania—awaiting trial as a traitor.

The Communist parties in all satellite states are in a ferment. The men on whom Malenkov has to rely are trying to penetrate the thoughts of the men in Moscow, trying to read the signs. They ask, will Malenkov remain top man? Will we be safe siding with him? Who are his enemies? May Beria not win out in the end, and will we not then be purged ourselves?

Malenkov knows that these questions are being asked. He has read the declarations of allegiance, but he cannot be sure. His tasks are enormous. Not only must he consolidate his power within the Soviet hierarchy, he must also impress his strength upon the satellite leaders. And while he is showing his strength, he must also be careful.

Once before he was not careful. Once before he cast away the caution which had served him so well throughout his successful career. In 1946 he had thought himself strong enough to defy Zhdanov and the Old Bolsheviks. He failed. It is a lesson he has remembered.

Strength, cautiously applied, might be the proper tactic— strength applied where there would be little resistance. The shooting down of the American and British fliers showed strength, but the risks were small—just "strongly worded" notes from Washington and London. Other actions must be taken that carry a similar aura of strength, but do not disturb a peace offensive.

Malenkov, looking out into the world, must feel that he needs time, but that he cannot afford to lose a minute. The loyalty of the Communist satellites, that would come first. But then also the loyalty of the Communist parties abroad. The old leaders are ill: Maurice Thorez of the French Communist Party, who has been in Moscow for years; Wilhelm Pieck of East Germany, overshadowed by younger men. Palmiro Togliatti's Italian party is losing support. The Communist Party of Greece trying to build an illegal underground machinery, is forced to operate from Bulgaria. Harry Pollitt and the British Communists are in retreat, particularly since the Prague purge trial of 1952. In the United States, William Z. Foster is old and ailing; most of the other top Communists are in jail.

In Latin America, the Communist Party of Argentina allied itself with the anti-United States policies of Premier Juan Perón; but their alliance has become too close. In Guatemala, a bright spot on the world Communist landscape, the party is expanding its influence; it is also gaining new strength in Cuba. In Brazil it is organizing in pseudosecrecy, causing food riots and unrest in the starving northern regions.

In Asia, of course, there is China and Mao Tse-tung. The stalemate in the Korean War has enabled the Chinese to strengthen their army. They are an important factor in a successful peace offensive that can split the Western allies and their friends in Asia.

Japan? There is a definite chance for increased Communist strength in Japan. American economic aid cannot support that overpopulated island nation indefinitely. The southern Asian nations of India, Pakistan, Burma, and Indonesia have learned that Communist parties consider their independent governments mere "bourgeois nationalists"; no different, really, from Chiang Kai-shek.

In the Near East, Iran promises a fruitful field for Communist activity. The Communist Tudeh (Masses) party forms a solid bloc within an unstable nation. The Arabs, generally, might be expected to endorse Moscow's revived anti-Zionism; Israel, seen from Malenkov's desk, has become an "outpost of American imperialism." In North Africa, Communist parties are allied with nationalist groups; their future potential is great. Africa is becoming an important target for Communist agitation.

The picture Malenkov sees from the Kremlin is contradictory. There is reason both for pessimism and optimism. As seen from Moscow, the splitting tactic is eminently sound, the tactic which Malenkov, backed by Stalin, advocated at the Nineteenth Party Congress in 1952. It was not a new tactic, but worth reviving. It means, this time, splitting the United States from its friends in Europe and Asia.

There are sufficient real disagreements between the United States and her allies, enough potential conflict to exploit. All that is needed, from Moscow's point of view, is the sharpening of what Stalin in his *Economic Problems of Socialism in the U.S.S.R.* called "the contradictions between capitalist countries." To contribute to this sharpening, *Red Star,* the Soviet army newspaper, has carried articles claiming that "a wave of hatred and resistance is rising among the millions of peoples against the American troops as world policemen." Radio Moscow has been saying that Canada is being absorbed into the United States, that "no foe has ever dealt Britain such heavy blows or has appropriated so much of her Empire as her United States 'friends' are doing today." Tass has carried a feature article, entitled "U.S. Monopolies Are Lording It over the Netherlands West Indies." In these and many other ways, Soviet propaganda services, and Communist parties throughout the world, represent the United States as the hypocritical exploiter, a tyrant disguised as friend.

Malenkov can profit from the experience of the past. He knows that French-German antagonism is likely to delay perfection of the North Atlantic Treaty Alliance. He knows that Italian-Yugoslav conflict over Trieste can endanger extension of the Yugoslav-Greek-Turkish military agreement. He knows that the Arab states, split among themselves, are united in resentment of United States support of Israel. He knows that French control in Indo-China is still resented among former colonial nations of southern Asia, although without French armies Vietnam, Cambodia, and Laos would be overrun by communism.

He knows that France in Morocco, Britain at the Suez Canal, American troops on Japanese soil, are causes for resentment and friction. He knows that the bulk of the American people dislike supporting the armies of other nations—and that these nations resent American prodding and American "charity." He can see the weak spots, one by one, the spots where cleavages between America and Europe, between Europe and the Near East, between America and Asia, between Europe and Asia, cleavages within Europe, within the Near East, within Asia, and even cleavages within each nation, may be widened by skillful agitation.

A peace offensive can cause the same confusion which the policy of a "united front," of an "outstretched hand" created in the 1930s. It may bring about the American depression—already anticipated as a "Malenkov depression" by some United States writers—which Malenkov's protégé Eugene Varga had forecast, but which war production caused by Soviet aggression may have postponed.

The job of world-wide agitation, from Malenkov's point of view, must continue unabated. In fact, so as not to suggest that any weakening might come with the transfer of power, agitation and propaganda must be stepped up. While cordially, softly speaking of "peaceful" negotiations, of "co-existence" between the Communist states and the West, Malenkov can hardly afford to relax the Soviet propaganda drive.

There is, then, ground for optimism from Malenkov's point of view, as he looks about the world. There are trouble spots in the West to make more troublesome, conflicts to sharpen, differences of opinion on which to capitalize.

But there is also ground for pessimism. Since the heyday of world communism, immediately after World War II, membership in Communist parties has gone down everywhere. Party newspapers, such as *Ce Soir* in Paris, have fallen by the wayside. Aggressive Kremlin policies have served to expose Communists operating in the free nations, have reduced their usefulness as channels for Kremlin propaganda. The deluded friends of Moscow, the fellow travelers or crypto-Communists, have dropped out one by one. When the impetuous Zhdanov forced the break with Tito, he helped destroy pro-Soviet affections as far away as Burma.

Ever since the Zhdanov policy of bold antagonism toward the United States emerged in 1947, the fortunes of world communism have gone down. This downward trend began, in fact, even earlier and can perhaps be traced to the summer of 1945, when the Communist Party of the United States ousted Earl Browder. It had been Browder's policy to take the pledges of cooperation, voiced by Stalin at Teheran, quite seriously. Browder was found guilty, in the words of the Communist Party of the United States, of "deserting to the side of the class enemy—American monopoly capital."

The "Teheran policy," the tactic of speaking and acting softly toward the temporary wartime allies, had paid off handsomely in such indispensable items as Lend-Lease shipments. It had contributed to the increase in membership and funds available to the Communist parties. It had strengthened the Communists of Western Europe—to the point where their leaders received cabinet posts. But the swift change to a policy of all-out antagonism toward the West had weakened the Communist parties abroad and strengthened Western unity against Soviet aggression.

Malenkov, viewing the world from the Kremlin, must weigh all this. More than anything else he needs time—time to consolidate his own position at home, time to knit together the frayed world Communist movement and to staff its key positions with reliable "Malenkovites." In turn, these new Malenkov men need time to purge their parties' leadership and membership of men who fail to adjust themselves to the new regime in the Kremlin, men who make a habit of nostalgia—who remember too often, and too keenly, the good old days when Stalin was alive.

Malenkov must favor a return to the Teheran policy, or something very much like it. After all, even during its most pronounced application, that policy had simply been organized hypocrisy; and it had worked. The capitalist countries had sent obliging ambassadors to Moscow. Writers who ignored the seamy side of Soviet society found a wide public. Soviet friendship societies blossomed. Communists, in those bygone days, had been respected nonconformists, dissenters who carried the aura of heroic rebels fighting for social reform.

As Malenkov, even temporarily, decides on a policy of hypocrisy—of speaking softly in the Teheran-policy manner—such a policy must constitute a grave danger to the West. As a "Malenkovism" develops that turns a hypocritical smile westward, the foundation of Western strength is being weakened.

This is true because the West has not really learned much since 1945. In much of Europe and Asia, the neutralist notion that the United States and the Soviet Union are twin dangers

is far from dead. The idea that there exists "two power blocs"
—one led by the United States and the other by Moscow, and
that there is little to choose between the two—is a prevalent
form of naïve sophistication. A knowing air of cynicism still
meets reports of forced labor and secret-police terror in the
Soviet Union, the same cynicism that sometimes greets American aid abroad, the cynicism that says, "surely there must be
some catch to it."

In the United States itself, anti-communism became fash-
ionable after such Soviet crudities as the coup d'état in
Czechoslovakia. Preferable though it is to the naïveté during
the Teheran period, this anti-communism is only skin-deep
with some. One kind word from the man in the Kremlin, and
wishful thinking can sweep some opinion makers in the
United States off their feet. When Malenkov addressed the
Supreme Soviet, shortly after he succeeded Stalin, he spoke
three slightly conciliatory sentences which might have sig-
naled the beginning of "Malenkovism," of a temporary effort
to lull the West into relaxing its vigilance, of slowing down
its rate of armament.

Quite possibly, Georgi Malenkov played a part in planning the invasion of the Korean Republic by Communist
forces in 1950. In fact, some scholars speculate that Malenkov went to Peiping in the fall of that year to persuade the
Chinese Communists to throw their full weight against the
United Nations counterattack that was driving north toward
the Yalu River. At any rate, Malenkov must know the mixed
lesson of Korea: that while it is advantageous to the U.S.S.R.
to have the Chinese and North Korean Communists fight the
battle for her, the southward plunge of Red troops on June
25, 1950, did much to unite anti-Communists the world over.

As he translates this lesson into active tactics, Malenkov

must realize that highhanded actions of the Korean type have consistently strengthened the free world's will to resist. The Czechoslovak coup d'état prompted the Marshall Plan. Korea brought about NATO, the American armament program, the Greek-Turkish-Yugoslav alliance, the plans for a European Defense Community, and the blueprint of a Middle East defense command. Here, quite clearly, are cause and effect. But the Prague coup was not necessary to dramatize Kremlin methods to those fully aware; no Korean invasion was needed to illustrate the aggressive tactics of the Soviet Union. Less dramatic actions have been equally outrageous.

Before the Czechoslovak coup d'état, many saw in Prague a successful "bridge between the West and the East." They were annoyed and disillusioned by the coup. Similarly, Premier Syngman Rhee of the Republic of Korea was imagined by some as the main cause for guerrilla unrest against his government, whereas, in reality, these guerrilla activities were the probing maneuvers of the invaders.

However, without Prague and Korea, without these crude and perhaps ill-considered Kremlin actions, the Soviet regime might still be able to masquerade as merely a force for social progress. Few steps would be necessary for Malenkov to turn back the clock of world opinion drastically. One action would be an offer of conciliation to Marshal Tito of Yugoslavia following a liquidation of the Korean War.

As Malenkov took power, Tito was making an unprecedented visit to Great Britain to settle political and military questions and strengthen Yugoslavia's ties with the West. But it should be remembered that it was the impetuous Zhdanov, Malenkov's adversary, who had pushed Tito too hard. Malenkov might derive tremendous satisfaction from repairing what his one-time rival had destroyed. Moreover, the evolving Malenkov-Mao relationship might well form a pattern for a possible Malenkov-Tito reunion.

After Stalin's death, Mao Tse-tung of China rose in importance. A Moscow-Peiping split is not indicated—if only because it would be disadvantageous to both regimes. But greater *de facto* equality between the two governments seems quite certain. As high priests at Stalin's shrine, Malenkov and Mao stand on equal footing; as heads of two populous nations, they can also benefit in terms of internal and external propaganda from such an adjustment in relationship. Emphasis on equality would strengthen Mao inside China, for it would rob anti-Communist and anti-Soviet forces in China of an important talking point: Mao's subservience to Moscow.

A Malenkov-Tito deal might follow a similar pattern. Again, equality would be the key concept. Internal opposition to such a development would give Malenkov the opportunity of purging a "Zhdanovite" opposition, of eliminating party officials with too marked a tendency toward nostalgia for the Stalin era. Externally, Malenkov would be able to represent himself as reasonable and willing to develop new relationships. Even if Tito did not accept such an offer—it would certainly be extremely difficult for him to do so—the new man in the Kremlin would have definitely affected world opinion by a gesture toward reconciliation with the Yugoslavs.

The possibility of a Malenkov offer to Tito is cited here, not because it is very likely, but as an illustration of the type of gesture that might cause the pendulum of world opinion to swing toward Malenkov, although nothing of substance would have changed. Malenkov can benefit most from a policy of keeping the West off balance; of blowing hot one day and cold the next; of, simultaneously, talking peace and stirring up guerrilla war, as in northern Iran; of answering the questions of a foreign journalist with great cordiality, while provoking riots in Japan. It is the technique of a magician, who distracts the attention of his audience with the clever gestures of one hand while he prepares his next trick with the other.

The situations in Iran and Japan have just been mentioned. Both nations are obvious targets of Moscow-inspired agitation. That is well realized in the case of Iran, because of the long controversy over the nationalized oil properties. But the potentially dangerous position of Japan is less well known, and it should therefore be emphasized.

However Malenkov may revise, speed up, or delay the timetable of Communist aggression, Japan is likely to be printed on it in large letters. This overpopulated island nation is heavily dependent on American aid; its economy would best be helped by trade with China, and the Peiping regime has made much of this. Also, in early 1953, seven and a half years after the war's end, 30,000 Japanese war prisoners were returned to Japan from China—many of them, no doubt, thoroughly indoctrinated Communists. The political-economic condition of Japan is potentially most explosive. Its Communist Party, after years of internal conflict, has been molded into a maneuverable and hard nucleus of revolution.

The Japanese Communist Party, like the Communist Party of India, looks simultaneously to Moscow and Peiping for support and guidance. Greater equality between the Soviet and Chinese Communists would, in these areas, merely confirm an already existing attitude. In addition to the repatriated war prisoners, Japan has the internal problem of a large

Korean minority heavily infiltrated with agents from North Korea.

Targets like Japan and Iran are inviting because they give the Kremlin an opportunity to show its satellites that revolutionary action is far from dead. Internal unrest in Near Eastern and Asian nations is one of the safest ways in which Malenkov can demonstrate his strength, while keeping risks at a minimum. *The Korean onslaught, an overt act of war which united the enemies of communism, must be a warning to Malenkov that underground and guerrilla operations are preferable to open acts of aggression.* Also, guerrillas create a dilemma for the United States. If guerrillas form among Iran's Kurds, a minority that is under constant propaganda attack from Moscow, there is no way in which the United States could intervene; the Iranian government is not likely to ask for outside help. Similarly, if trouble starts inside Japan, which regained her independence on April 28, 1952, she will doubtless try hard to put her own house in order.

The case of Indo-China illustrates the advantage which Malenkov can derive from using guerrilla warfare rather than armed invasion. In Korea, the Communists actually crossed a border in open violation of United Nations rulings. The issue was clear. But United Nations intervention against the Communists in Indo-China would encounter insuperable legal hurdles because Peiping intervention has been unobtrusive.

The Indo-Chinese Communists inside Vietnam are supported by Red China, but technically they represent an internal revolutionary force. Similar guerrilla movements might be fostered inside the Korean Republic, Japan, Iran, India, North Africa, or inside Latin American nations. In every case,

Malenkov could disavow Soviet involvement and repeat the time-honored clichés of coexistence and peace.

We cannot be certain, of course, whether Malenkov will choose exactly these tactical roads. But we must recognize the dilemma of the West, and above all of the United States, that has arisen with a change of emphasis in Kremlin policy. A Teheran-type policy can play down conflicts, just as Malenkov did when he said "there is not one dispute or undecided question that cannot be decided by peaceful means" and through "mutual understanding." Such a policy must seek to be disarming, both in the literal and the metaphoric sense of the word. In the United States latent pressures to reduce the expensive armament program have already sprung to the surface after a series of conciliatory gestures on Malenkov's part.

Details of a Malenkov "peace offensive" quickly followed the session of the Supreme Soviet. The Soviet government apologized for the shooting down of a British bomber over Germany. It also offered to obtain the release of British and French diplomats and civilians seized by Communist forces in Korea at the beginning of hostilities. Then, on March 28, the Korean Communists responded to a request made by UN Commander Gen. Mark Clark on February 22, and offered to exchange sick and wounded prisoners. Two days later, following his return from Moscow, Chinese Communist Premier Chou En-lai proposed that the future status of all prisoners might be settled and a Korean truce negotiated.

The Malenkov peace offensive exposed disastrous immaturities of political understanding in the United States, but even more so in nations such as France and India. It seems as if the free world has learned nothing in the seven years of Soviet aggression; seven years that showed the results of grave miscalculations during World War II. Wishful thinking, hopeful sentimentality, or the immature desire for immediate gains at the price of long-range world security— those were the world's reaction to Malenkov's tactical moves designed to lull the world into reducing its vigilance.

When Beria praised Malenkov before the Supreme Soviet, he described him as "a talented disciple of Lenin." It was Lenin who taught his revolutionary disciples to "retreat in good order when the forces of the enemy are obviously superior to our own, in order to prepare with the utmost energy for a new offensive."

We must recognize that a policy of Soviet hypocrisy is far more dangerous to the free world than is a policy of frank antagonism.

No peace offensive can change the Soviet regime's intent to achieve world-wide supremacy. Short-range tactics may change, but the long-range strategy does not. Malenkov's tactical moves put the free world's political maturity to a crucial test.

At such a moment in history, the free world must realize that the outstretched hand of the new man in the Kremlin is only a magician's clever gesture, seeking to detract attention from the danger of a poised bayonet.

APPENDIXES

APPENDIX I

The Soviet Table of Organization

STRUCTURE OF THE COMMUNIST PARTY
OF THE SOVIET UNION
(As of March 20, 1953)

First Secretary of the Presidium of the Central Committee
    Georgi M. Malenkov
Presidium of the Central Committee
    Georgi M. Malenkov, Lavrenti P. Beria, Vyacheslav M.
    Molotov, Klementi I. Voroshilov, Nikita S. Khrushchev,
    Nikolai A. Bulganin, Lazar M. Kaganovich, Anastas I.
    Mikoyan, Maxim Z. Saburov, Mikhail G. Pervukhin.
Secretariat of the Central Committee
    Nikita S. Khrushchev, Mikhail A. Suslov, Peter N. Pospe-
    lov, Nikolai N. Shatalin, Semyon D. Ignatiev.*
Central Committee of the C.P.S.U.
Congress of the C.P.S.U.

ADDITIONAL APPOINTMENTS
(As of March 15, 1953)

Klimenti E. Vororshilov
    Chairman of the Presidium of the Supreme Soviet.
Nikolai M. Pegov
    Secretary of the Presidium of the Supreme Soviet.
Nikolai M. Shvernik
    Chairman of the All-Union Central Council of Trade
    Unions.

---

* Ignatiev was dismissed on April 7, 1953.

STRUCTURE OF THE GOVERNMENT
OF THE SOVIET UNION
(As of March 15, 1953)

Premier; Chairman of the Council of Ministers
Georgi M. Malenkov

Deputy Premiers; First Deputy Chairmen of the
Council of Ministers
Lavrenti P. Beria, Minister of Internal Affairs; Vyacheslav
M. Molotov, Minister of Foreign Affairs; Nikolai A. Bul-
ganin, Minister of Defense and Marshal of the Soviet
Union; Lazar M. Kaganovich (no portfolio specified).
Council of Ministers of the U.S.S.R.
Anastas I. Mikoyan, Deputy Chairman of the Council of
Ministers and Minister of Domestic and Foreign Trade;
Alexei I. Kozlov, Minister of Agriculture and Procure-
ment; Panteleimon K. Ponomarenko, Minister of Cul-
ture; Alexei N. Kosygin, Minister of Light and Food
Industries; Alexander F. Zasyadko, Minister of Coal In-
dustry; Nikolai K. Baibakov, Minister of Oil Industry;
Ivan S. Tevosyan, Minister Metallurgical Industry; Sergei
M. Tikhomirov, Minister of Chemical Industry; Maxim Z.
Saburov, Minister of Machine Construction; Vyacheslav
A. Malyshev, Minister of Transport and Heavy-machine
Building; Mikhail G. Pervukhin, Minister of Electric
Power Stations and Electrical Industry; Colonel-General
Dmitri F. Ustinov, Minister of Defense Industry; Pavel A.
Yudin, Minister of Building Materials Industry; Georgi
M. Orlov, Minister of Timber and Paper Industry; Nikolai
A. Dygai, Minister of Construction of Machine Building
Enterprises; Boris P. Beshchev, Minister of Railway Trans-
port; Nikolai D. Psurtsev, Minister of Communications;
Zosim A. Shashkov, Minister of Sea and River Fleet;
Areseni G. Zverev, Minister of Finance; Andrei F. Tretya-
kov, Minister of Health; Konstantin P. Gorshenin, Minis-
ter of Justice; General Vsevolod N. Merkulov, Minister of
State Control.

Gregori P. Kosyachenko, Chairman of the State Planning Committee (Administration of the Five-Year Plan); Konstantin M. Sokolov, Chairman of the State Committee on Construction.

CHANGES IN GOVERNMENT AND PARTY

THE NINETEENTH COMMUNIST PARTY CONGRESS which took place in October, 1952, was the first such Congress since 1939. It greatly altered the structure of the party, replacing the 12-man Politburo with a 36-man Presidium and widening the 71-man Central Committee to include 125 full members and 110 nonvoting alternate members.

Announcements made on March 6, 1953, one day after Stalin's death, largely nullified the decisions of the Congress. These decisions affected both the government and the party; in every case, a marked tendency toward consolidation was evident. The Presidium's membership was reduced to ten, with four alternates. The number of ministries was reduced drastically by a series of mergers.

The fourth session of the Supreme Soviet, which approved the government changes, had originally been scheduled for Saturday, March 14, 1953. At the last moment, it was postponed by one day. Instead, the Saturday was devoted to a special high-level meeting that resulted in last-minute revisions, both in the government and in party structure.

Among the total results, the following may be considered as particularly notable:

Anastas I. Mikoyan, on March 6, had been named trade minister. On March 15 he was also named Deputy Chairman of the Council of Ministers (Deputy Premier)—but not *First* Deputy Premier, which would have placed him in the same category as Beria, Molotov, Kaganovich, and Bulganin. Mikoyan, in 1949, had shared the fate of Molotov when he was divested of his ministerial post, although retaining Politburo status. Zhdanov, Molotov, and Mikoyan had at one time formed an inner Politburo circle concerned with formulating foreign policy.

Andrei A. Andreyev, who in 1948 was considered Malenkov's

closest rival in succeeding to Zhdanov's position, was not listed as a minister on March 6. Although divested of all his government and party posts, Andreyev was on March 15 named to membership in the Presidium of the Supreme Soviet. Malenkov's attitude toward Andreyev was illustrated at the Nineteenth Party Congress, when he took occasion to criticize Andreyev for collective farm policies which Andreyev had publicly described as a mistake as long ago as January, 1950.

The following appointments may be regarded as strengthening Malenkov, as they affect men who are considered to be his close associates: the appointment on March 6 of Maxim Z. Saburov to head the Ministry of Machine Building; the appointment, at the same time, of Mikhail G. Pervukhin to head the Ministry of Electric Power Stations and Power Industry; the last-minute appointment, announced on March 15, of Alexi I. Kozlov to be Minister of Agriculture and Agricultural Procurement; the naming, at the same time, of Panteleimon K. Ponomarenko to head the new Ministry of Culture, a merger of the ministries of Higher Education, Cinematography, the Arts Committee, the Broadcasting Committee, the State Publishing House, and the Ministry of Labor Reserves. Ponomarenko, definitely a Malenkov protégé, had no previous experience in this field, as his career was largely devoted to industrial and agricultural affairs.

Changes in the Communist Party's secretariat, decided on Saturday, March 14, were announced six days later. Malenkov resigned as a member of the secretariat but retained his post as first secretary of the Presidium of the Central Committee, the party's highest policy-making body. The five men named to form the new secretariat, the central administrative body of the party, were: Nikita S. Khrushchev—possibly a brother of Malenkov's wife, Elena Khrushchev—Mikhail A. Suslov, Peter N. Pospelov, Nikolai N. Shatalin, and Semyon D. Ignatiev.

Khrushchev replaced Malenkov's antagonist Andreyev on the Council of Collective Farm Affairs and has served from 1938 to 1949 as First Secretary of the Ukrainian Communist Party and was Premier of the Ukraine from 1944 to 1947. A strong figure in his own right, he has differed with Malenkov on agricultural matters and may be close to Beria.

Suslov's association with Malenkov was dramatized on December 24, 1952, when he criticized a Soviet economist for hiding his earlier endorsement of economic ideas expressed by Nikolai A. Voznesensky, one of Malenkov's antagonists.

Pospelov served as *Pravda* editor in the 1940s, and as director of the Marx-Engels-Lenin Institute from 1949 on. He was associated with Malenkov in revising the Communist Party's program in 1952, but was, during Malenkov's period of power, merely reinstated as *deputy*-editor of *Pravda*.

Shatalin is a very close collaborator of Malenkov. He served in the Administration of Cadres as deputy director in 1946, and since then in the party's Organizational Bureau and as a party inspector.

Ignatiev, although appointed on March 7 to the Secretariat as a Malenkov man, was dismissed on April 7. He had been Minister of State Security in January, 1953, when his ministry charged nine doctors with plotting the death of high Soviet personalities. When Beria took control of the Security Ministry, he charged Ignatiev with "political blindness and gullibility" for permitting the false indictment of the doctors.

The re-emergence of Mikoyan and Andreyev, together with Malenkov's exit from the Secretariat and Ignatiev's removal, appeared as tactical moves designed to check Malenkov's power.

Malenkov's Important Addresses

MALENKOV'S REPORT TO THE NINETEENTH PARTY CONGRESS, 1952

From October 5 to 12, 1952, the Nineteenth Congress of the Communist Party of the Soviet Union (Bolsheviks) took place in Moscow. This Congress was the first since the Eighteenth Congress was held, prior to World War II, in 1939. The first item on the 1952 Congress agenda read, "1. Report of Central Committee of C.P.S.U. (B)—reporter, Comrade G. M. Malenkov, Secretary C.C."

Following Mr. Malenkov's keynote address to the 1952 Party Congress:

Comrades, the period since the Eighteenth Congress of the Party has been crowded with events of world-historic significance.

The Second World War shook to its very foundations the life of many nations and states and changed the face of the world. Engineered by the forces of international imperialist reaction and unleashed in the East by militarist Japan and in the West by Hitler Germany, the war upset the calculations of its instigators, and, thanks to the heroic struggle of the Soviet people, ended in a way unforeseen by the imperialists.

Instead of the destruction or weakening of the Soviet Union, the result was the strengthening of the U.S.S.R. and the growth of its international prestige. Instead of the weakening and defeat of democracy, the result was the dropping out of several countries in Central and Southeastern Europe from the capitalist system and the establishment in them of the people's democratic system.

162

Instead of further enslavement of the peoples in the colonies and dependencies, the result was a new powerful upsurge of the struggle for national liberation in these countries, with the crisis of the colonial system of imperialism becoming more acute. The historic victory of the great Chinese people was a telling blow to the entire world system of imperialism. Today one-third of humanity has already been delivered from imperialist oppression, liberated from the chains of imperialist exploitation.

In the capitalist world itself, the war deleted three large states—Germany, Japan, and Italy—from the list of the Great Powers, while France and Britain lost their previous positions.

The postwar period has been one of continuous weakening of the world capitalist system and of the growth of the forces of democracy and Socialism.

In the economic sphere the postwar years have been years of new and growing economic difficulties in the capitalist countries, of the development of American imperialist expansion with resultant sharpening of the antagonisms between the capitalist countries. These antagonisms have been agravated by the attempts of the imperialists to find a way out of the economic difficulties through militarization of the economy and preparation of another war.

In the political sphere the postwar period has been marked by the emergence of two camps—the aggressive, antidemocratic camp headed by the United States, and the camp of peace and democracy. A new center of reaction and aggression has taken shape in the capitalist world in this period. Its embodiment is the United States, from which now emanates the chief menace to the peace, freedom, and national independence of the peoples. Faced with this menace the peace forces have risen everywhere for determined struggle in defense of peace and the national independence of their countries.

In the postwar period the Soviet Union has continued its advance, interrupted by the war, along the path indicated by the Eighteenth Party Congress, the path of peaceful progress and gradual transition from Socialism to Communism. The postwar years have brought big achievements in industry, transport, and agriculture and in all branches of science, culture, and art. They have also brought further consolidation of the Soviet system, have strengthened the moral-political unity of Soviet society and the friendship of the peoples of our country.

Through all these years the Soviet Union has been waging an active struggle for the maintenance and consolidation of world peace.

Let us examine the principal aspects of the international situation.

"Two Trends of Development"

The present over-all world economic situation is characterized by two trends of development.

The first trend is represented by the steady advance of the peace economy of the Soviet Union and the People's Democracies, an economy which is free from crises and aims at securing maximum satisfaction of the material and cultural requirements of society. This economy ensures systematic raising of the standard of living of the masses and full employment. A feature of this economy is the friendly economic cooperation of the countries comprising the democratic camp.

The second trend is represented by the economy of capitalism, the productive forces of which are stagnant. This is an economy caught in the vice of the steadily deepening general crisis of capitalism and of constantly recurring economic crises; this is the trend of militarization of the economy and one-sided development of branches of industry producing for war, of rivalry between countries, and enslavement of some countries by others. This situation stems from the fact that capitalist economy aims not at promoting the interests of society, but at securing maximum profits for the capitalists through the exploitation, the ruin, and impoverishment of the majority of the people in the given country, through enslaving and systematically plundering the peoples of other countries, especially the backward countries, and lastly through wars and militarization of the national economy.

Industrial development in the U.S.S.R. and in the capitalist countries is characterized by the following figures:

*Growth of Industrial Output in the U.S.S.R.
and the Capitalist Countries for 1929–1951*

(in percentages of 1929)

	1929	1939	1943	1946	1947	1948	1949	1950	1951
U.S.S.R.	100	552	573	466	571	721	870	1082	1266
U.S.A.	100	99	217	155	170	175	160	182	200
BRITAIN	100	123	no fig-	112	121	135	144	157	160
FRANCE	100	80	ures	63	74	85	92	92	104
ITALY	100	108	published	72	93	97	103	118	134

As is seen from this table the volume of industrial output in the U.S.S.R. in 1951 was 1,266 per cent of 1929, which represents a nearly thirteenfold increase. Soviet industry in the postwar period, as was the case before the war, is making uninterrupted progress based on the development of peace production.

It will also be seen from the table that in the U.S.A. industrial production marked time in the period between 1929 and 1939; it afterward advanced but only due to a sharp increase in military output during the Second World War, then it slumped considerably and rose again only with the unleashing of war against the Korean people and the transition to an intensified arms drive and, as a consequence, rose in 1951 to double the 1929 figure.

Industrial output in Britain increased only 60 per cent in the same period while in several West European capitalist countries industry is still marking time around the 1929 level.

In the European People's Democracies, although they suffered much more damage in the war than the capitalist countries of Western Europe, the prewar level of industrial output was surpassed in 1951: in Poland 2.9 times, in Czechoslovakia 1.7 times, in Hungary 2.5 times, in Romania 1.9 times, in Bulgaria 4.6 times and more than fivefold in Albania. Agriculture, too, is making steady headway in these countries, progress being especially rapid in industrial crops; considerable achievements have been attained in livestock farming.

The German Democratic Republic has made impressive progress in economic development. By 1952, the prewar level of industrial output had not only been regained, it was surpassed by 36 per cent. The 1951 volume of industrial output was 2.4 times greater than in 1946. The iron and steel industry, engineering, and the chemical and power industries are developing from year to year. In agriculture prewar levels have been surpassed both in regard to the area sown to crops and in harvest yields.

The Chinese People's Republic is making rapid economic progress. Its people are working with great enthusiasm and are successfully eliminating the severe aftermath of many years of ruinous war against the Japanese invaders and Kuomintang reaction. Industrial development since the establishment of the people's democratic power in China has proceeded at a rapid rate: compared with 1949, the volume of industrial output in 1951 has more than doubled; rail transport has been rehabilitated and new railway lines are being built at an accelerated rate. The great agrarian reform, carried out by the People's Government of China, has resulted in a big advance in agriculture: the grain yield in 1951 was 128 per cent and cotton 252 per cent compared with 1949. Whereas the national finances of the old China were in a state of complete dislocation with inflation assuming colossal dimensions, the Chinese People's Government has consolidated the country's finances and stabilized its currency.

Big economic advances were made in the Korean People's Democratic Republic following its liberation from the Japanese colonizers. Already in 1949 the volume of industrial output was four times that of 1946. The agrarian reform carried out by the people's democratic Government was followed by a nearly 25 per cent increase in the area sown to crops, and harvest yields of all crops increased considerably. The American imperialist attack interrupted the peaceful constructive labor of the masses in the Korean People's Democratic Republic. American and other troops, operating under the United Nations flag, are savagely destroying North Korea's peaceful towns and villages, its industry and agriculture.

Important successes have been won by the Mongolian People's

Republic in developing its economy, which is gaining in strength and scope with every passing year. The material well-being of the Mongolian people is improving and their culture developing. The country's basic occupation, livestock farming, is making steady headway; flocks and herds have increased 2.5 times since the establishment of the Republic, and all the livestock now belongs to the working peasantry. Output of state-owned and cooperative industries has nearly trebled in the last ten years.

All the data on industrial development in the capitalist countries and in the countries of the democratic camp show that as regards rate of development, industrial output in the capitalist countries, the United States included, is considerably behind the rate of industrial development in the U.S.S.R. and the People's Democracies.

"Contradiction of Capitalism"

Another thing that emerges from these data is that industrial output in the capitalist countries rose somewhat, solely due to war preparations and to the servicing of the war machine during war.

Far from eliminating the economic and political contradictions of capitalism, the Second World War aggravated these contradictions still more, undermined the economies of the capitalist countries and deepened the general crisis of the world capitalist system. The Second World War failed to justify the hopes of the big bourgeoisie of the imperialist countries. Each of the two belligerent capitalist groups calculated on redividing the world by armed force, on seizing new raw material sources and expanding the markets for its goods, that is, on strengthening its own economic position at the expense of its adversaries and establishing world domination.

But these calculations miscarried. Although Germany and Japan were knocked out as the chief rivals of the three main capitalist countries—the United States, Britain, and France—the hopes of these countries, especially the United States, of being thus able to increase industrial output four or fivefold, were shattered. In addition, China and the European People's Democracies dropped out of the capitalist system, and, together with the Soviet Union, formed a united and powerful camp of peace and democracy which stands opposed to the camp of imperialism.

The economic result of the rise of two opposing camps, as Comrade Stalin has pointed out, was the disintegration of the single, all-embracing world market and the emergence of two parallel world markets: that of the countries of the camp of peace and democracy, and that of the aggressive, imperialist camp. The disintegration of the single world market is the most important economic outcome of the Second World War and its economic consequences.

The two world markets are developing in opposite directions. The new, democratic world market experiences no sales difficulties because its capacity increases from year to year in conformity with the crisis-free development of industry in the democratic camp, because uninterrupted growth of output in all the countries of the democratic camp makes for steady extension of the capacity of the democratic market. In contrast to this, there is the other world market, the imperialist market, which is not connected with the U.S.S.R. and the other democratic countries and because of this has been narrowed down and is suffering from sales difficulties caused by breaks and crises in production, unemployment and impoverishment of the masses, and by the severance of its ties with the democratic countries. Moreover, it should be borne in mind that disintegration of the single world market has drastically reduced the spheres in which the chief capitalist countries (United States, Britain, France) could obtain access to the world's resources. As a result the capitalist world market is steadily shrinking, conditions for the sale of goods in this market have deteriorated and continue to do so.

The capitalist countries emerged from the Second World War with varying results, and this has substantially changed the economic relations between them. The economies of many of the countries which took part in the war were greatly undermined by the protracted hostilities and losses in manpower and material values. This applies primarily to Germany, Italy, and Japan. Much damage was caused also to France, Holland, Belgium, and several other countries. Britain came out of the war very seriously weakened.

The United States of America waxed rich on the war and the American billionaires strengthened their economic positions. Nevertheless, the United States did not succeed in attaining its goal; it did not succeed in establishing the domination of American capital over the world market. With Germany and Japan out of the running, the United States expected to increase its industrial output four or five times over. However, it managed only to double output and is now sliding into economic crisis. It is a fact that there are at least three million wholly unemployed in the United States and even more working part time. Mass strikes are adding to the complications of the American billionaires. This is all traceable to the fact that America's industry has been deprived of such markets as the U.S.S.R., China, and the European People's Democracies, and for this the United States ruling circles are to blame.

"American Imperialism"

American imperialism acts now not only as an international exploiter and enslaver of the peoples, but also as a force disorganizing the economies of all the other capitalist countries. Taking advantage of the weakened state of its rivals, American monopoly capital has, since the war, seized a substantial share of the capitalist world market. It is destroying the traditional multilateral economic ties between the capitalist countries and replacing them with unilateral ties between these countries and the United States. The American monopolies are adding to the dislocation on the capitalist world market by boosting their own exports by means of the most unscrupulous dumping, simultaneously sealing off their home market from foreign goods, with the result that the American people are made to bear the brunt of high prices. American imperialism is depriving the West European countries of the possibility of acquiring food in their former East European markets to which West European countries traditionally exported large quantities of manufactured goods in exchange for food and raw materials.

This economic policy of American imperialism could not but

sharpen the antagonisms between the United States and the other capitalist countries. The chief of these remains the antagonism between the United States and Britain, taking the form of open struggle between the American and British monopolies for sources of oil, rubber, nonferrous and rare metals, sulfur and wool, and for markets.

To this should be added the very serious antagonisms between the United States and Japan, the United States and Italy, the United States and Western Germany—the countries subjected to the occupation yoke of the United States dictators. It would be naïve to think that these vanquished countries will agree to remain indefinitely under the heel of the American occupationists. It would be folly to think that they will not attempt, in one way or another, to throw off the American yoke and live free and independent lives.

The antagonisms between the United States and Britain, and between the United States and France, are becoming increasingly acute and will become still more acute accordingly as American capitalism, to the accompaniment of noise about "aid," and by granting credits, insinuates itself into the economies of Britain, France, and Italy, seizing raw-material sources and markets in the British and French colonies. Britain and, following her, France and the other capitalist countries are endeavoring to break away from subordination to the United States in order to secure for themselves an independent position and high profits. Even now British capitalists are putting up a stubborn fight against American dictation in world trade.

The economic difficulties which have gripped the capitalist countries since the war have been further aggravated by the fact that the imperialists have themselves shut the door to the democratic world market. The United States of America has reduced its trade with the Soviet Union and the European People's Democracies to practically nil, and has cut off trade with China. It has virtually forbidden not only the vanquished countries (Japan, Western Germany, and Italy), but also Britain, France, Holland, Denmark, Norway, Belgium, and other capitalist countries to sell or buy goods in the market of the countries of the democratic camp. In 1951 United States trade with the countries that now comprise the democratic camp was only one-tenth of the 1937 figure; British trade with these countries has dropped to one-sixth, and French trade—by more than fourfold.

The United States, as well as Britain and France, thought that their economic "blockade" of the U.S.S.R., China, and the European People's Democracies would strangle these countries. Actually the effect has been not the strangling but the strengthening of the new democratic world market. The imperialists have thereby delivered a telling blow to their own export trade and have aggravated still more the contradiction between the production potential of their industry and the possibilities for the sale of its products.

All this signifies that even deeper contradictions have arisen in the capitalist economy, and that the world system of capitalist economy as a whole has become considerably narrower and weaker and even less stable than before the war.

Conscious of these economic difficulties, the United States capitalists are endeavoring to overcome them by means of the war in Korea, the armaments drive, and the militarization of industry.

"War Hysteria"

Having launched a reactionary war against the Korean people, and whipping up war hysteria against the democratic camp, the United States, British, and French imperialists have converted their economies to a war footing and have carried militarization of the economy and the arms drive to colossal dimensions in their countries. An ever-increasing proportion of industrial output in these countries is now used for equipping the armed forces. War contracts play a decisive role in all major industries in the United States and other capitalist countries. Direct and indirect expenditure on armaments accounts for a steadily increasing share of the budgets of the capitalist countries. Direct military expenditure in the United States rose from one billion dollars in the 1937–1938 fiscal year to 58.2 billion dollars in 1952–1953 and now accounts for 74 per cent of the U.S. budget compared with 14 per cent in 1937–1938. In Britain, military expenditure has grown from 197 million pounds to 1,634 million pounds in the same period, constituting 34 per cent of the total budget as compared with 17 per cent before the war; in France military expenditure now accounts for nearly 40 per cent of the total budget.

This unprecedented rise in military expenditure is leading to a nonstop rise in taxation and to larger inflationary emissions of paper money. The severe weakening of the financial systems of the capitalist countries—the result of the war and of the policy of the ruling circles of the United States—is becoming more pronounced. Currency depreciation has assumed unparalleled dimensions. In 1951 the purchasing power of the dollar, according to official and obviously doctored figures, was only 43 per cent of 1939; the pound sterling had dropped to 32 per cent, the French franc to 3.8 per cent, and the Italian lira to less than 2 per cent.

The switch to a war economy has enabled the United States and other capitalist countries to raise industrial output for the time being. On this basis bourgeois economists are trying to prove that big war orders can keep "business activity" at a high level indefinitely. But real life gives the lie to these assertions. Now, in the third year of the particularly intensified militarization of the capitalist economy, its fatal consequences are becoming increasingly apparent. The war and inflation factors, while producing temporary booms, have imparted a one-sided war character to economic development in the capitalist countries. An increasing share of goods and raw materials is swallowed up by unproductive military consumption or becomes a dead weight in the shape of enormous strategic stockpiles. At the same time the militarization of the economy results in the population being robbed of their money through higher taxes. All this turns the budgets of the capitalist countries into a means by which the billionaires rob the people; it substantially lowers the purchasing power of the population, reduces the demand for manufactured goods and agricultural produce, drastically curtails civilian production, and creates the conditions for the onset of a severe economic crisis.

Militarization of the national economy does not do away with but, on the contrary, increases the disproportion between production capacity and the diminishing purchasing power of the population, which the ruling clique in the capitalist countries is reducing to the very minimum, and this in turn leads to a steady contraction of the capitalist market. Thus the expansion of war production is inevitably leading to the maturing of a new deepgoing economic crisis.

The armaments drive is a particularly heavy burden on the economy of the satellites of the United States of America. Having unleashed the war in Korea, the United States increased its pressure on the West European states, demanding that they gear their industry to war in ever-increasing measure and allocate excessive appropriations for war preparation, depriving their civilian industries of the necessary raw materials and auxiliaries. American imperialism has once and for all discarded the mask of "restorer" of the economy of capitalist countries. American "aid" is now given only for armaments, for the preparation of a new war. The armaments drive conducted by the rulers of Britain, France, Italy, Western Germany, Belgium, Norway, and other capitalist countries on orders from the American monopolies, is ruining the economy of these countries and pushing them towards disaster.

The billionaires, having subordinated to themselves the bourgeois state and dictating to it the policy of armaments drive and preparation for another war, are making colossal profits. The armaments drive has become a source of unprecedented enrichment for the billionaires, and in the first place for the monopolies and billionaires of the U.S. Even according to official underestimated data, the profits of American capitalist monopolies rose from 3.3 billion dollars in 1938 to 42.9 billion dollars in 1951 or thirteen times over. Tremendous profits are being piled up by the British monopolist money-bags, as well as by the capitalist monopolies of France, Italy, Japan, and other countries, despite the fact that the economy of these countries is in a state of protracted stagnation.

At the same time militarization has led to a sharp decline in the conditions of the masses. Increased taxes, rising prices for goods of mass consumption, and inflation have increased the relative and absolute impoverishment of the working people. In the United States of America, even if we allow for the devaluation of currency, direct taxation of the population in the present fiscal year amounts to more than twelve times the 1937–1938 level. In the West European countries, where the taxpayer carried a heavy enough burden even before the Second World War, taxes have increased, doubling in Britain and increasing in France 2.6 times and in Italy—1.5 times.

Even the obviously doctored official cost-of-living and retail price indices testify to the steady rise in the cost of living, particularly after the launching of American aggression in Korea. In these conditions the policy of "freezing" wages, implemented by the capitalists with the support of the right-wing socialists and reactionary trade-union leaders, has resulted in a substantial reduction in real wages for factory and office workers. In France and Italy real wages this year are less than half the prewar figure, and in Britain—20 per cent less than before the war. In the United States, according to figures released by the United Electrical Workers Union, the cost of living has risen nearly threefold compared with the 1939 level. Despite growing war production, the number of unemployed and part-time unemployed is rising in the capitalist countries. In Italy and Western Germany unemployment exceeds the level of the most difficult years of the 1929–1933 world economic crisis; Italy has over 2 million unemployed and a still greater number of part-time unemployed; nearly three million are unemployed and part-time unemployed in Western Germany. In Japan nearly 10 million people are completely without work or have only part-time employment. The U.S.A. has no less than 3 million wholly unemployed and 10 million part-time unemployed. Unemployment is rising in Britain, too, where the figure already exceeds half a million. In such a small country as Belgium, there are more than 300,000 unemployed.

The steady deterioration of the material conditions of broad strata of the population caused by the armaments drive is leading to ever greater discontent among the masses and to intensified struggle on their part against lowering the standard of living and the entire policy of preparing for a new war. Class contradictions between the imperialist bourgeoisie, on the one hand, and the working class and all the toiling people, on the other, are rapidly becoming more acute. A strike wave is spreading wider and wider throughout the capitalist world.

The situation in which the world capitalist system finds itself is complicated by the fact that, as a result of the war and the new upsurge of the national-liberation struggle in the colonial and dependent countries, the disintegration of the colonial system of imperialism is actually taking place.

As a direct result of the defeat of fascist Germany and imperialist Japan, the imperialist front was breached in China, Korea, and Vietnam, where People's Republics have arisen in place of the former semi-colonies and colonies. The victory of the Chinese people revolutionized the East still more and helped to stimulate the liberation struggle waged by the peoples oppressed by imperialism.

The contradictions between the colony-owning countries and the colonies became still more pronounced after the war. Britain, France, Belgium, and the other colonial powers are seeking to recoup at the expense of the colonies for the burdens which the militarization of their economy and United States expansion have imposed on them. At the same time the American imperialists are penetrating into the colonies and spheres of influence of these colonial powers, capturing positions for themselves in these areas, and intensifying the exploitation of the peoples of the colonial and dependent countries. In the course of this struggle the American plunderers are fomenting conspiracies against their British and French "allies," thus further aggravating the crisis of the imperialist colonial system. The territory of many colonial and dependent countries (Egypt, Iran, Syria, Morocco, Tunisia, etc.) is used for military bases and their population prepared for the role of "cannon fodder" in a future war.

As a result of protracted imperialist oppression and feudal survivals, the economy and particularly the agriculture of the colonial and dependent countries is in a state of decline. Tens of millions of people in India, Indonesia, Iran, and the countries of Africa live in conditions of chronic hunger, and enormous numbers die of starvation. The rapacious exploitation of the colonial and dependent countries by the imperialist powers retards the develop-

ment of the productive forces in these countries, keeps the purchasing power of the population at an exceedingly low level, and
curtails markets for manufacturers. All this weighs like a millstone
on the economy of the capitalist world, aggravating the internal
contradictions of the world capitalist system as a whole.

The peoples of the colonial and dependent countries are putting
up ever more determined resistance to the imperialist enslavers.
That the scale of the national-liberation movement is expanding
is evident from the struggle being waged by the peoples of Vietnam, Burma, Malaya, the Philippines, and Indonesia, and from
the growth of national resistance in India, Iran, Egypt, and other
countries.

"Preparations for a New War"

The postwar activity of the U.S., British, and French ruling
circles in the sphere of international relations too has been marked
by preparations for a new war.

Almost immediately after the Second World War, the United
States of America renounced the line of policy agreed upon and
pursued by the wartime allies and laid down in the decisions of
the Teheran, Yalta, and Potsdam conferences of the powers. By a
series of aggressive acts the U.S.A. aggravated the international
situation and brought the world face to face with the danger of a
new war.

The rulers of the U.S. have been quite candid in formulating
the aims of their aggressive policy. As far back as 1945, shortly
after he became President of the United States, Truman declared
that "victory . . . has placed upon the American people the continuing burden of responsibility for world leadership." Subsequently Truman and other American politicians repeated time
and again the claim to "U.S. world leadership." This course, which
aims at establishing world domination, at subjugating all other
countries, is the keynote of the entire policy pursued by the U.S.
imperialist ruling clique.

The U.S. tycoons knew, of course, that it would be impossible
to establish domination over other nations by peaceful means.
They knew from the experience of the Hitlerites, who also sought

to establish their rule over other countries, that world dominion was unthinkable without force, without unleashing a new war; and they decided to violate the peace, to prepare a new war. Since the U.S.S.R. is the main opponent of another war, the principal bulwark of peace, the U.S. magnates concluded that the war should be spearheaded against the U.S.S.R. and the other countries standing for peace. In this way the North Atlantic aggressive bloc, formed without knowledge of the U.S.S.R. and behind its back, came into being. And in order to conceal the aggressive aims of this bloc, to deceive the peoples, they proclaimed it a "defensive" bloc against "Communism," against the Soviet Union which, allegedly, is getting ready to attack the U.S., Britain, France, and the other members of the bloc.

With this same criminal end in view, American military bases are being created in different countries situated near the Soviet frontiers.

With this same criminal end in view, the U.S. ruling circles are remilitarizing Western Germany and Japan.

By remilitarizing Western Germany and Japan, the ruling circles of the U.S.A. and their adherents are reviving, in full sight of the whole world, the two hotbeds of the Second World War to eradicate which the peoples shed their blood in that war.

The U.S. attack on the Korean People's Democratic Republic marked the transition of the U.S.-British bloc from preparation of aggresive war to direct acts of aggression. The Korean people, who in close cooperation with the valiant Chinese volunteers are heroically defending the freedom and independence of their homeland and giving a rebuff to the violators of peace, enjoy the warmest sympathy of all democratic and peace-loving mankind.

At present the international situation taken as a whole bears a number of specific features and peculiarities of which it is necessary to note the following.

United States, "Principle Aggressive Power"

The principal aggressive power—the United States of America —is whipping the other capitalist countries towards war at an accelerated rate, primarily those belonging to the North Atlantic bloc, as well as the countries which were defeated in the Second World War—Western Germany, Italy, and Japan. Dictating their will to others, the U.S. rulers are defining for all the members of the bloc the aims of the war, the theaters of hostilities, the forces that are to take part, and decide other questions pertaining to the preparation for war.

The rulers of the U.S. claim that they are inspired by ideals such as the creation of a "community of free countries." Time and again they come out with the declaration that the U.S., Britain, France, Turkey, Greece represent this "community of free countries," while the U.S.S.R. and the People's Democratic Republics are, allegedly, "not free." Our understanding of this is that the U.S., Britain, France, Turkey, and other capitalist countries really do have "freedom," not freedom for the people, however, but freedom to exploit and plunder the people. As regards the U.S.S.R. and the People's Democratic Countries, this kind of "freedom" certainly does not exist, for in these countries freedom to exploit and plunder the working people was abolished long ago. Here, then, is what the advocates of the "American way of life" boast of.

In actual fact the policy of the U.S. in regard to its West European and other capitalist "friends" is not a democratic policy, but an imperialist one. Under the label of "anti-Communism" and "defense of freedom" the old, long-established bourgeois countries and their colonies are virtually being subordinated to the United States and plundered. Just as Hitler did before them, the U.S. imperialists need the "struggle against Communism" as a smoke screen in order to divert attention from their real schemes of conquest. While pursuing an imperialist policy in regard to Britain, France, and other capitalist countries, the United States of America has, moreover, the effrontery, to put it mildly, to pose as the genuine friend of these countries. A fine friend! After bridling and saddling its junior partners and lashing and whipping them, it plunders and shackles them, repeating all the time "let us be friends," which, in the language of the American money-bags means: first you carry me, then I ride you.

Once-free capitalist states, Britain, France, the Netherlands,

Belgium, and Norway are now in fact abandoning their own national policy and carrying out a policy dictated by the U.S. imperialists, yielding their territories for American bases and military springboards, thereby endangering their own countries in the event of hostilities breaking out. On American bidding they conclude alliances and blocs directed against their own national interests. A striking example of this is seen in the actions of the French ruling circles who, with their own hands, are helping to revive France's most bitter and age-old enemy, German militarism. British leaders, both Conservative and Labour, have committed themselves for a long time to the role of junior partner of the United States, thereby pledging to pursue not their own national policy but an American policy. As a result of this policy the British people already bear a heavy burden and the British Empire has been shaken to its foundations.

In spite of this, British propaganda organs claim that it is the Communists who are wrecking the British Empire. Yet the ruling circles of the British Empire cannot be blind to the obvious facts which leave no doubt that the possessions of the British Empire are being seized not by the Communists but by the American billionaires.

Was it the Communists and not the American billionaires who seized Canada, who are seizing Australia and New Zealand, who are ousting Britain from the Suez Canal Zone and from the markets of Latin America and the Near and Middle East, and laying their hands on the oil areas owned by Britain?

The facts show that no enemy of Britain has ever dealt her such heavy blows or took from her Empire, part by part, as is now being done by her American "friend." This "friend" belongs to the same bloc as Britain and has built air bases on British soil, thereby placing her in a grievous and, I would say, dangerous position; and yet it has the audacity to pose as Britain's savior from "Soviet Communism."

As for such "free" countries as Greece, Turkey, and Yugoslavia, they have already been turned into American colonies, while the rulers of Yugoslavia—all these Titos, Kardeljs, Rankovics, Djilases, Pijades, and others—who long ago became American agents engage in espionage and subversion against the U.S.S.R. and the People's Democracies on assignments from their American "bosses."

The ruling circles of France, Italy, Britain, Western Germany, and Japan have harnessed themselves to the chariot of U.S. imperialism and have renounced a national, independent foreign policy of their own. True, in this way the ruling cliques of these countries betray the national interests of their countries and admit their own bankruptcy. But these cliques prefer to sacrifice the national interests of their states in the hope of obtaining the aid of the transatlantic imperialist patrons against their peoples, whom they fear more than foreign imperialist slavery.

The Right-wing Social Democrats, and the top leaders of the British Labour Party, of the French Socialist Party and of the Social Democratic Party of Western Germany in the first place, also bear direct responsibility for this antinational policy of the ruling circles. The Right-wing Socialists of Sweden, Denmark, Norway, Finland, Austria, and other countries are following in the footsteps of their colleagues, and, ever since the Second World War, have been waging a frenzied struggle against the peace-loving and democratic forces of the peoples. Present-day right-wing social democracy, in addition to its old role of lackey of the national bourgeoisie, has become an agency of foreign, U.S. imperialism, carrying out its foulest assignments in preparing for war and in fighting against its own people.

"Strategy of United States Imperialism"

A distinctive feature of the strategy of U.S. imperialism is that its bosses base their war plans on the utilization of the territory of others and the armies of others—primarily the West German and Japanese armies, as well as the British, French, and Italian— on utilization of other peoples who are to serve, according to the schemes of the U.S. strategists, as blind instruments and cannon fodder in the conquest of world dominion by the U.S. monopolists.

But even now the more sober and progressive politicians in the European and other capitalist countries, men who have not been blinded by hatred of the Soviet Union, see clearly the abyss into which the American adventurists, who have run amok, are plunging them; they are beginning to take a stand against war. It should be assumed that genuine peace-loving democratic forces will be found in the countries that are doomed to the role of pawns in the hands of the U.S. dictators, forces which will follow their own independent, peaceful policy and will find a way out of the impasse into which they have been driven by the U.S. dictators. The European and other countries taking this new path will meet with complete understanding in all the peace-loving countries.

In their endeavors to mask their policy of conquest, the ruling circles of the United States seek to pass off the so-called "cold war" against the democratic camp as a peaceful defensive policy and frighten their own peoples with the nonexistent danger of attack from the U.S.S.R. Masking the aggressive plans and the military operations now in progress with demagogic phrasemongering about peace is a characteristic feature of the policy of the bosses of the Atlantic bloc. The crux of the matter is that today it is not so easy to drive peoples who only recently bore the full brunt of a bloody shambles, into a new war, a war against the peace-loving peoples. Hence all the efforts of the aggressive Atlantic wolf to appear in sheep's clothing.

In these circumstances it would be dangerous to underestimate the harm of the pharisaical peace camouflage resorted to by the present-day aggressors.

War preparations are accompanied by an unprecedented wave of unbridled militarism which affects every aspect of the life of the people in the countries of the imperialist camp, by a frenzied offensive of reaction against the working people, and by fascization of the entire regime in these countries.

If the Hitler imperialists in preparing for the Second World War installed fascism in their country, now the American imperialists who are engaged in preparations for a new war, are installing a brutal fascist regime not only in the United States, but in other countries as well, and above all in those countries where the forces of peace and democracy are particularly strong, for instance, in France, Italy, and Japan. The ruling circles of these countries, carrying out the ignominious mission dictated by the American militarists, have declared war on their peoples. Moreover, the U.S. armed forces stationed outside the boundaries of the United States are performing the duties of punitive gendarme troops.

U.S. imperialism is at present not only the aggressor, it is the world gendarme seeking to strangle freedom wherever possible and to implant fascism.

Against this world gendarme there is rising even now a wave of hatred and resistance on the part of the peoples suppressed by it.

All this testifies to the weakening of the positions of the imperialists and leads to a sharp intensification of the struggle waged inside the imperialist camp between the forces of fascist reaction and the democratic forces of the people of the imperialist countries. Such a situation is fraught with exceedingly serious consequences for the warmongers.

In connection with the growing danger of war a popular peace movement is developing, an antiwar coalition is being created of different classes and social strata interested in ending the international tension and preventing a new world war. The warmongers will not succeed in their efforts to label this nonparty, peaceful, democratic movement a party, allegedly communist, movement. The fact that the Stockholm Appeal was signed by 500 million people and the Appeal for the conclusion of a peace pact among the five Great Powers by over 600 million is the best rebuff to this claim of the warmongers and an indication of the tremendous scale of the nonparty, democratic movement for peace. This peace movement does not pursue the aim of abolishing capitalism, for it is not a socialist, but a democratic movement of hundreds of millions of people. The peace partisans are advancing demands and suggestions which are bound to contribute to preserving peace and preventing another war. The achievement of this goal would, in the present historical conditions, be a tremendous victory for the cause of democracy and peace.

The present correlation of forces between the camp of imperialism and war and the camp of democracy and peace makes this prospect a completely real one. For the first time in history there exists a mighty and united camp of peace-loving states. In the capitalist countries the working class is better organized than before, powerful democratic international organizations of workers, peasants, women, and the youth have been established. The Communist parties, fighting heroically for the cause of peace, have grown in numbers and strength.

The peoples of all countries, including the broad masses in the United States of America—for in the event of war they would suffer no less than the population of other countries—are interested in combating the danger of a new war. The war in Korea despite the vast preponderance of American technique, has already taken from the American people a toll of hundreds of thousands in killed and wounded. It is not difficult to visualize how enormous the sacrifices of the American people would be should the bloated financial tycoons of the U.S.A. hurl them into war against the peace-loving peoples.

The task now is to activate the popular masses still more, to strengthen the organization of the partisans of peace, to expose the warmakers tirelessly and not allow them to enmesh the peoples in a web of lies. To bridle and isolate the gamblers of the camp of the imperialist aggressors who seek to embroil the peoples in a sanguinary slaughter for the sake of their profits—such is the principal task of all progressive and peace-loving mankind.

Soviet Foreign Policy

The basic line of the Party in the sphere of foreign policy was and remains a policy of peace among nations and of guaranteeing the security of our socialist homeland.

Since the first days of the existence of the Soviet state the Communist Party has proclaimed, and has pursued in practice, a policy of peace and friendly relations among nations. Throughout the period between the two world wars the Soviet Union persistently upheld the cause of peace and fought on the international arena against the danger of another war; it worked for a policy of collective security and collective rebuff to aggressors. It was no fault of the Soviet Union that the reactionary circles in the United States and the countries of Western Europe frustrated the policy of collective security, encouraged Hitlerite aggression and led to the unleashing of the Second World War.

While unswervingly upholding a policy of peace, our Party, keeping in mind the hostile encirclement, tirelessly strengthened the country's defense in order to meet the enemy fully prepared.

At the Eighteenth Party Congress in 1939, when the conflagration of war had already flared up, Comrade Stalin stressed the basic principles of Soviet foreign policy, pointing out that "We stand for peace and the strengthening of business relations with all countries. That is our position; and we shall adhere to this position as long as these countries maintain like relations with the Soviet Union, and as long as they make no attempt to trespass on the interests of our country." At the same time Comrade Stalin issued a warning to the aggressors. "We are not afraid," he declared, "of the threats of aggressors, and are ready to deal two blows for every blow delivered by instigators of war who attempt to violate the Soviet borders."

And when Hitler Germany treacherously attacked our homeland, the Soviet people gave the enemy an annihilating rebuff and smashed him completely. The whole world saw that our Party does not throw words to the winds.

After the Second World War, the Party continued to pursue a foreign policy of ensuring a lasting and stable peace and of promoting international cooperation. The Soviet Government advanced its widely known program of measures to avert war.

The peacefulness of the Soviet Union is illustrated not only by its proposals but also by its deeds. After the war the Soviet Union considerably reduced its armed forces, which are now numerically not superior to the forces it had before the war. In the briefest space of time after the war the Soviet Government withdrew its troops from the territory of China, Korea, Norway, Czechoslovakia, Yugoslavia, and Bulgaria, whither those troops had been moved in the course of military operations against the fascist aggressors. The Supreme Soviet of the U.S.S.R., holding that the fight against the man-hating propaganda for another war plays a big role in easing international tension, adopted, on March 12, 1951, the Law in Defense of Peace and proclaimed war propaganda the gravest of crimes against humanity. It thereby set an example for other countries.

During the most serious complications on the international arena in recent years, it was the Soviet Union that advanced proposals providing a basis for a peaceful settlement of outstanding questions. It suffices to recall that it was the Soviet side which advanced the proposals that served as the basis for the truce talks in Korea.

The Government of the U.S.S.R. attaches much importance to the United Nations organization, holding that it could be an important instrument for maintaining peace. But at present the United States is turning the United Nations from the organ of international cooperation, which it should be according to the Charter, into an organ of its dictatorial policy in the struggle against peace and is using it as a screen for its aggressive actions. However, notwithstanding the tremendous obstacles put in its way by the voting machine which the United States has set up in the United Nations, the Soviet Union upholds peace there and works for the adoption of realistic proposals arising from the present-day international situation; proposals aimed at curbing the aggressive forces, at preventing another war, and at stopping hostilities where they are already in progress.

It would be incorrect to consider that war could be directed only against the Soviet state. The First World War, as we know, was unleashed by the imperialists long before the U.S.S.R. came into being. The Second World War began as a war among capitalist states, and the capitalist countries themselves suffered heavily from it. The contradictions which today rend the imperialist camp may lead to war between one capitalist state and another. Taking all these circumstances into consideration, the Soviet Union is working to prevent any war among states and is acting for a peaceful settlement of international conflicts and disagreements.

However, in pursuing its policy of ensuring lasting peace, the Soviet Union finds itself up against the aggressive policy pursued by the ruling circles of the United States of America.

Moreover, bellicose American circles are endeavoring to put the blame where it does not belong. They are inflating in every possible way their propaganda of lies about a supposed threat on the part of the Soviet Union. As for these lies and inventions about the Soviet Union, it would be ridiculous to go into them, for they completely lack foundation. Indisputable facts show who really is the aggressor.

Everybody knows that the United States of America is intensifying its armaments drive, refuses to ban the atomic and germ weapons, and to reduce conventional armaments, while the Soviet Union proposes a ban on the atomic and germ weapons and a reduction of other armaments and armed forces.

Everybody knows that the United States refuses to conclude a peace pact, while the Soviet Union proposes the conclusion of such a pact.

"The United States Attacked Korea"

Everybody knows that the United States is forming aggressive blocs against the peace-loving peoples, while the exclusive object of the treaties concluded between the Soviet Union and foreign states is to combat revival of Japanese or German aggression.

Everybody knows that the United States attacked Korea and is trying to enslave it, while the Soviet Union has not conducted any hostilities anywhere since the end of the Second World War.

The United States is carrying out aggression also against China. It has seized ancient Chinese territory—the island of Taiwan. Its air force is bombing Chinese territory in violation of all accepted standards of international law. Everybody knows that the air force of the U.S.S.R. is not bombing anybody and that the U.S.S.R. has not seized any foreign territory.

Such are the indisputable facts.

Passing over to our relations with Britain and France, it must be said that these relations ought to be in keeping with the spirit of the treaties we concluded with those countries during the Second World War and which stipulate cooperation with them in the postwar period. However, the British and French governments are grossly violating these treaties. Contrary to the solemn pledges of postwar cooperation which they gave to the Soviet Union at the time it was waging a sanguinary war to liberate the peoples of Europe from German-fascist enslavement, the rulers of Britain and France have joined completely in carrying out the American imperialists' aggressive plans against the peace-loving states. It is clear that in view of such a stand taken by the governments of Britain and France, our relations with these countries leave much to be desired.

The position of the U.S.S.R. as regards the United States, Britain, France, and the other bourgeois states is clear, and our side has stated that position on many occasions. Now, as well, the U.S.S.R. is ready for cooperation with these states, having in mind the observance of peaceful international standards and the guaranteeing of a stable and lasting peace.

With regard to the defeated countries—Germany, Italy, and Japan—the Soviet Government pursues a policy entirely different in principle from the policy of the imperialist powers. The fact that the Soviet socialist state was among the victors has created an absolutely new, unprecedented situation and possibilities for the peoples of the defeated countries. For every country which signed an unconditional surrender the policy of the Soviet state opens up the possibility of peaceful, democratic development, of progress for civilian industries and agriculture, of selling goods on foreign markets, and of creating national armed forces essential for the country's defense. In conformity with the Potsdam Agreement, the Soviet Union unswervingly pursues a policy aimed at the speediest conclusion of a peace treaty with Germany, the withdrawal of all occupation forces from Germany, and the establishment of a united, independent, peace-loving, democratic Germany, having in mind that the existence of such a Germany, together with the existence of the peace-loving Soviet Union, excludes the possibility of new wars in Europe and makes the enslavement of European countries by the world imperialists impossible.

It is to be hoped that the German people, who are faced with the dilemma of either taking that path or of being turned into mercenary soldiers of the American and British imperialists, will choose the correct path—the path of peace.

The same must be said with regard to Italy, to whose fraternal people the Soviet Union wishes complete restoration of their national independence.

The Soviet Government considers that Japan should also become an independent democratic peace-loving state, as envisaged by joint decisions of the Allies. The Soviet Government refused to sign the one-sided treaty which the American dictators forced upon the San Francisco Conference, since that treaty tramples upon the principles of the Cairo and Potsdam declarations and the Yalta Agreement, and is aimed at turning Japan into an American Far Eastern military base. The peoples of the Soviet Union have deep respect for the Japanese people, who have to endure the yoke of foreign bondage, and they believe that the Japanese people will achieve national independence for their homeland and take the path of peace.

The Soviet policy of peace and security of the peoples proceeds from the fact that the peaceful coexistence and cooperation of capitalism and Communism are quite possible provided there is a mutual desire to cooperate, readiness to adhere to commitments entered into, and observance of the principle of equality and non-interference in the internal affairs of other states.

The Soviet Union has always stood, and stands today for the development of trade and cooperation with other countries notwithstanding differences in social systems. The Party will pursue this policy in the future, as well, on the basis of mutual advantage.

While American and British bellicose circles keep reiterating that only the armaments drive keeps industry in the capitalist countries going at full capacity, there is in actual fact another prospect—the prospect of developing and extending trade relations between all countries, irrespective of differences in their social systems which could keep the factories and mills in the industrially developed countries working to capacity for years, that could ensure markets in other countries for the goods in which some countries are rich, promote economic advance in the underdeveloped countries and thereby establish lasting economic cooperation.

In pursuing its policy of peace the Soviet Union is in complete unanimity with the other democratic peace-loving states: the

Chinese People's Republic, Poland, Romania, Czechoslovakia, Hungary, Bulgaria, Albania, the German Democratic Republic, the Korean People's Democratic Republic, the Mongolian People's Republic. The relations between the U.S.S.R. and these countries are an example of completely new relations among states, relations such as have never been witnessed in history. They are based on the principles of equality, economic cooperation, and respect for national independence. True to its treaties of mutual aid, the U.S.S.R. has rendered and will render aid and support in the further strengthening and development of these countries.

We are confident that in peaceful competition with capitalism, the socialist system of economy will prove its superiority over the capitalist system more and more vividly year by year. We have no intention, however, of forcing our ideology or our economic system on anybody. "Export of revolution is nonsense," says Comrade Stalin. "Every country will make its own revolution if it wants to, and if it does not want to there will be no revolution."

While it steadfastly pursues its policy of peaceful cooperation with all countries, the Soviet Union takes into account the existence of the threat of new aggression on the part of the warmongers who have lost all restraint. Hence, it is strengthening its defense capacity and will continue to strengthen it.

The Soviet Union is not frightened by the threats of warmongers. Our people have experience in fighting aggressors and are not novices at giving them a drubbing. They gave the aggressors a drubbing way back at the time of the civil war, when the Soviet state was young and comparatively weak, they gave them a drubbing in the Second World War, and they will give future aggressors a drubbing too if they dare to attack our homeland.

"The Prospect of a War"

The facts of history cannot be ignored. And the facts show that as a result of the First World War Russia dropped out of the system of capitalism, while as a result of the Second World War a whole series of countries in Europe and Asia dropped out of the system of capitalism. There is every reason to assume that a third world war would bring about the collapse of the world capitalist system.

That, so to speak, is the prospect of a war and its consequences if war is forced on the peoples by the warmongers, by the aggressors.

But there is another prospect, the prospect of preserving peace, the prospect of peace among nations. That prospect calls for prohibition of war propaganda in accordance with the resolution adopted by the United Nations, a ban on atomic and germ weapons, consistent reduction of the armed forces of the Great Powers, conclusion of a peace pact among the powers, extension of trade among countries, restoration of the single international market, and other analogous measures in the spirit of strengthening peace.

Implementation of these measures would strengthen peace, rid the peoples of fear of the war danger, put an end to the unparalleled expenditure of material resources on armaments and preparation for a war of annihilation, and provide the possibility of diverting them for the welfare of the peoples.

The Soviet Union stands for implementation of these measures, for the prospect of peace among nations.

Tasks on Foreign Policy

The tasks of the Party in the sphere of foreign policy:

1. To continue the struggle against the plotting and unleashing of another war, to rally the powerful antiwar, democratic front for the strengthening of peace, to strengthen the bonds of friendship and solidarity with peace supporters all over the world, persistently to expose all the preparations for another war, all the machinations and intrigues of the warmongers;

2. To continue to pursue a policy of international cooperation and promotion of business relations with all countries;

3. To strengthen and develop inviolable relations of friendship with the Chinese People's Republic, with the European People's Democracies—Poland, Czechoslovakia, Romania, Hungary, Bulgaria, Albania, with the German Democratic Republic, with the Korean People's Democratic Republic, and with the Mongolian People's Republic;

4. Tirelessly to strengthen the defense might of the Soviet state and to increase our preparedness to give any aggressor a crushing blow.

"Internal Position" of the Soviet Union

The period under review is characterized by a further consolidation of the internal position of the Soviet Union, by a growth of the entire national economy and socialist culture.

In the first two years following the Eighteenth Party Congress the working people of our country continued successfully to carry out the third Five-Year Plan and achieved a further strengthening of the Soviet Union. In these years new successes were scored in advancing the national economy.

The peaceful labor of the Soviet people was interrupted by the perfidious attack of fascist Germany on the U.S.S.R. A difficult period began in the history of the Soviet state—the period of the Great Patriotic War. In the course of this war the working class, the collective-farm peasantry, and Soviet intelligentsia both at the front and in the rear displayed a high sense of duty and devotion to their homeland.

Having brought the war to a close with a historic victory, the Soviet Union entered a new, peaceful period of its economic development. The Soviet state in a short time, drawing upon its own means and resources, without outside assistance, restored the war-ravaged economy and pushed it ahead, leaving prewar economic standards behind.

Progress in restoring industry and agriculture made it possible already in 1947 to abolish rationing of food and manufactured goods and to carry out a monetary reform. These measures, and the five cuts effected in the prices of food and manufactured goods, increased the purchasing power of the Soviet rouble and ensured a rise in the material well-being of the working people. In 1950 the rouble was put on a gold basis and its rate of exchange raised in relation to foreign currency.

The achievements scored in restoring and advancing the economy enabled the Soviet state to begin the practical realization of new important national-economic tasks, including the construction of powerful hydroelectric stations on the Volga and the Dnieper, the building of big canals for shipping and irrigation, and the planting of shelter belts on vast stretches of the country.

The historic events that have taken place in the period under review have revealed the Soviet social and state system not only as the best form of organization for the economic and cultural advancement of the country in the years of peaceful construction, but also as the best form for mobilizing all the energies of the people to repel the enemy in wartime. These events have likewise shown the tremendous growth of the political activity of the working people, the further consolidation of the moral-political unity of the Soviet people rallied around the Communist Party, the further consolidation of the fraternal cooperation of the peoples of the U.S.S.R., and the development of Soviet patriotism.

Our people are determined to go ahead working selflessly for the good of their socialist homeland and to fulfill with honor the historic task of building Communist society.

"Socialist Industrialization"

During the prewar Five-Year Plans socialist industrialization was carried out in the U.S.S.R. The powerful industry was the basis for the development of the entire national economy and of preparing the country for active defence. The war years particularly demonstrated the correctness of our Party's general line of industrializing the country. The implementation of the industrialization policy was of decisive significance for the Soviet people's destiny and saved our homeland from enslavement.

In the difficult conditions of the war the Party was able quickly to switch industry to a war footing. The equipment of all the more important industrial plants was evacuated from the zone of hostilities to the eastern areas. In the war years the Soviet state mustered sufficient forces and resources not only for the rapid commissioning of the evacuated enterprises, but also for the speedy construction of new enterprises, chiefly heavy-industry plants. Despite the temporary occupation of economically important areas of the country by the fascist invaders, industry in the course of the war produced for the front, year by year, all types of armaments and munitions in ever-growing quantities.

With the termination of the war, industry was reconverted from war production to civilian production. The Party set the task of primarily developing heavy industry on a large scale, especially the iron and steel, fuel and electric-power industries, for without heavy industry it was impossible to cope with the tasks of restoring and further advancing the national economy. At the same time the Party focused particular attention on expanding the production of consumer goods in order to raise the living standard of the people.

A certain period of time was needed to restore the national economy to the prewar level. The level of the prewar year 1940 for over-all annual volume of industrial production was reached and surpassed in 1948; for coal output it was reached in 1947; for steel and cement, in 1948; for pig iron and oil, in 1949; for footwear, in 1950; for cotton textiles, in 1951. This means that the war delayed the development of our industry for eight or nine years, that is, roughly for two Five-Year Plan periods.

As a result of the successful restoration and development of industry in the postwar years, we now have a much higher level of industrial production than in the prewar period. Here are the data:

Growth of Industrial Production in U.S.S.R.

(in percentages of 1940)

	1940	1944	1945	1946	1947	1948	1949	1950	1951	1952
										(plan)
Industry as a whole respectively	100	104	92	77	93	118	141	173	202	223
Of which:										
Group A. Output of means of production respectively	100	136	112	82	101	130	163	205	239	267
Group B. Output of consumer goods respectively	100	54	59	67	82	99	107	123	143	156

It can be seen from these figures that in 1945 and 1946 there was a drop in the level of industrial production. This was due to the fact that production of military equipment was sharply curtailed after the war and the reconversion of industry to a peacetime footing required a certain amount of time. The postwar readjustment of industrial production was in the main completed during 1946 after which the output of our industry began to mount rapidly, and in 1951 its gross volume was more than double the 1940 output. In 1952 new progress has been made in advancing our industry. As is known, the plan for the current year with regard to industry as a whole is not only being successfully fulfilled, but is being overfulfilled; there is every reason to believe, therefore, that industrial output in 1952 will be approximately 2.3 times the 1940 output.

Particularly rapid progress is being made by industry manufacturing means of production; its 1951 total output volume exceeded the prewar level 2.4 times, and the 1952 output is to exceed that level by approximately 2.7 times. This year's output is to be as follows: 25 million tons of pig iron, or roughly 70 per cent more than in 1940; 35 million tons of steel, or roughly 90 per cent more than in 1940; 27 million tons of rolled metal, or more than double the 1940 output; 300 million tons of coal, or over 80 per cent more than in 1940; 47 million tons of oil, or over 50 per cent more than was produced in 1940; 117 thousand million kilowatt hours of electric power, or 2.4 times more than in 1940; and more than three times as much machinery and equipment will be produced as in 1940.

As for the annual increase in the output of the major industries, we have had a considerably greater increase in recent years than in the prewar period. Thus, in the past three years—1949–1951—that is when the prewar level of industrial production had been not only restored but surpassed, the increase in the output of pig iron amounted to 8 million tons, of steel 13 million tons, and of rolled metal 10 million tons, whereas in prewar years it had taken eight years to achieve an increase of this size in the output of pig iron, nine years for steel, and twelve years for rolled metal. The increase in the coal output in these three years

amounted to 74 million tons and the increase in the oil output
to 13 million tons; before the war it had taken six years to
achieve an increase of this size in the output of coal and ten
years for oil. The increase in the output of electric power in those
three years amounted to 37 thousand million kilowatt hours; before the war it had taken nine years to obtain an increase of this
size in the output of electric power.

The growth in output of means of production and of agricultural production has provided a sound basis for the development
of industry producing articles of consumption. The total output of
this industry in 1951 was 43 per cent greater than in 1940, and
in 1952 it will be approximately 60 per cent greater than the 1940
output. The 1952 output is to be as follows: over 5 thousand million meters of cotton textiles, or roughly 30 per cent more than in
1940; nearly 190 million meters of woolen fabrics, or roughly
60 per cent more than in 1940; 218 million meters of silk fabrics,
or 2.8 times the 1940 output; 250 million pairs of leather footwear,
or roughly 20 per cent more than in 1940; 125 million pairs of rubber footwear, or 80 per cent more than was turned out in 1940;
over 3,300,000 tons of sugar, or over 50 per cent more than in
1940; over 380 thousand tons of dairy-produced butter (leaving
out of account the considerable amount of homemade butter),
which will be over 70 per cent more than the prewar figure of
dairy-produced butter.

As a result of the successful rehabilitation and development of
industry in the postwar period, industrial production in the
U.S.S.R. per capita of population now exceeds the prewar level.
Thus, production of electric power per capita in 1951 was more
than double the 1940 output, pig iron 50 per cent, steel 70 per
cent, and coal 60 per cent greater; production of cement was
more than double, cotton textiles 20 per cent greater, woolens
more than 60 per cent greater, and paper 70 per cent greater, etc.

During the period under review, especially in the postwar
years, there has been a considerable expansion and consolidation
of the production and technical base of our industry, brought
about both by the building of new and the reconstruction of existing plants. In 1946–1951 alone over 320 thousand million roubles

out of total capital investments of about 500 thousand million roubles in the national economy were invested in industry. During this period about 7,000 big state industrial enterprises were rehabilitated, built anew, and commissioned. Compared with 1940 basic production plant of industry had increased 77 per cent by 1952.

"Advanced Soviet Science"

But it is not only that basic production plant has grown quantitatively. The past period was also characterized by industry's continued technical progress. In contrast to the situation in capitalist countries where there are periodical gaps in technical development, gaps accompanied by the destruction of productive forces of society through economic crises, in the U.S.S.R., which does not experience such crises, production is constantly being perfected on the basis of higher technique and on the basis of the achievements of advanced Soviet science. In the postwar years all branches of industry have been equipped with new machines and mechanisms, more advanced technological processes have been introduced, and a more rational organization of production effected. The machine-tool park was increased 2.2 times during this period by the addition of new, more productive machines. In the past three years alone the Soviet engineering industry has produced about 1,600 new types of machines and mechanisms.

Our science plays an important role in promoting further technical progress; by its discoveries it is helping the Soviet people to disclose the wealth and forces of nature more fully and to make better use of them. In the postwar period our scientists have successfully solved many scientific problems of great national-economic significance. A most important achievement of Soviet science in this period has been the discovery of ways of producing atomic energy. Thereby our science and technology have put an end to the United States' monopoly position in this field and have dealt a serious blow to the instigators of war, who tried to make use of the secret of producing atomic energy and their possession of the atomic weapon as a means of blackmailing and intimidating other peoples. While possessing real possibilities for producing atomic energy, the Soviet state is deeply interested in seeing this new type of energy used for peaceful purposes, for the good of the people, since such a use of atomic energy vastly extends man's dominion over the elements and opens up before humanity colossal opportunities for increasing the productive forces, for technical and cultural progress, and for multiplying the social wealth.

Major achievements by Soviet science and technology are attested to by the annual award of Stalin Prizes for outstanding scientific works, inventions, and radical improvements in methods of production. Eight thousand four hundred and seventy persons engaged in science, industry, transport, and agriculture have been honored with the title of Stalin Prize Winner.

An important result of the development of industry during this period has been the rapid advance of industry in the eastern regions of the U.S.S.R., as a consequence of which the distribution of our industry has been greatly changed. A powerful industrial base has been established in the eastern parts of the country—along the Volga, in the Urals, Siberia, the Far East, the Kazakh Soviet Socialist Republic, and in the Union Republics of Central Asia. By 1952 the total volume of industrial output in these areas had trebled in comparison with 1940. In 1951 the eastern areas accounted for about a third of the entire industrial output of the U.S.S.R., more than half of the steel and rolled metal, nearly half of the coal and oil, and over 40 per cent of the electric power.

Such are the principal results of the development of industry in the U.S.S.R. in the period under review.

The tasks in the sphere of advancement of our industry for the next few years are outlined in the draft directives of the fifth Five-Year Plan for development of the U.S.S.R., which have been presented for the consideration of this Congress. These tasks are to raise the level of industrial output in 1955 to about 70 per cent above 1950, with the output of means of production to increase by roughly 80 per cent and production of consumer goods by approximately 65 per cent. This assignment for increasing industrial output signifies that in 1955 the volume of industrial output will be three times the 1940 figure.

The fifth Five-Year Plan means another major forward stride in our country's advance from Socialism to Communism.

Our industry has every opportunity to accomplish the assigned tasks. Today all branches of industry are equipped with the very latest machinery, they have skilled workers, engineers, and technicians, and industrial enterprises experience no shortage of raw materials or other supplies. Now it is a matter of utilizing these opportunities to the full, of resolutely eliminating all shortcomings in work, of disclosing latent reserves in industry and transforming them into a mighty source for advancement of the national economy.

"Poorly Operating Establishments"

Each year industry not only fulfills state plans, but it over-fulfills them. But the general indices of good work for industry as a whole conceal poor work by many establishments which do not fulfill state assignments, as a result of which the national economy does not get the stipulated quantity of products. Ministries, however, do not take the proper measures to ensure fulfillment of plan by every establishment and, instead, frequently shift assignments from poorly operating establishments to efficient establishments. Consequently, the poorly operating enterprises live at the expense of the efficient enterprises.

One of the chief reasons for the failure to fulfill state plans is the uneven flow of output at enterprises during the month. The Party has more than once drawn the attention of executives in the economic field to this shortcoming. Yet even today many establishments operate by fits and starts, producing nearly half of the month's output in the last ten days, which leads to under-capacity operation, overtime, more waste, and upsets the work of allied enterprises.

Some establishments, in an effort to fulfill the gross output plan, resort to a practice that is inimical to the interests of the state, producing articles of secondary importance above the plan while failing to meet state plan assignments in respect to major items.

Some industries violate state discipline in relation to quality of goods. There have been cases of the consumers being supplied with low-grade articles and goods which are not up to the established standards and technical conditions. Machine-building plants not infrequently begin to manufacture machines before the design has been fully completed and which do not permit proper operation. Light-industry enterprises still turn out large quantities of inferior quality goods. All this is detrimental to the national economy.

Such shortcomings in the work of industry cannot be tolerated. The state plan is a law. All establishments must carry out the state assignments fixed for them and ensure the national economy the items it needs. Executives in the economic field and Party organizations are duty-bound to ensure fulfillment of plan by every enterprise not only for volume of gross output but absolutely for production of all items in accordance with the state plan, to strive for systematic improvement in the quality of the output, and to disclose and completely to eliminate the factors preventing the normal work of the enterprises.

Special attention should be given to the task of ensuring continued maximum advance in the productivity of labor in all branches of industry.

At all stages of socialist development our Party has worked steadfastly for a systematic rise in labor productivity as the major condition for the growth and perfection of socialist production. This is the explanation, in the main, for the tremendous progress that has been made in industrial development in the U.S.S.R. Between 1940–1951 labor productivity in industry increased 50 per cent; and the growth in the productivity of labor accounted for 70 per cent of the increase in industrial output for this period. In the building trades labor productivity went up 36 per cent in the same period.

The rapid growth in the productivity of labor in the U.S.S.R. is chiefly a result of the extensive introduction of new machinery and advanced technological processes in the national economy, of the mechanization and electrification of production, particularly, the mechanization of labor-consuming and heavy work, and also of better organization of the work, the higher general educational level and cultural level of the working people and greater skill on the job. The socialist system of economy offers unlimited opportunities for using the most up-to-date machinery. Besides saving labor, machinery in the U.S.S.R. also makes work easier. For this reason in a socialist economy workers are very eager to use machinery in the labor process, which is not the case under capitalism. The Soviet worker is directly interested in higher productivity of labor, because he knows that this makes for the increased economic might of the U.S.S.R. and a higher living standard. The high productivity of social labor under Socialism is based on the unity of interests of the state and the people.

However, the possibilities for raising labor productivity in our industry are far from being fully utilized as yet. This is indicated, firstly, by the failure of many enterprises to fulfill their plans for labor productivity. It should be noted that ministries are not giving sufficient attention to this important matter. Instead of making certain that every enterprise fulfills its assignment for labor productivity, ministries often rest content with the average results obtained by an industry as a whole, without taking the proper measures to bring the lagging enterprises up to the level of the leading ones.

At many enterprises higher labor productivity is hampered by poor utilization of the means of mechanization at hand. There have been intolerable cases of a neglectful and wasteful attitude toward equipment. Mechanization of production at any enterprise should certainly release some of the workers so that they might be employed either for the expansion of production at the particular enterprise or for work at new plants. Yet some industrial executives, instead of seeing to it that the means of mechanization are properly used so as to obtain higher labor productivity, not infrequently run the enterprise in the old way, extensively employing manual labor.

"Serious Shortcoming"

Another serious shortcoming in the sphere of mechanization is the fact that in the mechanization of production processes some departments are either not mechanized at all or insufficiently mechanized. At many enterprises, where the principal production processes are highly mechanized, the auxiliary operations including such labor-consuming jobs as bringing up, carrying over, and loading of raw material, supplies, and finished articles are slightly mechanized. All this diminishes the over-all economic effect of mechanization and disrupts normal production.

Higher labor productivity is also hampered by the fact that at many enterprises and construction sites the work is unsatisfactorily organized, with the result that much time is wasted. Ministries often fix the number of workers for establishments or building sites without making a sufficient study of the real requirements, or verifying whether the labor force is properly utilized. "Fluctuation" of labor at enterprises and especially at construction sites still obtains, causing great harm to production.

Technical norms are very important in raising productivity of labor. Yet at many establishments they are in an unsatisfactory state. There still prevail norms fixed at lower standards, so-called experimental-statistical norms, which do not correspond to the present level of technique, do not reflect the experience of foremost workers, and do not stimulate higher labor productivity. The proportion of experimental-statistical norms is very high, exceeding at many enterprises 50 per cent of all the norms in operation.

It is the task of the Party, economic and trade-union organizations speedily to eliminate the causes hampering the growth in labor productivity and to ensure fulfillment and overfulfillment of targets for higher labor productivity in all branches of the national economy, at every enterprise, and in every production sector. The shortcomings in utilizing the wealth of machinery at our disposal must be vigorously eradicated, the program for integrated mechanization and automatization of production processes must be persistently carried out, the latest achievements of science and technology must be more extensively introduced in all branches of the national economy, the forms and methods of organization of labor and production must be systematically improved, and better utilization must be made of labor power.

Comrades, our industry is expanding, developing, and growing stronger and becoming more perfected technically all the time. We shall continue to develop in every way the productive forces of our socialist industry as the foundation of the might of our country and of the growth in the material well-being of the Soviet people.

"Collective Farm System"

By the beginning of the period under review, *i. e.* by the time of the Eighteenth Party Congress, the collective-farm system in our country had been firmly established, the collective farms had been consolidated, and the socialist system of economy had established itself as the only form of agriculture.

The war temporarily held up the development of agriculture and inflicted great damage upon it, especially in the areas that were occupied, where the Hitlerite invaders ravaged and plundered the collective farms, the machine and tractor stations, and the state farms. Despite the enormous wartime difficulties, however, the collective and state farms of the eastern areas uninterruptedly supplied the Army and the population with food, and the light industry with raw materials. Without the collective-farm system, without the selfless work of the men and women collective farmers, without their high political consciousness and high level of organization, we would not have been able to cope with this most difficult task.

With the switch to peaceful construction the Party was confronted with the task of effecting the speediest possible restoration and further development of agriculture. A particular concern of the Party in the postwar period was to strengthen the collective farms organizationally and economically, to assist them in restoring and further developing their commonly owned economy and, on this basis, to improve the material well-being of the collective-farm peasantry. A significant factor in the further development of the productive forces of agriculture was the amalgamation of the small collective farms, for big collective farms can more easily expand and improve their commonly owned economy. At the present time there are 97,000 amalgamated collective farms instead of the 254,000 small collective farms as of January 1, 1950.

As a result of the steps taken by the Party and the Government, the difficulties in agriculture caused by the war and the severe drought that followed in 1946 were successfully overcome, the prewar level of agricultural production was restored and surpassed in a short period.

There has been a rapid restoration of crop areas in postwar years, harvest yields have been rising and the gross production of grain, industrial, fodder, vegetable, and melon, and other crops has been increasing. The total area under cultivation in 1952 exceeded the prewar level by 5.3 million hectares.

In the third year after the war, the prewar level of grain production was restored, and in subsequent years it increased, the production of marketable grain rising considerably at the same time. In the current year, 1952, the total grain harvest amounted to 8,000 million poods with the total harvest of the most important food crop, wheat, 48 per cent bigger than in 1940.

The grain problem, formerly considered the most acute and gravest problem, has thus been solved successfully, solved once and for all.

Particularly rapid has been the development of cotton and sugar-beet production in the postwar period; in 1951 the gross output of raw cotton exceeded the prewar level by 46 per cent, sugar beet—31 per cent. This year an even richer harvest of these most important crops was gathered. The prewar level has been surpassed in oil-bearing plants, potatoes, and fodder crops; moreover, the gross harvest of rich feeds (root fodder crops, melon fodder crops, and silage) was in 1951 already 25 per cent greater than in 1940. The postwar years have seen a considerable increase in the production of flax, vegetable, and melon crops. However, owing to insufficient attention by Party, government, and agri-

cultural bodies to the production of these essential crops, the output of flax and vegetables in a number of regions has still not
reached the prewar level.

This year, as in previous years, the state plans for the delivery
of grain, cotton, sugar beet, oil-bearing seeds, potatoes, vegetables,
and other farm produce, as well as the products of animal husbandry, are being carried out successfully.

"Grain Problem . . . Solved"

Our agriculture is becoming more and more perfected, more
productive, and is turning out more and more produce for the
market. This vital feature of the development of our agriculture
must be appreciated. Now that the grain problem has been successfully solved, the results attained in agriculture can no longer
be gauged in the old way, solely by the amount of grain produced. As can be seen from the data given, apart from achievements in grain production, we have made great headway in developing the production of cotton, sugar beet, oil-bearing, fodder,
and other crops. Our agriculture today has changed in quality; it
differs basically from the old low-productive, extensive agriculture. Whereas the area under all agricultural crops in the U.S.S.R.
in 1952 is 1.4 times more than in 1913, the area under grain crops
having increased 5 per cent, the area under industrial, vegetable
and melon crops has increased more than 2.4 times, and the area
under fodder crops, more than 11 times. At present industrial
crops account for more than 40 per cent of the total value of marketable field crops. Consequently, it would be a grave error to
assess the achievements attained in agriculture solely by the level
of grain production.

Much attention has been paid in the postwar years to equipping
agriculture with new technique. Otherwise we could not have
solved the task of restoring and further developing agriculture in
a short period. During this time machine and tractor stations have
been supplied with large numbers of new, improved caterpillar
tractors with diesel engines, self-propelled harvester combines,
mowers, sugar-beet harvester combines, flax harvester combines,
cotton picking and other highly efficient machines. The aggregate

horsepower of the tractors belonging to machine and tractor stations and state farms has risen 59 per cent above the prewar level, that of harvester combines has risen 51 per cent. Agriculture has been supplied with many new machines for labor-consuming jobs in animal husbandry. In connection with the considerable increase in mechanization in agriculture and forestry in the postwar years, the network of machine and tractor stations has been extended, a large number of forestry stations for mechanizing the work of tree planting, land-amelioration stations for mechanizing the work of draining and improving meadows and pastures, and animal-husbandry machine stations for mechanizing labor-consuming operations in animal husbandry have been organized. All in all, during this period 1,546 new machine and tractor, forest planting, land improvement and animal-husbandry machine stations have been established, bringing the total number of such stations to 8,939 at present.

The postwar achievements in agricultural development have created conditions making possible the accomplishment of still greater tasks in agriculture. The interests of the national economy and the tasks of further improving the well-being of the Soviet people call for the further expansion of agricultural production. The draft directives of the fifth Five-Year Plan envisage the following increase in the gross harvest in the course of the five years: grain 40–50 per cent, including wheat 55–65 per cent; raw cotton 55–65 per cent; flax 40–50 per cent; sugar beet 65–70 per cent; sunflower 50–60 per cent; potatoes 40–45 per cent; and the production of fodder crops will be approximately doubled or tripled.

Now that the prewar level of crop acreage has been restored and surpassed the only correct line in increasing agricultural production is that of further raising crop yield in every possible way. Raising the crop yield is the main task in agriculture. To solve this task successfully it is necessary to improve the quality and reduce the duration of field work, to improve efficiency in the utilization of tractors and agricultural machines, to complete the mechanization of the basic farm work, to ensure the speediest possible introduction of crop rotation with the sowing of perennial grasses on collective and state farms, to improve seed selection, to introduce a correct system of soil cultivation everywhere, to increase the use of fertilizer and increase the area of irrigated land. It is necessary to enhance the organizing role of machine and tractor stations in the collective farms, heighten the responsibility of machine and tractor stations for fulfillment of plans for yields and gross harvests of agricultural crops and for the development of animal husbandry.

Our agriculture must be raised to a higher plane of productivity and perfected, with highly developed grass cultivation and correct crop rotation, and a greater share of the arable land planted to industrial and fodder crops, vegetables, and potatoes.

"Animal Husbandry"

In connection with the notable progress made in soil cultivation, the utmost development of animal husbandry became the cardinal task of the Party and the Government in the advancement of agriculture in the postwar years. In the period from July 1945 to July 1952 the increase of large-horned cattle in the U.S.S.R. was 13.4 million head, sheep 41.8 million head, pigs 21.2 million head and horses 5.6 million head. The level of the prewar year of 1940 for the number of large-horned cattle for all categories of farming was attained in 1948, for sheep—in 1950, and for pigs, this year. To place the production of animal husbandry on a solid foundation, the Party has been giving special attention to the development of commonly owned collective and state farm productive livestock. Now the animal husbandry of the collective farms and the state farms constitutes the predominant proportion of the country's animal husbandry both with regard to total livestock and output of product of animal husbandry. The gross and marketable output of meat, milk, butter, eggs, wool, and hides in the U.S.S.R. as a whole has surpassed the prewar level.

To meet the growing requirements of the population for produce of animal husbandry and of light industry for raw materials, animal husbandry must be further advanced considerably. The draft directives of the fifth Five-Year Plan envisage an 18–20 per cent increase in the herds of cattle for agriculture in general in the five-year period, while the envisaged increase in the commonly owned herds of cattle belonging to collective farms is 36–38 per cent; the total increase envisaged for head of sheep is 60–62 per cent, while for collective farm herds it is to be 75–80 per cent; for pigs the total increase is to be 45–50 per cent, and for collective farms 85–90 per cent; the number of horses is to increase on the whole by 10–12 per cent, while for collective farms the increase is to be 14–16 per cent; the increase for poultry on collective farms is to be 3–3.5 times. The draft directives provide for the following increase in production: meat and lard 80–90 per cent; milk 45–50 per cent; wool 2–2.5 times; eggs (in collective and state farms) 6–7 times.

This augmentation of the herds of commonly owned collective-farm and state-farm livestock with the simultaneous substantial increase in its productivity remains the main task in the development of animal husbandry. To fulfill this task successfully the first thing to do is to create a stable fodder base in all collective and state farms, provide proper facilities for housing cattle, and also to mechanize work in animal husbandry on a large scale. Animal husbandry must aim to become a highly productive, profitable industry, producing much output for the market. More must be done to improve the quality of the collective- and state-farm cattle, to ensure the rapid reproduction of highly productive strains of farm animals, and to create new highly productive ones. The sound development of animal husbandry is possible only provided the growth of the herds is properly coordinated with qualitative improvement and increase in livestock productivity on a large scale.

The state farms have been considerably developed and consolidated in the postwar years; they have considerably increased their area under crops as compared with the prewar period, enlarged the herds of productive cattle, and have increased the output of farm produce. There are, however, serious shortcomings in the work of the state farms. One of the major shortcomings in the work of a large number of state farms is the high production cost of grain, meat, milk, and other produce. By developing diversified farming, improving the organization of production,

introducing integrated mechanization of all the most labor-consuming operations, increasing crop yields and livestock productivity the state farms must ensure a further increase in output for
the market and considerably reduce production costs.

"Irrigation, Afforestation"

Highly important for the further development of agriculture
is irrigation and protective afforestation. Many big irrigation systems equipped with modern machinery were built before the war,
and old irrigation systems were reconstructed; as a result, the area
of actually irrigated land in the republics of Central Asia and
other parts of the U.S.S.R. rose one and a half times, which made
it possible to accomplish so important a task as that of considerably increasing cotton production. The planting of shelter belts
was begun.

In the postwar years the construction of irrigation systems and
the planting of forest shelter belts assumed still greater proportions. Extensive irrigation systems are being built in the republics
of the Transcaucasus, where the area of actually irrigated land
will, as a result of this work, increase more than one and a half
times in the next few years. The work of irrigating the highly fer-
tile but drought-ridden land in the central black-earth zone—the
Kursk, Orel, Voronezh, and Tambov regions—so that guaranteed
harvests of grain, industrial, and other crops may be obtained, has
been in progress since 1947. The work of creating extensive state
shelter belts in the steppe and forest-steppe regions of the European part of the U.S.S.R., windbreaks on collective and state farms,
and ponds and reservoirs, has been in progress on a large scale
since 1948. In the past three and a half years the collective and
state farms and forestries have effected protective afforestation
on an area of 2.6 million hectares and built over 12 thousand ponds
and reservoirs. In the areas of excessive moisture, primarily in
Byelorussia and the Baltic republics, a great deal is being done,
as was the case before the war, to drain swamps and marshland.

Broad horizons open up before agriculture in consequence of
the construction of the gigantic hydroelectric stations and irrigation systems on the Volga, the Don, the Dnieper, and the Amu

Darya and of the commissioning of the Volga-Don Navigation Canal named after V. I. Lenin. The construction of these stations and irrigation systems will make it possible to irrigate more than 6 million hectares of land and to bring water to pastures, by sectional irrigation, on 22 million hectares; it affords extensive opportunities for the electrification of farming, the introduction of electric plowing, the use of power combines and other electrically-driven agricultural machines.

In addition to large-scale irrigation construction, a new system of irrigation is being introduced successfully on all the irrigated lands; under this system the irrigated sectors are considerably enlarged by improving the distribution of the branch canals of the irrigation network, reducing the number of permanent irrigation canals on the fields, and replacing them by temporary canals, thus making possible fuller use of the irrigated land and of the water and creating more favorable conditions for the mechanization of farming on the irrigated land.

The accomplishment of the outlined large-scale work for developing irrigation, creating shelter belts, and draining marshland will lift our agriculture to a higher plane, and the country will be protected forever against the vagaries of the weather. The task is to carry out the work of developing irrigation, of planting forest shelter belts, and draining swamps successfully and within the periods specified. Party, Soviet, and economic organizations must give this work special attention.

It is also very important to take measures to improve crop yields in the non-black-earth regions of the European part of the U.S.S.R. It is well known that the non-black-earth regions have great possibilities for the successful development of soil cultivation and animal husbandry, since they have favorable climatic conditions and a sufficient amount of moisture. However, crop yields in the non-black-earth belt are still low. To obtain big and stable harvests here it is necessary, first of all, to organize on a large scale the liming of acid soils with the simultaneous introduction of sufficient amounts of organic and mineral fertilizers, to develop the sowing of grasses in every way, and improve soil cultivation.

In the process of restoring and developing agriculture, our

Party, Soviet, and agricultural bodies have in the postwar years improved their guidance of the collective farms, machine and tractor stations, and state farms. However, there are still mistakes and shortcomings in this work.

"Mistakes and Shortcomings"

What are these mistakes and shortcomings in the guidance of agriculture and what are the tasks in this connection?

First of all, it must be said that some of our leading workers, especially in connection with the merging of the smaller collective farms, were guilty of a wrong, narrow, utilitarian approach to questions of collective-farm development. They proposed the hasty, mass resettlement of villages to form big collective-farm towns, the scrapping of all the old farm buildings, and the farmers' homes, and the setting up of big "collective-farm towns," "collective farm cities," "agro-cities" on new sites, regarding this as the most important task in the organizational and economic strengthening of the collective farms. The error these comrades make is that they have forgotten the principal production tasks facing the collective farms and have put in the forefront subsidiary, narrow, utilitarian tasks, problems of amenities in the collective farms. Amenities are, undoubtedly, of great significance but, after all, they are subsidiary, subordinate, and not principal tasks and can be solved successfully only on the basis of developed common production. Forgetfulness or underestimation of the principal production tasks may lead all our practical work in the countryside along incorrect lines, may impede the further development of the collective farms, and do harm to both amenities and to the entire work of socialist construction. The Party took measures in good time to overcome these incorrect tendencies in the sphere of collective-farm development. The Party, Soviet, and agricultural bodies must continue to show constant concern for strengthening and developing the common enterprise in the collective farms, which is the collective farms' main strength, and on this basis ensure an increase in collective-farm production for the market and a further rise in the material and the living conditions of the collective farmers in general.

It must be noted further that the practice of setting up subsidiary enterprises producing bricks, tiles, and other industrial items has become widespread in many collective and state farms. Experience has shown that this increases the cost of building materials and manufactured goods and, what is most important, it distracts the collective and state farms from the solution of agricultural production problems and is an impediment to the development of agriculture. This state of affairs must be rectified and all the efforts of the collective and state farms must be concentrated wholly on the further development of diversified farming in order to fully utilize their economic potentialities and natural conditions for the utmost increase in output of grain, cotton, sugar beet, flax, potatoes, meat, milk, eggs, wool, vegetables, fruit, tea, and other farm produce. As for building materials and other manufactured goods, our state industry and producer cooperatives are in a position to provide and must fully provide the collective and state farms with all these at cheaper prices.

"Squandered . . ."

It must further be admitted that there still are instances of collective-farm property being squandered and of other violations of the Rules of the Agricultural Artel. Some workers in Party, Soviet, and agricultural bodies instead of guarding the interests of the collective farms' common enterprise themselves engage in pilfering collective-farm property, flagrantly violate Soviet law, engage in arbitrary practices, and commit lawless acts in relation to collective farms. These workers take advantage of their official position to occupy collective-farm land, make collective-farm boards and chairmen supply them with grain, meat, milk, and other commodities free of charge or at low price; they exchange their own low-productive stock for high-productive and more valuable cattle belonging to the collective farms, and so on. All these anticollective farm, antistate actions inflict serious harm on the collective-farm peasantry, impede the further organizational and economic consolidation of the collective farms, and undermine the prestige of the Party and Soviet state. It is necessary resolutely to put an end to violations of the Rules of the

Agricultural Artel, to punish as enemies of the collective-farm system persons guilty of pilfering collective-farm property with all the severity of the laws of the socialist state.

It must further be noted that Party, Soviet, and agricultural bodies are dealing unsatisfactorily with such important questions as the organization of labor in the collective farms. In the field of collective-farm labor organization some leading workers, as is known, followed an incorrect course by introducing detached teams in the collective farms and doing away with production brigades, which was actually directed against the mechanization of grain farming and led to weakening of the collective farms. The work done to eliminate these mistakes and distortions made it possible considerably to improve the organization of labor in the collective farms and to strengthen the production brigade. Nevertheless there are still essential shortcomings in this field. In many collective farms there are no permanently composed production brigades; means of production are not attached to particular brigades and this leads to the elimination of personal responsibility; much working time is wasted because of faulty administration which lowers the labor productivity of the collective farmers and leads to a lag in farm work. Party, Soviet, and agricultural bodies must exert themselves daily to improve the organization of labor in collective farms. A more progressive system of distributing incomes should be introduced in the collective farms under which the collective farm's income is distributed among its members in accordance with the number of work-day units credited to the collective farmer and directly depending on the actual amount of farm produce obtained by the brigade, team, or individual collective farmer. This will considerably increase the collective farmers' labor productivity, completely eliminate leveling in payment, and further enhance the value of the work-day unit.

It must be pointed out furthermore that a stereotyped, formal approach to many practical questions has not yet been eliminated in the leadership of agriculture. Party, Soviet, and agricultural leaders not infrequently disregard local, concrete conditions and issue the same instructions for all districts, collective farms, ma-

chine and tractor stations, and state farms regarding agrotech-
nique, livestock farming, labor organization and other questions
relating to agriculture; such instructions, correct and necessary
for certain districts and farms, are often useless, and, at times,
even harmful for other districts and farms. There are still quite
a few people among Party, Soviet, and agricultural functionaries
who judge agriculture and try to direct it on the basis of so-called
average indices. These people judge crop yields by average sta-
tistics, and livestock productivity in the same way. Anyone satisfied with average indices cannot notice the districts, collective
farms, and state farms lagging behind, whose affairs are in a bad
state; it is impossible to take timely and effective measures to give
them the necessary assistance. On the other hand, behind these
average indices it is impossible to see the districts, collective and
state farms that have advanced far ahead, for whom assignments
based on average indices are not a stimulus to better work, but
a retardment and hindrance to their development.

"Antiscientific and Reactionary . . ."

Finally, mention must be made of the existence of substantial
shortcomings in introducing the achievements of science and advanced methods in farming. We have many leading collective
farms, machine and tractor stations, and state farms; there are
thousands of foremost workers in agriculture who are making
big headway in raising yields and productivity of livestock by
creatively applying the achievements of science. However, the
popularization and application of the best experience in collective-
and state-farm production are still unsatisfactory. Our agricultural science has made a big contribution ensuring the advance
of agriculture. Antiscientific and reactionary ideas have been exposed and defeated in agricultural science which is now developing on the only correct basis—on a materialistic, Michurin basis—
equipping our workers in their efforts to advance agriculture. But
notwithstanding the achievements registered, agricultural science
still lags behind the needs of collective-farm and state-farm production. The socialist system of agriculture opens wide vistas to
science, it makes it possible rapidly to disseminate the achieve-

ments of science and advanced experience and to make them
available to all collective farms, machine and tractor stations, and
state farms. It is a most important duty of Party, Soviet, and agricultural bodies to foster in every way the creative initiative of
scientists and workers in agriculture, to swell the ranks of farmers noted for obtaining big yields and high productivity in livestock farming, to uphold all that is advanced and progressive,
to accelerate the application of the achievements of science and
advanced experience in agriculture in all spheres of collective-
farm and state-farm production.

Comrades, we all rejoice at the colossal growth of our socialist
agriculture. Our field and stock farming is now on a new, powerful upgrade. There is no doubt that within the next few years our
collective farms, machine and tractor stations, state farms, well
equipped with machinery, will score still more significant success in developing agriculture, and we shall have an abundance of
foodstuffs for the people and plentiful supplies of raw materials
for the rapidly growing light industry.

Trade, Transport, Communications

With the development of the country's industry and agriculture
there was also an advance in trade. In the postwar years state and
cooperative trade has increased 2.9 times and considerably surpassed the prewar level. In 1951, compared with 1940, the state
and cooperative stores sold the population: 80 per cent more meat
and meat products, 60 per cent more fish and fish products,
80 per cent more butter, nearly twice as much vegetable oil
and other fats, 70 per cent more sugar, 80 per cent more fabrics,
and 50 per cent more footwear. The network of retail state and
cooperative trade expanded, the assortment of goods was substantially increased and the quality improved. However, there are still
many serious shortcomings in our trade. The trading organizations
still make little study of the public demand; they commit mistakes
in the delivery and distribution of goods among the regions and
republics. Service is poor in a number of places. The task is, in a
short time to eliminate the shortcomings and to elevate Soviet
trade to a new, higher plane. The draft directives of the fifth Five-

Year Plan provide for an increase in retail state and cooperative trade by the end of the Plan by approximately 70 per cent compared with 1950.

The growth in production and trade was accompanied by the development of all types of transport and freightage.

During the years of the Great Patriotic War our transport, railroad transport in particular, coped successfully with the difficult task of ensuring the conveyance of freights for the Army as well as the freight for the national economy. In the postwar years all types of transport have not only been restored but have made considerable advances as against prewar. In the current year compared with 1940 the rail freight carriage is approximately 80 per cent greater, riverborne and seaborne freight carriage—60 per cent greater, road transport 3.1 times as great, airborne freight carriage increased 9.2 times. The average daily car loadings on the railroads in the current year is 40 per cent above 1940.

Today all forms of transport have a more solid technical base. The carrying capacity of the major trunk lines has been increased by the restoration and new construction of second tracks, the expansion of sidings, the laying of heavy rails, the extension of automatic bloc systems, and other measures; new railroads have been built and commissioned; the work of electrifying lines with the heaviest freight traffic has been continued; the rolling stock has been greatly increased, especially with regard to powerful locomotives and cars of large freight-carrying capacity.

In water transport the length of the inland waterways utilized for navigation in 1951 was greater than that of 1940 by 23,000 kilometers. Sea and river transport has been augmented with new cargo and passenger ships. The degree of mechanization of loading and unloading work has considerably increased since 1940; in 1951 it was 83 per cent higher for the Ministry of the Inland Waterways and 90 per cent higher for the Ministry of the Merchant Marine.

Road transport is equipped with new and better lorries and passenger cars. The network of motor roads with improved surface has expanded by 3.1 times compared with 1940.

In the postwar years such means of communication as the

post, telegraph, telephone, and radio have been further developed. The country's telephone and telegraph system has been expanded and the capacity of urban telephone exchanges increased. Today all the district centers have telephone and telegraph connections with the regional centers; and the equipment of village Soviets and machine and tractor stations with telephones has in the main been completed. The radio-receiving network is at present nearly twice as large as in 1940. The postal service has considerably expanded; the length of the postal air lines increased 2.5 times.

Along with the achievements, there are serious shortcomings in transport and communications. Many railway lines and shipping and motor agencies do not fulfill the plans assigned them for loading and carrying freight. There is still much idle time in the loading and unloading of railroad cars and vessels. Irrational and exceedingly distant rail freighting has not yet been eliminated. The work of road transport is as yet poorly organized, the idle time of the lorry park excessive and empty runs too frequent. Among the shortcomings in communications should be classed the still inadequate service rendered to the national economy and the population by the communication agencies.

It is necessary further to develop and improve the work of all modes of transport and communications, to take care of transport facilities and constantly see to it that they are kept in good order, to develop and strengthen the technical facilities of all types of transport, and to improve in every way the work of the post, telegraph, and telephone services.

"The National Economy"

The development of the national economy in the U.S.S.R. is effected by means of its own resources, by means of its internal sources of accumulation. For this reason our Party has always given and gives now close attention to observing the strictest economy, regarding a regime of economy as a vital condition for creating accumulations within the national economy, and for correct utilization of the means accumulated. The exercise of economy as a method of socialist management played a big role in the industrialization of the country. Now that in our country a new, powerful advance of the national economy is being effected and simultaneously with this prices of consumer goods systematically reduced, the exercise of economy acquires still greater significance. The more fully and rationally the resources of industry are utilized, the more thriftily and economically we manage our affairs —the greater will be our successes in developing all branches of the national economy and the greater the results in raising the material and cultural level of the people.

Yet, there are serious shortcomings in mobilizing and properly utilizing the internal resources of the national economy.

First of all, it is necessary to point to the heavy losses and unproductive expenditure in industry. In a number of branches production capacities are still poorly utilized. Many ministries determine the capacities of enterprises with an eye on the "bottle-necks" in production. When capacities are computed, low norms of productivity of the equipment are often fixed; quotas for the amount of labor required in the production of articles are established with no consideration shown for the advanced technology and improved methods of labor organization. Instead of increasing output by making more efficient use of the internal resources of the enterprises, the ministries not infrequently demand capital investments by the Government for the construction of new enterprises. Many enterprises tolerate heavy losses arising from mismanagement and irrational use of materials, raw materials, fuel, electric power, tools, and other material values; the established quotas for expenditure, moreover, are often violated; perfectly good substitutes are not used in adequate measure; there is still a great deal of spoilage in production. During 1951, for example, losses and unproductive expenditure in establishments of national significance totaled 4,900 million roubles, including 3,000 million due to spoilage.

As a result of the unsatisfactory use of production capacities, and heavy losses owing to mismanagement, many industrial enterprises do not fulfill their assignments as regards lowering production costs and they allow excessive expenditure. Serious violations in the matter of planning production costs occur in enterprises. Some executives motivated by narrow interests of their own particular line, and to the detriment of state interests, artificially create "reserves" in the plans for production costs by raising the quotas for expenditure of raw materials and auxiliaries and by increasing, needlessly, the quotas of labor required for the production of various items. This way of planning production costs at some enterprises, which is harmful to the state interests, indicates that the ministries do not exercise proper control over this matter. Instead of making a real study of production conditions at each enterprise and adopting the measures necessary for ensuring systematic cuts in production costs, the ministries allow production costs to be planned without verification and without approval of planned computations.

Furthermore, it should be noted that the exercise of economy is especially unsatisfactory in building. Our construction is still expensive. The builders lag considerably behind industrial workers in the matter of lowering production costs. There are major shortcomings in the organization of building work: unsatisfactory use is being made of the machinery, labor productivity is low, irrational use of materials is tolerated, overheads are extremely high. A major shortcoming in capital construction is the dispersal of forces and means among numerous building organizations, which include a great many small building organizations that do not make effective use of machinery. All this leads to higher building costs, to inflating office staffs, to heavy overhead charges; in 1951, for example, the overhead expenses in building in excess of estimates amounted to more than 1,000 million roubles, and instead of a planned profit of 2,900 million roubles, the construction organizations incurred in that year a loss of 2,500 million roubles.

Further. Big losses and unproductive expenditure occur also in agriculture. Agriculture is at present equipped with machines on a far greater scale than before the war. But there still are major shortcomings in the use of tractors and agricultural machines. Matters are unsatisfactory in many machine and tractor stations and state farms with respect to maintenance of the machine and tractor fleet, as a result of which agricultural machinery is prematurely worn out and considerable excess expenditure on the repair of machines is incurred; there is heavy excess expenditure of fuel and lubricants. All this raises the cost of tractor work. Mismanagement has not yet been done away with in many machine and tractor stations, collective farms, and state farms; poor organization of work leads to harvests being below plan and to big crop losses; care of collective-farm property is unsatisfactory; owing to poor care of cattle there are big losses in stock and low productivity of animal husbandry in many collective farms.

In transport, too, there are heavy losses and unproductive expenditure. On many railways, shipping lines, and motor transport organizations, owing to failure to fulfill freightage plans, considerable idle time of cars, ships, and trucks, to excess expenditure of fuel and losses due to mismanagement, there have been considerable excess expenditure and losses. There are still many cases of a negligent attitude towards rolling stock, ships, and trucks, with great damage to the state.

"Heavy Overhead Expenditure"

Furthermore, extremely heavy overhead expenditure is incurred in purchasing, storing, and marketing agricultural products; marketing expenses of trade organizations are also large. Staffs of the purchasing, selling, and distribution organizations are unduly inflated. At the center and in the localities there are many purchasing and distributive organizations frequently engaged in the purchase and sale of the same products and raw materials. Shortcomings in planning the purchasing and selling of goods lead to irrational and unduly long-distance shipments. High overhead expenditure in purchasing, storing, and marketing agricultural products is due to the fact that the ministries in charge of the purchasing and distributing organizations do not give the proper attention to the matter of reducing overhead expenditure, do not verify the costs of the purchased products. Lack of control on the part of the ministries creates the ground for various abuses, makes it possible for purchasing organizations to include all losses and waste in the purchasing expenses and thus camouflage their mismanagement. The lack of proper order, and failure to exercise economy in organizing purchasing, supply, and marketing cause a loss of several billion roubles to the state.

Lastly, overhead administrative expenditure is still high. Office staffs in a number of state administration organs have been cut repeatedly in recent years. But this was done mainly on orders from the top, from the administration. The question of cutting expenditure on office staffs has not yet become a matter of daily concern to the executives of the establishments and organizations. Many ministries and departments permit the employment of personnel in excess of stipulated staffs. There is considerable excess personnel also in the offices of the regional, city, and district establishments and organizations.

Experience shows that improvement in the work of managerial and office staffs, as well as improvement in the organization of purchasing and marketing, result and will continue to result in the release of a part of these workers. It is the duty of the economic and Party organizations to make the proper use of the released workers in the interests of developing the national economy. The corresponding ministries, the Ministry of Labor Reserves, the Party, and trade-union organizations must see to it that these cadres acquire the necessary industrial skill and are able to apply their abilities in those branches of economy whose development requires more personnel.

The excessive expenditure of materials, money, and labor resources observed in all branches of the national economy, indicates that many executives have forgotten the need for exercising economy, that they do not concern themselves with the rational and economical expenditure of state funds, that they do not devote proper attention to improvements in financial and managerial matters in the enterprises and establishments in their charge, while the Party organizations do not notice these shortcomings and do not correct these executives.

The task is to put an end to the indifferent attitude of the economic executives and Party organizations to mismanagement and squandering; the question of enforcing the strictest economy must always be the focal point in all our economic and Party activities. We must constantly be concerned with educating the Soviet people in the spirit of a careful attitude towards public, socialist property. It is necessary to eliminate all excess expenditure of materials, labor, and monetary resources, and systematically to ensure fulfillment and overfulfillment of the assignments for lowering production costs. It is necessary to intensify the struggle against mismanagement, to effect drastic cuts in overhead expenditure in industry, building, transport, agriculture, in the trading, purchasing, and marketing organizations, to take resolute steps to simplify the state and economic apparatus and reduce the cost of its maintenance, to strengthen, through the medium of the financial departments, the control exercised by the trouble over fulfillment of economic plans and observance of economy; our executive personnel must master to perfection the methods of socialist management, they must enhance their technical and economic knowledge, systematically improve production methods, seek, find, and utilize the reserves latent in the national economy.

"Socialist Emulation"

For the successful accomplishment of the tasks of developing the national economy, the further unfolding of socialist emulation is of enormous importance. The Party has always devoted great attention to organizing this emulation and held that the main thing in socialist emulation is to raise the lagging workers to the level of the best, to emulate the example of the latter. In the conditions prevailing in our society, good example in labor plays a most important part in every sector of socialist construction. The Soviet people are convinced daily through their own experience that the best example of production organization, the introduction of new machinery, of various improvements and inventions inevitably lightens labor and leads to a rise in the standard of living of the people. On all sectors of socialist construction we have numerous examples of the creative initiative of the working people aimed at ensuring uninterrupted growth and improvement of socialist production. Our people have long been famed for their creative initiative, resourcefulness, and inventiveness.

The enemies of Socialism and their yes men of all hues portray

Socialism as a system for crushing individuality. Nothing could be more primitive and vulgar than these assertions. It has been proved that the socialist system has emancipated the individual, ensured the flowering of individual and of collective endeavor, and that it has created favorable conditions for the all-round development of the talent and abilities latent in the very depths of the popular masses.

In our country honest work is highly valued and readily encouraged. The Party and the government widely practice the system of bonuses and awards to working people for achievements and successes in their work in all fields of national economy and culture. Since the end of the Patriotic War orders and medals of the U.S.S.R. have been awarded to 1,346,000 workers, collective farmers, scientists, engineers and technicians, office employees, doctors, teachers, and other workers. And in recognition of the outstanding innovations made by 6,480 working people of our country they were honored with the high title of Hero of Socialist Labor.

It is the task of the Party, Soviet, and economic organizations, of the trade-union and Komsomol organizations to extend the emulation movement in all sectors of socialist construction, to give every encouragement to good examples in work and to progressive undertakings by leading workers and innovators, to promote the most widespread use of advanced experience by the masses of the workers in order to help bring up the lagging workers to the level of the advanced. In the struggle between the new and the old, between the advanced and the backward, it is important not only to see the forces which create the new social system, but to develop these forces constantly, to work for their all-round advancement, tirelessly to organize and perfect them in the interest of the successful march forward.

"Standards of Soviet Society"

The achievements in all branches of the national economy brought about further improvement in the living and cultural standards of Soviet society. This is quite natural. There could have been no other result because in our country socialist production is developed for the purpose of satisfying to the highest degree the constantly growing material and cultural requirements of society.

The main index of the rising standard of living of the Soviet people is the steady growth of the national income. Between 1940 and 1951 the national income of the U.S.S.R. rose by 83 per cent. As distinct from the capitalist countries, where more than half the national income is appropriated by the exploiting classes, in the Soviet Union the entire national income is the property of the working people. About three-quarters of the national income is used for satisfying the personal material and cultural needs of the working people of the U.S.S.R. and the remainder goes for expanding socialist production and for other state and social needs.

A vital source of the growth of the real earnings of industrial and office workers and of the real incomes of the peasants is the policy of reducing prices on general consumer goods consistently pursued by the Government. As a result of the five reductions in state retail prices effected in 1947–1952, prices of foods and manufactured goods are at present on the average 50 per cent lower than in the fourth quarter of 1947.

As is known, industrial and office workers in our country receive, at state expense, social insurance benefits, pensions, accommodation in sanatoriums, rest homes, and child establishments free of charge or at a considerably reduced cost, and paid annual vacations. All working people of town and country receive free medical assistance. The state pays, in town and country, allowances to mothers of large families and to unmarried mothers; it ensures free tuition in the elementary and seven-year schools and allocates stipends to students. The sum of 40.8 billion roubles was paid out in 1940 and the sum of 125 billion roubles in 1951 in the above-mentioned benefits and allowances to working people in town and country.

As a result of the rise in nominal wages and salaries and in the incomes of the peasants in cash and in kind, as a result of the reductions in prices of general consumer goods and of the increase in other state payments to the population, real incomes of the industrial and office workers increased, per worker, by about

57 per cent in 1951 as against 1940, and the corresponding real incomes of peasants, assessed per working peasant, rose approximately 60 per cent.

The draft directives of the fifth Five-Year Plan provide for an increase of at least 60 per cent in the national income of the U.S.S.R. during the five-year period, for an increase of at least 35 per cent in real wages and salaries, taking into account the retail price reductions, and for an increase in the incomes of the collective farmers in cash and in kind (expressed in terms of money) of at least 40 per cent.

Large-scale housing and municipal construction is being carried out in our country. During the postwar years alone new dwellings with a total of more than 155 million square meters of floor-space have been built in the cities and industrial settlements, and over 3.8 million homes—in rural localities. The scale of housing construction has been especially large in districts which were under occupation during the war. But notwithstanding the large scale of housing construction, an acute shortage of housing is still felt in our country. Many ministries and local Soviets have failed year after year in carrying out the plans set them for house building, and the funds allocated by the state for this purpose have not been fully utilized. The default in the last two years alone due to nonfulfillment of the housing program was more than four million square meters. We still have economic executives and Party functionaries who are inclined to regard the housing needs of the working people as a secondary matter, and who take no steps to carry out plans for the construction and repair of dwellings. The task is to expand housing construction to the utmost. The draft directives of the fifth Five-Year Plan provide for approximately a twofold increase in capital investments in state housing construction as compared with the fourth Five-Year Plan.

The Party and the Government have always displayed, and continue to display, great concern for the health of our people. State expenditure on health protection, including the expenditure for this purpose from the social insurance funds, rose from 11.2 billion roubles in 1940 to 26.4 billion roubles in 1951. On this basis, further improvement and expansion of the medical and health services for the population have been achieved. In 1951 there were 30 per cent more hospital beds in the towns and rural localities than in 1940. The network of sanatoriums has been enlarged. The number of doctors in the country has increased by 80 per cent.

Population Increase: 9,500,000

As a result of the rise in the material and cultural level of the people and the improvement of the public health services, the mortality rate in our country has dropped. In the last three years the net population increase was 9,500,000.

Expenditure on education increased from 22.5 billion roubles in 1940 to 57.3 billion roubles in 1951, that is, by more than two and a half times. In the postwar years alone, 23,500 school buildings have been erected. The number of people attending school in the U.S.S.R. is now 57 million, or nearly eight million more than in 1940. Seven-year and ten-year schooling has been considerably expanded; from 1940 to 1951 inclusive, the number of pupils in 5–10 grades increased by 25 per cent. The number of pupils in secondary technical schools and other specialized secondary schools increased by 40 per cent, and the number of students attending establishments of higher learning increased by 67 per cent. In 1952 alone the higher-education establishments graduated 221 thousand young specialists for the various branches of the national economy and enrolled 375 thousand new students. Now working in the Soviet Union are approximately 5.5 million specialists with diplomas from higher schools and specialized secondary schools, that is, 2.2 times more than before the war.

Taking into account the ever-increasing significance of science in the life of our society, the Party displays daily concern for its development. The Soviet state launched the construction and equipment of a big network of scientific research institutions and has created the most favorable conditions for the flowering of science; it has ensured large-scale training of scientific personnel. The number of research institutes, laboratories, and other scientific institutions in the U.S.S.R. increased from 1,560 in 1939 to 2,900 by the beginning of 1952. The number of scientific workers almost doubled during the same period. State expenditure for the promotion of science between 1946–1951 amounted to 47.2 billion roubles.

During the period under review the network of cultural and educational establishments in the towns and rural localities was expanded on a broad scale. At the present time the country has 368,000 libraries of various types. Since 1939 the number of libraries has increased by more than 120,000. Annual book printings have reached 800 million copies, an increase of 1.8 times since 1940. In the period since 1939 the number of sound-film installations in the towns and villages has been almost trebled.

Literature: "Big Shortcomings"

Literature and art constitute an integral and most important component of Soviet culture. We have recorded major achievements in developing Soviet literature, the fine arts, the theater, and the cinema. A striking illustration of this is the annual award of Stalin Prizes to numerous gifted workers in these spheres. The high title of Stalin Prize Winner has been conferred upon 2,339 men and women of literature and art.

It would, however, be incorrect not to see, because of the great achievements, the big shortcomings in our literature and art. The point is that despite important successes in developing literature and art, the ideological and artistic level of many works is still not high enough. Many mediocre and dull works, and sometimes simply potboilers which distort Soviet reality, still crop up in literature and art. In the work of some writers and artists, the vibrant and variegated life of Soviet society is portrayed in a spiritless and boring manner. The shortcomings in the cinema, that important and popular form of art, have not been eliminated. Our film people know how to make good pictures, pictures of high educational value, but their number is still small. Our cinematography has every possibility for making plenty of good films of various kinds but this possibility is poorly utilized.

The fact that the ideological and cultural level of the Soviet man has risen immeasurably must be taken into account; the Party helps him to improve his tastes by placing at his disposal the best works of literature and art. The Soviet public does not tolerate dull, empty, and false works, and it makes high demands on our writers and artists. In their works our writers and artists should pillory the faults, shortcomings, and unhealthy phenomena to be met with in society; they must create positive artistic images of the men and women of the new type in all their splendor and human dignity, and thereby promote the inculcation in the people of our society of traits, habits, and customs free from the ulcers and vices to which capitalism gives rise. Yet in our Soviet fiction and dramaturgy, just as in cinematography, such types of works as satire are nonexistent to this day. It would be incorrect to think that our Soviet reality does not provide any material for satire. We need Soviet Gogols and Shchedrins whose scorching satire would burn out all that is negative, decaying and moribund, everything that acts as brake on our march onward.

Our Soviet literature and art must boldly portray life's contradictions and conflicts, must skillfully employ the weapon of criticism as an effective means of education. The strength and the significance of realistic art are that it can and must bring to the fore and disclose the lofty spiritual qualities and typical positive traits of character of the ordinary man, create a vivid artistic image of him that would be worthy of being an example and an object of emulation to others.

In creating artistic images, our artists, writers, and art workers must always remember that the typical is not only that which is most frequently encountered but that which most fully and pointedly expresses the essence of the given social force. In the Marxist-Leninist understanding, the typical by no means signifies some sort of statistical average. Typicalness corresponds to the essence of the given social-historical phenomenon; it is not merely the most widespread, frequently occurring, and ordinary phenomenon. Conscious hyperbole and accentuation of an image does not exclude typicalness but discloses it more fully and emphasizes it. The typical is the basic sphere of manifestation of the Party approach in realistic art. The problem of typicalness is always a political problem.

The lofty and noble task confronting workers in literature and art can be successfully resolved only if we conduct a decisive battle against hack-work by our artists and writers, if falseness and rottenness are mercilessly rooted out of works of literature and art. A tremendous responsibility in the great struggle to nurture that which is new and radiant and to extirpate that which is decrepit and moribund in the life of society, rests with our workers in literature and art. It is the duty of our writers, artists, composers, and cinema workers to study the life of Soviet society more deeply, to create major works of art worthy of our great people.

Comrades, we have won big successes in improving the Soviet people's material well-being and in advancing their culture. But we cannot rest content with what has been achieved. The task is, on the basis of the development of the entire national economy to ensure a further steady rise in the material and cultural level of the Soviet people. Our Party will continue to display unceasing concern for satisfying to the maximum the constantly growing requirements of the Soviet people, because their welfare and their prosperity is the supreme law for our Party.

"Workers, Peasants, and Intelligentsia"

In the period since the Eighteenth Party Congress, our Soviet state has continued to grow, develop, and gain strength.

The economic foundation of our state—socialist ownership of the means of production—has grown and gained in strength. In this period the friendly cooperation of the workers, peasants, and intelligentsia, comprising the Soviet socialist society, has become still stronger.

In the face of the greatest difficulties, our social and state system proved, as the experience of the war showed, to be the firmest, the most resilient and stable in the world. The indestructible might of the Soviet socialist system is due to the fact that it is a genuinely people's system, created by the people themselves, that it enjoys their powerful support and ensures the progress of all the material and spiritual forces of the people.

The enemies and vulgarizers of Marxism advocated the theory, most harmful to our cause, of the weakening and withering away of the Soviet state in conditions of capitalist encirclement. Smashing and rejecting this rotten theory, the Party advanced and substantiated the thesis that in conditions when the socialist revolution has been victorious in one country while capitalism dominates in the majority of others, the country where the revolution has triumphed must not weaken, but strengthen its state to the utmost, that the state is preserved even under Communism should the capitalist encirclement remain. We could not have achieved the successes in our peaceful construction of which we are proud today had we allowed our state to be weakened. We would have found ourselves disarmed in the face of the enemy and in danger of military defeat if we had not strengthened our state, our Army, our punitive and security organs. The Party has made the Soviet land an indestructible fortress of Socialism because it strengthened in every way and continues to strengthen the socialist state.

When the fascist invaders attacked our country, they counted on the internal instability of the Soviet social and state system, on the weakness of the Soviet rear. But, as is known, the war upset these calculations. The historic statement of Comrade Stalin that in the event of war the front and rear in our country, owing to their oneness and internal unity, would prove to be stronger than in any other country, was fully confirmed. In the course of the war the armed forces and the rear of the Soviet power grew stronger. The selfless labor of Soviet men and women in the rear and the heroic struggle of the Soviet Army and Navy at the front have gone down into history as an unprecedented exploit of the people in defense of the homeland. Our Army and Navy were built up and they grew strong and fought under the direct leadership of Comrade Stalin. A captain of genius and organizer of the historic victories of the Soviet people in the Great Patriotic War, Comrade Stalin created the advanced Soviet military science, and taught our Army the art of victory. Our people love their Army and Navy, and accord them constant solicitude and attention. The armed forces of the Soviet Union were, are, and will always be the reliable bulwark of the security of our homeland.

The Great Patriotic War and the ensuing years of peaceful development showed once more that the Soviet social system, built under the leadership of the Party, is the best form of organization of society, that the Soviet state system is a model of a multinational state. Many of our enemies and ill-wishers in the bourgeois camp endlessly repeated that the Soviet multinational state was an unstable state, they placed their hopes on dissension between the peoples of the U.S.S.R., and predicted the inevitable collapse of the Soviet Union. They judged our state by the standard of their own bourgeois countries, in which national contradictions and strife are inherent. The enemies of Socialism are unable to understand that as a result of the Great October Revolution and of the socialist transformations all the peoples of our country are linked with one another by ties of firm friendship on the basis of complete equality. Our Party, unswervingly implementing the Lenin-Stalin national policy, strengthened the Soviet multinational state, developed friendship and mutual cooperation among the peoples of the Soviet Union, supported, ensured, and encouraged in every way the progress of the national cultures of the peoples of our country, waged an uncompromising struggle against all and sundry nationalist elements. The Soviet state system, which withstood the severe trials of the war and became for the whole world an example and a model of genuine equality and cooperation among nations, demonstrates the great triumph of the Lenin-Stalin ideas on the national question. Our Party guards and will continue to guard as the apple of the eye the unity and friendship of the peoples of the U.S.S.R., it has strengthened and will continue to strengthen the Soviet multinational state.

In the period under review, the Soviet family was joined by other peoples. The Lithuanian, Moldavian, Latvian, and Estonian Soviet Socialist Republics were formed. The entire Ukrainian nation was reunited in a single state. Byelorussia brought together the entire Byelorussian nation into a single family. In the North-

west we now have new borders which are more just and more
in conformity with the interests of the country's defense. In the
Far East the Soviet Union regained Southern Sakhalin and the
Kurile Islands, formerly severed from Russia. Now the state frontiers of the Soviet Union correspond as never before to the his-
torically evolved conditions in which the peoples of our country
have developed.

With the assistance of the peoples of the fraternal republics,
the new union republics have within a short space of time not
only advanced far ahead in the matter of industrialization, they
have also effected the transfer of small peasant economy onto
the path of Socialism, have completed collectivization and are
successfully developing socialist agriculture.

In the postwar period the basic function of our state—the function of economic-organizational and cultural-educational work
—has been developed and strengthened still more. The sweeping
advance of socialist construction and the tasks of bringing the
Party and Soviet leadership still closer to the districts, towns, and
villages, made it necessary to introduce a number of changes
in the administrative-territorial system of our state by forming
new regions, areas, and districts. The growth of the national economy called for further changes in the organizational forms of
state administration of various branches of industry, agriculture,
and other aspects of the national economy. This found reflection
in the reduction in size of central bodies of state administration
and in the creation of new ones.

Of the greatest significance for strengthening our state was
the unswerving observance of the principles of socialist democracy which underlie the Stalin Constitution. Elections were held
twice in the postwar period to the Supreme Soviet of the U.S.S.R.,
the Supreme Soviets of the Union and Autonomous Republics, and
the local Soviets of working people's deputies. These elections
were marked by a great political upsurge and served as a new
expression of the unity of our people, of the boundless confidence
the people place in our Communist Party and the Soviet Government.

Internal Party Tasks

The tasks of the Party in the sphere of internal policy are:

1) To continue steadfastly to strengthen the economic might of our state, organizing and directing the peaceful labor of the Soviet people towards fulfillment and overfulfillment of the great tasks set forth in the fifth Five-Year Plan for the development of the U.S.S.R., which constitutes an important stage in the transition from Socialism to Communism;

2) To promote the further advance of industry and transport. Introduce more widely into industry, building, and transport the latest achievements of science and technology, to increase in every way the productivity of labor, strengthen discipline in fulfilling state plans, ensure high-quality production. To reduce steadily costs of production, this being the basis for systematic reduction of wholesale and retail prices for all goods;

3) To bring about a further advance in agriculture in order to create in our country within the briefest space of time an abundance of foodstuffs for the population and of raw materials for light industry; to ensure the implicit fulfillment of the principal task in agriculture—the utmost increase in yields of all crops and growth in the head of livestock while simultaneously raising its productivity, an increase in gross and marketable production of crop growing and animal husbandry. To improve the work of the machine and tractor stations and state farms. To raise the labor productivity of the collective farmers, further strengthen the commonly owned economy of the collective farms, multiply their wealth and on this basis ensure further improvement of the material well-being of the collective-farm peasantry;

4) To effect the strictest regime of economy in all spheres of the national economy and in all branches of administration;

5) To develop further the advanced Soviet science with the object of advancing it to first place in world science. To direct the scientists' efforts toward a more rapid solution of scientific problems pertaining to utilization of the tremendous natural resources of our country, to strengthen the creative cooperation of scientists

and industrial workers, remembering that this cooperation enriches science with practical experience, and helps practical workers to solve more rapidly the tasks facing them;

6) To develop to the utmost the creative initiative of the working people of our country, broaden the socialist emulation movement, work tirelessly for the purpose of multiplying the positive model examples of organization of labor in a new way in all fields of socialist construction, disseminate these examples of model work persistently among all working people so that the example of the best workers of our society is followed by more and more men and women on the labor front;

7) To improve further the material well-being of our people; to increase steadily the real wages of industrial and office workers, improve housing conditions for the working people; to help in every way to increase the incomes of the peasants. To develop Soviet culture; to improve public education and the health services; to give constant attention to the further development of Soviet literature and the arts;

8) To strengthen to the utmost our social and state system. To further the political activity and strengthen the patriotism of Soviet people, strengthen the moral-political unity and friendship of the peoples of our country;

9) To keep vigilant watch for machinations by the warmongers. To strengthen in every way the Soviet Army, Navy, and security organs.

"Correct Policy of the Communist Party"

The steady growth in the might of our Soviet homeland is the result of the correct policy of the Communist Party and of its organizational work in implementing that policy. The Party, the leading and guiding force of Soviet society, saw to it that the country prepared in good time for active defense, directed the people's efforts toward smashing the enemy during the war years, and to the cause of ensuring a new, powerful economic upsurge in the postwar period.

The historic victory of the Soviet people in the Great Patriotic

War, preschedule fulfillment of the fourth Five-Year Plan, the
continued development of our national economy, the rise in the
material well-being and cultural level of the Soviet people, the
reinforcing of the moral-political unity of Soviet society and of
the friendship of the peoples of our country, the rallying of all
the forces of the camp of peace and democracy around the Soviet
Union—such are the main results confirming the correctness of
our Party's policy.

The period under review has been one of continued strengthening of the Party and of consolidation of the complete unity and
oneness of its ranks. This unity of the Party won in fierce struggle
against the enemies of Leninism, is the characteristic feature of
the position inside the Party, of its inner life. Therein lies the
source of our Party's strength and invincibility.

The unity of the Party ranks was the decisive condition for
the victory of the Soviet people in the Great Patriotic War. In the
most trying and difficult days of that war, when the destinies of
our homeland were in the balance, our Party acted as a single
fighting organization, knowing neither vacillation nor differences.
In the light of the results of the war, there stands out in all its
greatness the significance of the irreconcilable struggle which our
Party waged for many years against each and every enemy of
Marxism-Leninism, against the Trotskyite-Bukharinite degener-
ates, against the capitulators and traitors who endeavored to divert the Party from its correct path and disrupt the unity of its
ranks. It has been proved that these foul traitors and treason-
mongers were only waiting for a military attack on the Soviet
Union, calculating that at the most difficult moment they would
stab the Soviet state in the back, and thus play into the hands
of the enemies of our people. By crushing the Trotskyite-Bukharinite underground, which was the rallying center for all the anti-
Soviet forces in the country, by purging our Party and Soviet
organizations of enemies of the people, the Party thereby destroyed, in good time, any possibility of a "fifth column" appear-
ing in the U.S.S.R. and prepared the country politically for active
defense. It will readily be understood that had we not done this
in good time then our position during the war would have been

that of people under fire from the front and the rear, and we might have lost the war.

For the unshakable unity of its ranks the Party is indebted in the first instance to our leader and teacher, Comrade Stalin, who upheld the Leninist unity of the Party. Unity of the Party ranks was, is, and always will be the foundation of its strength and invincibility. Tempered in the crucible of the grim ordeal of the war and in the struggle to overcome the postwar difficulties, the Party has come to this Congress with even greater strength and unity, rallied as never before around its Central Committee.

The strength of our Party lies in its organic ties with the broad masses, in the fact that it is a genuine people's party whose policy corresponds to the vital interests of the people. Such mass organizations as the Soviet trade unions and the Komsomol [Young Communist League] are now playing a much bigger role in rallying the working people around the Party and in training them in the spirit of Communism. In the struggle for freedom and independence of our homeland, for the construction of Communist society, our Party has come into even closer kinship with the people and has strengthened its contact with the broad masses of working people. The Soviet people unanimously support the policy of the Party and repose complete confidence in it.

Striking evidence of the closer contact between the Party and the masses, of its growing prestige among the Soviet people, is provided by the growth of Party membership. At the time of the Eighteenth Congress the Party had 1,588,852 members and 888,814 probationer members, making a total of 2,477,666. On October 1, 1952 the figure was 6,882,145, of whom 6,013,259 are members, and 868,886 probationer members.

During the Great Patriotic War, despite the heavy losses of the Party on the battlefronts, its membership, far from declining, actually increased by more than 1,600,000. The Party was joined by the staunchest Soviet people from the ranks of the Soviet Army and Navy who displayed valor in battle, by advanced members of the working class, of the collective-farm peasantry, and of the Soviet intelligentsia whose self-sacrificing labor in the rear paved the way for victory over the enemy.

"Lowering of the Level"

After the war, the Central Committee of the Party decided to slow down somewhat admittance of new members, but still admittance proceeded at an accelerated pace. The Party could not but notice that this rapid growth of its ranks had certain negative features, leading to a certain lowering of the level of political consciousness of the Party ranks and to a certain decline in the qualitative composition of the membership. A certain disparity appeared between the quantitative growth of the Party and the level of political training of its members and probationer members. To eliminate this disparity and to further improve the qualitative composition of the Party, the Central Committee decided not to force growth of membership and to concentrate the attention of Party organizations on raising the political level of members and probationer members. On the instructions of the Central Committee, Party organizations began more carefully to select new members, raising the requirements for applicants and undertaking extensive work to promote political training of the Communists. The result has been an undoubted advance in the political level of Party members, in the Marxist-Leninist consciousness of our cadres. However, it cannot be said that the task set by the Party of eliminating the lag in the political training of Communists compared with the growth of the Party's ranks has already been accomplished. Consequently we must continue the policy of restricting admission and improving the work of political training and Party tempering of the members, for the strength of the Party lies not only in the size of membership, but above all in its quality.

Strengthening of the Party bodies, improving their activity and intensifying the work of the Party organizations acquired a special significance in the postwar period.

The new tasks that confronted the country in connection with the conclusion of the war and the transition to peaceful construction, called for a big improvement in inner-Party work and a higher standard of leadership by the Party organizations of state and economic work. The fact of the matter is that wartime conditions had necessitated certain specific methods of Party leadership and had given rise to serious shortcomings in the work of the Party bodies and Party organizations. This found expression above all in the fact that the Party bodies devoted less attention to Party organizational and ideological work, with the result that in many Party organizations this work was neglected. There was a certain danger of the Party bodies losing contact with the masses, and that from militant organs of political leadership, displaying their own initiative, they would turn into something in the nature of administrative-management offices incapable of countering the sundry local, narrow-departmental, and other antistate tendencies, and failing to notice outright distortions of the Party's policy in economic upbuilding and violations of state interests.

To avert this danger and successfully to cope with the work of strengthening the local Party bodies and of advancing the activities of the Party organizations, it was necessary to do away with the neglect of Party organizational and ideological work and to put an end to such practices as introducing administrative methods of leadership in the Party organizations, leading to bureaucratization of Party work and to slackened activity and initiative on the part of the membership.

The Central Committee focused the attention of Party organizations on the task of consistently adhering to inner-Party democracy, of unfolding criticism and self-criticism, and, on this basis, to enhance control by the Party membership over the work of Party bodies, since this was the key to heightening the entire work of the Party, to raising the activity and initiative of the Party organizations and Party members. The measures carried out by the Party to develop inner-Party democracy and self-criticism helped its organizations to overcome, to a considerable degree, the defects in Party-political work and played an important part in raising this work to a higher level. This led to greater activity and initiative by the Party members, strengthened the lower Party organizations in industry, on the collective farms, and in offices, invigorated their activities, enhanced control by the membership over the work of leading Party bodies, and elevated the role played by the plenary meetings of Party committees and by the meetings of the Party Active.

However, it would be a mistake not to see that the level of Party-political work still lags behind the requirements of the situation and the tasks set by the Party. It must be admitted that there are shortcomings and errors in the work of the Party organizations; that there are still not a few negative, and very often, unhealthy practices in the life of our Party organizations which it is necessary to know, to see and expose so that they can be eliminated and overcome and the way cleared for further successful progress.

"Unhealthy Practices"

What are these shortcomings, mistakes, negative and unhealthy practices and what are the Party's tasks in this connection?

1. Self-criticism and particularly criticism from below have by no means been developed in full measure and by no means in all Party organizations, as the principal method of disclosing and eliminating our mistakes and shortcomings, our weaknesses and our ills.

Underestimation of the role of criticism and self-criticism in the life of the Party and state and persecution and reprisals for criticism are still to be met with in Party organizations. Often one meets functionaries who never tire of professing their devotion to the Party, but who in actual fact are intolerant of criticism from below, stifle it and wreak vengeance on the critics. Not a small number of facts is known of a bureaucratic attitude toward criticism and self-criticism, causing much damage to the Party's work, killing the initiative of Party organizations, undermining the prestige of the leadership among the Party membership and, in the case of individual Party organizations, leading to the assertion of anti-Party customs and practices by bureaucrats, sworn enemies of the Party.

The Party cannot ignore the fact that where criticism and self-criticism are neglected, where mass control over the activities of the organizations and establishments is weakened, the inevitable result is such ugly developments as bureaucratism, rottenness, and even disintegration in individual links of our apparatus. Such things, of course, are not widespread. Our Party is strong and healthy as never before. But we must realize that these dangerous illnesses have not become widespread only because the Party, using the weapon of criticism and self-criticism, openly and boldly, and in good time, disclosed these evils and dealt resolute blows at concrete manifestations of conceit, bureaucracy, and decay. The wisdom of leadership consists precisely in being able to discern the danger in the embryo and to prevent it from developing to a degree that it becomes a menace.

Criticism and self-criticism are the Party's tried and tested weapon in the battle against shortcomings, mistakes, and unhealthy phenomena which undermine its sound organism. Criticism and self-criticism do not weaken, but strengthen the Soviet state, the Soviet social system, and this is a sign of its vigor and vitality.

It is particularly important at this juncture to develop self-criticism and criticism from below, relentlessly to combat, as the Party's bitterest enemy, everyone who obstructs the development of criticism of our shortcomings, stifles criticism, and permits persecution and reprisals for criticism. The fact of the matter is that as a result of the victorious conclusion of the war and the big achievements in postwar economic development, there has appeared in the Party an uncritical attitude toward shortcomings and mistakes in the work of Party, economic and other organizations. Facts show that the successes have engendered in the ranks of the Party sentiments of complacency, ostentation, and philistine smugness, a desire to rest on one's laurels and live on past services. No small number of functionaries have appeared who believe that "everything is easy," "a walk-over," that "all is well" and that there is no need to indulge in so unpleasant a task as disclosing shortcomings and mistakes in the work, or combating negative and unhealthy practices in our organizations. These sentiments, harmful in their consequences, have got the better of some of our cadres who lack proper training and party staunchness. Leaders of Party, Soviet, and economic organizations not infrequently turn meetings, meetings of activists, plenary sessions, and conferences into ceremonial affairs, into occasions for self-praise with the result that mistakes and shortcomings in the work, maladies, and defects are not disclosed and not subjected to criticism, and this simply adds to the complacency and smugness. Careless attitudes have found their way into Party organizations. There have been cases of blunting of vigilance by functionaries of Party, economic, Soviet, and other organizations, cases of carelessness, and of Party and state secrets being divulged. Some functionaries have become so engrossed in economic matters and are so carried away by the successes, that they begin to forget that the capitalist encirclement still exists and that the enemies of the Soviet state are persistently trying to smuggle their agents into our midst and to use the unstable elements in Soviet society for their sordid purposes.

To ensure the further advance of our cause we must resolutely combat all negative practices and concentrate the attention of the Party and of all Soviet citizens on eliminating shortcomings in our work. This requires that self-criticism, and particularly criticism from below, be extensively developed.

"Criticism from Below"

The active participation of the broad masses of the working people in the struggle against shortcomings in our work and negative sides in the life of our society is striking evidence of the genuine democratism of the Soviet system and of the high degree of political awareness of the Soviet people. Criticism from below is an expression of the creative initiative and activity of millions of working people, of their concern for strengthening the Soviet state. The wider we develop self-criticism and criticism from below, the fuller will we bring out the creative potential and energies of our people and the greater and stronger will be the feeling of the masses that they are the masters of the country.

The view that criticism from below can develop of itself, automatically, is erroneous. It can develop and extend in scope only on the condition that every person who offers sound criticism can be confident that he will find support in our organizations and that the shortcomings he reveals will actually be eliminated. What we need is that Party organizations and Party functionaries, all our leading workers, give guidance in this and set an example of a sincere and conscientious attitude to criticism. Every leading worker, and especially Party worker, is in duty bound to create the conditions that will enable all honest Soviet citizens boldly and fearlessly to criticize shortcomings in the work of our organizations and establishments. Meetings, plenary sessions, meetings of activists, and conferences arranged by all organizations must become real open forums for bold and trenchant criticism of shortcomings.

Persistent struggle to eliminate shortcomings and unhealthy practices in the work of Party, Soviet, economic, and other organizations must be the daily task of the entire Party. A Communist has no right to be indifferent to unhealthy practices and shortcomings in our work, let alone conceal them from the Party. Every Party member is in duty bound, if he finds that one or another organization is not functioning properly, if damage is being done to the interests of the Party and state, to bring all such shortcomings, irrespective of whom it may concern, to the notice of the leading Party bodies, right up to the Central Committee of the Party. That is the duty of every Communist, his supreme obligation to the Party. Some leading workers take the view that if their subordinates report shortcomings to the Central Committee of the Party, they are thereby hampering them in their work of leadership and undermining their prestige. We must resolutely put an end to these harmful and profoundly anti-Party views.

The Party's task is to develop criticism and self-criticism to the utmost, to eliminate everything that hampers and obstructs them. The more we draw the masses of people into this effort to eliminate shortcomings in our work, and the stronger the rank and file control over the work of all our organizations, the more successfully will we advance in every field. Consistent implementation of the slogan of criticism and self-criticism calls for resolute struggle against all who obstruct the development of criticism and who visit reprisals on the critics. Functionaries who do not promote criticism and self-criticism are a hindrance to our forward movement. They have not matured for the function of leaders and cannot count on the confidence of the Party.

2. Party and state discipline is still lax among a section of
Party, Soviet, economic, and other functionaries.

Among our cadres we have not a few functionaries who take a
formal attitude to decisions of the Party and the Government, display no activity and persistence in carrying them out. Nor are they
perturbed by the fact that their work proceeds unsatisfactorily
and the country's interests suffer thereby. A formal attitude to
Party and Government decisions and a passive attitude to their
implementation are evils which must be eradicated in the most
merciless manner. What the Party needs is not officials steeped in
routine, indifferent people who place their personal tranquillity
above the interests of the job entrusted to them, but men who
place state interests above all and who work devotedly and inde-
fatigably in carrying out the directives of the Party and the Government.

One of the most dangerous and pernicious infringements of
Party and state discipline is concealment by some functionaries of
the true state of affairs in the enterprises and offices under their
charge, and the practice of embellishing the results of their work.
The Central Committee and the Government have brought to
light instances of some functionaries who, placing narrow de-
partmental and local interests above the interests of the state and
concealing from the Government, on the pretext of looking after
the enterprises in their charge, material resources at their disposal,
took the path of violating Party and state laws. Facts are also
known of business executives, with the connivance of Party organizations, submitting obviously inflated lists of required raw
materials and supplies, and of doctoring output reports to conceal
nonfulfillment of production programs. Quite a few functionaries,
forgetting that the enterprises entrusted to their supervision and
leadership are state enterprises, try to turn them into their own
private domains where this sort of an executive, if such he can be
called, does everything that "his left leg tells him." Another major
evil is that we have not a few officials who seem to think that Party
decisions and Soviet laws are not binding on them and imagine
that we have two kinds of discipline: one for the rank and file, and

the other for the leaders. These "leaders" think that everything is permitted them, that they can disregard state and Party regulations, violate Soviet law, and engage in all kinds of arbitrary action.

The Party demands of all its members, and even more so of leading cadres, that they be truthful and honest, that they scrupulously discharge their duty to the Party and the state. The Party cannot have confidence in men whose actions are inimical to the interests of the state, who try to be too clever for the Government, who try to deceive the Party and the state. Any deception of the Party and the state, no matter in what form, any attempt at deceit, whether by concealing or distorting the truth, cannot but be regarded as the gravest of crimes against the Party. It is high time to realize that our Party has one discipline, binding alike on rank and file members and leaders, that Soviet laws are equally binding on all Soviet citizens, whatever office they may hold. High office does not carry with it exoneration for executives guilty of an unscrupulous attitude to Party and Government decisions or of committing unlawful and arbitrary actions.

"Irresponsibility and Laxity"

The task is resolutely to put an end to all breaches of Party and state discipline, acts of irresponsibility and laxity, of a formal attitude toward decisions of the Party and Government, constantly to raise the sense of duty to the Party and the state of all our functionaries, to eradicate ruthlessly untruthfulness and dishonesty. Any attempt to conceal the truth from the Party and to deceive the Party is incompatible with Party membership. It is the paramount duty of every Party and Government worker constantly to watch over the interests of our homeland, actively and tirelessly to carry out Party and Government decisions.

3. **The precept of the great Lenin to the effect that the main thing in organizational work is the correct selection of people and verification of fulfillment of decisions, is not yet being carried out satisfactorily.**

Facts prove that the correct selection of people and verification of fulfillment of decisions are a long way from being the main thing in the leading activities of the central and local Party, Soviet, and economic organizations.

Poor organization of actually carrying out directives from the center and of their own decisions, lack of proper verification of their fulfillment is one of the most widespread and deeply rooted shortcomings in the practical work of Soviet, economic, and Party organizations. Our organizations and establishments issue decisions, directives, and orders in far greater numbers than is required, but they are little concerned about whether and how these decisions are carried out. And yet the essence of the matter is that they should be carried out correctly and not bureaucratically. An unconscientious, irresponsible attitude toward fulfillment of directives issued by leading bodies is the most dangerous and evil manifestation of bureaucratism. Experience shows that even good workers, when left to themselves, without control and without verification of their activities, tend to deteriorate and to become bureaucratic.

It is a most important task of the Party to strengthen to the utmost control and verification of fulfillment of decisions in the entire system of leadership, in the work of all organizations and establishments, from top to bottom. To this end, it is necessary to increase the personal responsibility of the leaders of all organizations and establishments for verifying fulfillment of decisions of the Party and the Government, seriously to improve the work of the control and inspection apparatus both at the center and in the localities, to reinforce its personnel with the object of assigning this work to authoritative, experienced, and politically astute people, capable of strictly protecting the interests of the state. It is necessary greatly to enhance the role of Party control, to concentrate the attention of the Party bodies on verifying fulfillment of Party and Government decisions. In all their activities connected with verifying fulfillment of decisions, our leading organs must rely on the broad masses of the working people, on the Party, trade-union and Komsomol organizations, on the Active of the local Soviets. Only verification of fulfillment from the top combined with control from below by the Party and non-Party masses will ensure the timely elimination of shortcomings in the work of our organizations and establishments and give rise to a situation in which decisions and directives are carried out in time and with precision, in a Bolshevik manner.

Cadres are the decisive force in Party and state leadership: without proper selection and training of cadres it is impossible successfully to implement the political line of the Party. The main task in selecting cadres is to improve in every way the qualitative composition of the Party workers, to reinforce our Party, Government and economic organizations with people devoted to the interests of the Party and state, people thoroughly versed in their work and capable of advancing it.

As a result of the work done by the Party the composition of the leading personnel has improved considerably. This, however, does not mean that the problem of improving the qualitative composition of the leading personnel has been solved completely. Now that all branches of economy have been equipped with up-to-date technique and that the cultural level of the Soviet people has been raised beyond measure, the demands made on leading cadres have changed, have become greater. At the helm in industry and agriculture, in the Party and state apparatus, we must have cultured people, experts in their work, capable of infusing fresh vigor, of promoting all that is advanced and progressive, and of developing it constructively. We have all the possibilities for doing this, because the base for selecting and promoting leading cadres corresponding to these standards has become broader than formerly.

"Distortion of the Party Line"

Today the further strengthening of the body of leading cadres depends mainly on properly organizing the study and selection of workers, and for this it is necessary first of all to eliminate the shortcomings, mistakes, and distortions in the work with cadres. And in this respect we have not a few shortcomings.

The main shortcoming is that in selecting cadres some executives are guided not by their political and professional qualifications, but by considerations of kinship, friendship, and cronyship. It often happens that honest workers, people who know their job but who are critical and refuse to tolerate shortcomings, thereby causing annoyance to the leadership, are dismissed on various pretexts and replaced by people of dubious worth, or by people entirely unsuited for the work, but advantageous and pleasing to some leaders. Such distortions of the Party line in selecting and promoting cadres have given rise in some organizations to the formation of a closed circle of people who shield one another and who place the interests of their group above those of the Party and state. Small wonder that such a situation usually leads to corruption and decay, as was the case, for example, in the Party organization in Ulyanovsk, where a section of the economic, Soviet, and Party workers in the leadership of the regional organization became demoralized and took the course of embezzlement, of stealing and pilfering state property.

A formal, bureaucratic approach to the matter of studying and selecting workers is highly detrimental to efforts to further improve the composition of the leading bodies. Workers are frequently selected on the basis of questionnaires and formal papers without serious verification of their professional and political qualities. The faulty practice of approving appointments or appointing people to jobs without seeing them has become rooted in the work of selecting cadres. Clearly on the basis of such a formal bureaucratic approach to the selection of cadres it is impossible to decide correctly whether the given person is suitable for the work for which he is recommended. Without establishing the merits and shortcomings of a person it is impossible to decide which post affords the greatest scope for his individual abilities.

It is the duty of the Party organizations to see that the principles established by our Party with regard to selecting and allocating cadres are strictly observed in all the links of our apparatus. An uncompromising struggle must be waged against relations based on nepotism and mutual guarantee, an end must be put to the bureaucratic attitude to the matter of studying and selecting cadres. The work of the Party bodies in studying and selecting cadres must be raised to a higher level, and Party control over the state of affairs in this sphere in Soviet and economic organizations must be strengthened considerably.

The task is to make the selection of people and verification of fulfillment of decisions really the main thing in the executive activities of central and local Party, Government, and economic organizations. It should be remembered that the purpose of verifying fulfillment is primarily to disclose shortcomings, to bring to light lawless acts, to assist honest workers with advice, to punish the incorrigible, and to secure fulfillment of adopted decisions, to study experience and on this basis to ensure the most correct, advantageous, and economical solution of the given task. A bureaucratic approach to the question of verifying fulfillment must not be permitted; we must not be afraid to cancel or correct any decision if it transpires that it was a wrong or inaccurate decision. Verification of fulfillment is inseparably connected with the task of eliminating shortcomings in the matter of selecting cadres; in accordance with the results of verification, inefficient, unsuitable, backward, unconscientious workers should be removed and be replaced by better, suitable, advanced, honest people; the verification of fulfillment should help bring forward new people capable of advancing the work, people who stand guard over the interests of the state.

4. In many Party organizations there are instances of underestimation of ideological work, with the result that this work lags behind the tasks of the Party, and in some organizations is in a state of neglect.

Ideological work is a primary duty of the Party, and underestimation of this work may cause irreparable damage to the interests of the Party and the state. We must always remember that any weakening of the influence of socialist ideology signifies strengthening of the influence of bourgeois ideology.

In our Soviet society there is not nor can there be a class basis for the domination of bourgeois ideology. Dominant in our country is socialist ideology, the unshakable foundation of which is Marxism-Leninism. Nevertheless, we still have survivals of bourgeois ideology, hangovers of private-property psychology and ethics. These survivals do not die away of themselves; they are highly tenacious and capable of growth, and a resolute struggle must be waged against them. Likewise we are not ensured against the penetration of alien views, ideas, and sentiments emanating from without, from capitalist states, or from within, from the remnants of groups hostile to Soviet rule and not yet completely eradicated by the Party. It must not be forgotten that the enemies of the Soviet state seek to spread, foster, and fan all kinds of unhealthy sentiments, to corrupt ideologically unstable elements in our society.

Some of our Party organizations, immersed in economic affairs, forget ideological questions, put them aside. Even in such leading Party organizations, as, for instance, the Moscow organization, insufficient attention is paid to ideological work. And this is not without its consequences. Wherever there is relaxation of attention to questions of ideology, favorable soil is created for reviving views and concepts hostile to us. People alien to us, all types of elements from the dregs of anti-Leninist groups smashed by the Party, seek to lay their hands on those sectors of ideological work which for one reason or other are neglected by Party organizations and where Party leadership and influence have weakened, in order to utilize these sectors for dragging in their line and reviving and spreading various kinds of non-Marxist "viewpoints" and "conceptions."

Underestimation of ideological work is in large measure the result of the failure of some of our leading personnel to deepen their consciousness, broaden their knowledge of Marxism-Leninism, to draw on the historical experience of the Party. Without this one cannot become a fully valid mature leader. He who lags behind ideologically and politically, who lives according to formulas learned by rote, and who does not have any sense of the new, is unable correctly to appraise the internal and external situation, he cannot head and is unworthy of heading the movement, and sooner or later he will be thrust aside by life. Only a leader who constantly improves his education, masters Marxism-Leninism creatively, trains and perfects in himself the qualities of a leader of the Lenin-Stalin type—only such a leader can measure up to the tasks of our Party.

Party organizations still devote inadequate attention to the matter of improving the ideological and political training of mem·

bers and probationer members, they do not properly organize and control their study of the Marxist-Leninist theory with the result that many members lack the necessary knowledge of Marxism-Leninism. Improving the political knowledge of members and candidate members is an indispensable condition for enhancing their leading role in all fields of life, for further activizing the Party ranks and improving the work of the Party organizations.

"Insufficient Leadership"

Owing to insufficient leadership of ideological work and lack of control over its content, serious errors and distortions often creep into books, newspapers, and magazines and into the work of scientific and other establishments in the ideological field. As a result of interference by the Central Committee of the Party, habits and traditions alien to Soviet people have been disclosed in many branches of science, instances of caste exclusiveness and intolerance toward criticism have been brought to light, and diverse manifestations of bourgeois ideology and all kinds of distortions by vulgarizers exposed and rooted out. The generally known discussions in relation to philosophy, biology, physiology, linguistics, and political economy revealed serious ideological flaws in various spheres of science; they gave an impetus to the development of criticism and conflict of opinions and played an important part in advancing science. The Arakcheyev regime which held sway on many sectors of the scientific front has been done away with. Nevertheless, in a number of branches of science the monopoly of separate groups of scientists who hold up the advance of the growing, fresh forces, barricade themselves against criticism and seek to decide scientific questions by administrative means, has not yet been completely eradicated. No branch of science can successfully develop in the musty atmosphere of mutual praise and of hushing up mistakes; attempts to establish monopolies of separate groups of scientists inevitably give rise to stagnation and regression in science.

The ideological work of the Party is called upon to play an important role in ridding the minds of men of the survivals of capitalism, of prejudice, and of the pernicious traditions of the old society. In the future, too, it will be necessary to develop in the masses a high sense of public duty, to educate the working people in the spirit of Soviet patriotism and friendship of the peoples, in the spirit of concern for the interests of the state, to develop the finest qualities of the Soviet people—confidence in the victory of our cause, and readiness and ability to overcome any difficulty.

It is the task of the Party organizations to put a resolute stop to this harmful underestimation of ideological work and to intensify this work in all spheres of Party and state activity, tirelessly to expose all manifestations of ideology alien to Marxism. It is necessary to develop and perfect socialist culture, science, literature, and art, to mobilize all means of ideological and political education, our propaganda, agitation, and the press, for improving the ideological training of the Communists, for raising the political vigilance and the political consciousness of the workers, peasants, and the intelligentsia. All our Party workers without exception must study in order to raise their ideological level and master the wealth of the party's political experience so as not to lag behind life and to be equal to the tasks of the Party. The Party organizations must conduct constant work among the members and probationer members, raise their ideological level, teach them Marxism-Leninism, and develop them into politically educated, conscious Communists.

Tasks Within the Party

Our tasks in the matter of further strengthening the Party are as follows:

1. To continue to improve the qualitative composition of the Party, not to permit any drive for numbers but to concentrate on raising the political level and Marxist tempering of the members and probationer members; to enhance the political activity of the members; to make all members staunch fighters for implementation of the policy and decisions of the Party, irreconcilable in relation to shortcomings in work, and capable of persistent work for the elimination of these shortcomings; to improve and perfect the work of the trade unions and of the Komsomol organization, daily to strengthen contact with the masses, remembering that the

strength and invincibility of our Party lie in its unbreakable bonds of kinship with the people;

2. To put an end to self-satisfaction and smugness which are harmful and dangerous for our cause, eliminate manifestations of ostentation and complacency in the ranks of the Party; boldly and resolutely to disclose and eliminate shortcomings and weaknesses in our work; consistently to implement inner-Party democracy, extend the unfolding of self-criticism and criticism from below, ensure for all honest Soviet people the possibility to criticize boldly and without fear shortcomings in the work of our organizations and establishments, to wage relentless struggle against all attempts at suppressing criticism, against persecution, and reprisals for criticism; to strengthen in every way Party and state discipline, to eradicate the formal approach to decisions of the Party and the Government, to wage relentless struggle against lack of discipline, against violation of state interests;

3. To elevate to a higher plane the work of the Party organs as regards correct selection, allocation, and training of cadres, observe strictly the principles laid down by the Party for the correct selection of cadres, wage an irreconcilable struggle against those who violate these principles, mercilessly combat any bureaucratic approach in selecting cadres, improve the qualitative composition of the leading cadres, to promote more boldly to leading posts people devoted to the interests of the Party and the state, who know their work well and are able to advance it further, to remove bad, unsuitable, backward, and unconscientious workers; to strengthen in every way control and verify fulfillment of decisions in the entire system of leadership from top to bottom, raise the personal responsibility of the heads of all organizations and establishments for verifying fulfillment of Party and Government decisions, combine such verification from above with verification from below on the part of the Party and non-Party masses; to ensure that correct selection of people and verification of fulfillment of decisions really become the main element in the guiding activity of the central and local Party, Soviet, and economic organizations;

4. To put an end to underestimation of ideological work, to wage

resolute struggle against liberalism and complacency in regard
to ideological mistakes and distortions, systematically to improve
and perfect the ideological and political training of our cadres; to
direct all means of exerting ideological influence, our propaganda,
agitation, and the press, for the Communist education of the Soviet
people; to elevate to a still higher level Soviet science, promoting
criticism and the conflict of opinions in scientific work, remembering that only in this way can Soviet science fulfill its mission—to
occupy first place in world science.

5. To continue to guard as the apple of the eye the Leninist
unity of the Party ranks which is the foundation of the strength
and invincibility of our Party.

"Theoretical Foundations of Marxism"

Comrades!

In our epoch the great teaching of Marx, Engels, Lenin, and
Stalin lights for all mankind the path of development of world
civilization.

Our Party is strong because in all its activities it is guided by
the theory of Marxism-Leninism. Its policy is based on scientific
knowledge of the laws of social development.

The historic role of our great teachers, Lenin and Stalin, is that,
having profoundly studied the theoretical foundations of Marxism
and having acquired perfect mastery of the dialectical method,
they defended and upheld Marxism against all distortions and
brilliantly developed the Marxist teaching. At every new turn of
history, Lenin and Stalin always applied Marxism to the specific
practical tasks of the epoch, demonstrating by their creative approach to the teaching of Marx and Engels that Marxism is not a
dead dogma, but a living guide to action.

The Marxist-Leninist theory has been the object of Comrade
Stalin's unremitting concern. During the whole of the past period,
Comrade Stalin's activities in the theoretical field have centered
on problems of world-historic significance—the development of
socialist economy and the gradual transition to Communism. By
creatively enriching and developing the science of Marxism-Len-

inism, Comrade Stalin equips the Party and the Soviet people ideologically in the struggle for the triumph of our cause.

Comrade Stalin's *Economic Problems of Socialism in the U.S.S.R.,* just published, is of the greatest importance for Marxist-Leninist theory and for all our practical work. This work contains an all-round investigation into the laws of social production and the distribution of material benefits in socialist society. It defines the scientific principles of the development of socialist economy and indicates the ways and means for the gradual transition from Socialism to Communism. By his elucidation of the problems of economic theory, Comrade Stalin has greatly advanced Marxist-Leninist political economy.

Comrade Stalin has formulated the program theses about the basic preliminary conditions for preparing for the transition to Communism. To prepare the way for the actual transition to Communism, Comrade Stalin teaches us, at least three basic prerequisites are required.

"It is necessary, first, firmly to ensure . . . the uninterrupted growth of social production as a whole, with priority to the growth of means of production. Priority to the growth of means of production is necessary not only because it will supply equipment to its own enterprises and to the enterprises in all other branches of the national economy, but also because without it extended reproduction is, in general, impossible." (J. Stalin. *Economic Problems of Socialism in the U.S.S.R.*)

"It is necessary, second, by means of gradual transitions, carried out in a way that is advantageous to the collective farms and, consequently, to society as a whole, to elevate collective-farm property to the level of national property, and to replace commodity circulation, likewise through gradual transitions, by a system of exchange of products, so that the central authority, or some other social-economic central body, will be in a position to embrace the whole of social production in the interests of society." (*Ibid.*)

Certainly, at the present stage, commodity circulation and collective-farm property are being used successfully to develop socialist economy and undoubtedly are advantageous to our society.

Their usefulness will continue in the near future too. But we must see our development in perspective.

". . . Neither an abundance of products capable of meeting all the requirements of society," Comrade Stalin points out, "nor transition to the formula, 'to each according to his needs,' can be achieved so long as such economic facts as collective-farm group property, commodity circulation, etc., remain in force." (*Ibid.*)

"Commodity Circulation"

So long as the socialist economy retains its two basic productive sectors—the state sector and collective-farm sector—commodity circulation with its "money economy" must continue to operate as an essential and useful element in our national-economic system. The existence of commodity production and commodity circulation determines also the existence under Socialism of the law of value, although under our system it has ceased to be the regulator of production.

But commodity circulation, like the law of value, is not eternal. When the two basic forms of socialist production—national and collective farm—give way to a single all-embracing productive sector, commodity circulation will disappear, together with its "money economy" and the law of value. The view held by some that commodity circulation will persist under Communism has nothing in common with Marxism. Commodity circulation is incompatible with the perspective of the transition from Socialism to Communism.

Comrade Stalin has theoretically substantiated the question of the measures necessary to elevate collective-farm property to the level of national property, and the gradual transition to a system of exchange of products between state industry and the collective farms. The present embryonic forms of exchange of products, as expressed in "remuneration" in goods for the output of cotton-growing, flax-growing, beet-growing and other collective farms, will develop into a comprehensive system of exchange of products.

"Such a system," Comrade Stalin points out, "will require a tremendous increase in the output of goods with which the city supplies the countryside, and for this reason will have to be introduced without undue haste, commensurate with the accumulation of city-made products. But introduced it must be, persistently and without hesitation, reducing step by step the sphere of commodity circulation and extending the sphere in which exchange of products operates.

"Such a system, by reducing the sphere of commodity circulation, will facilitate the transition from Socialism to Communism. In addition, it will make it possible to include the basic property of the collective farms and their products into the over-all system of national planning.

"This will be the effective and decisive means of elevating collective-farm property to the level of national property under our contemporary conditions." (*Ibid.*)

The system of exchange of products is undoubtedly advantageous to the collective-farm peasantry because they will receive from the state much more goods, and at lower prices, than under commodity circulation. Those collective farms now exchanging their products for manufactures—and this is the embryo of the exchange of products—are receiving tangible evidence of the tremendous gains and superiority of this system. It is known that many of these collective farms rank among the wealthiest.

In order to prepare the basic prerequisites for the transition to Communism, Comrade Stalin points out, "it is necessary, thirdly, to achieve such a cultural growth of society as will ensure all its members an all-round development of their physical and mental powers, enable members of society to acquire an education sufficient for active participation in the process of social development, and allow them freely to choose a profession and not be tied down all their lives, as is the case under the existing division of labor, to any particular profession.

"To achieve this, it is necessary first of all to reduce the working day to at least six and subsequently to five hours. This is essential in order that the members of society have sufficient free time for acquiring an all-round education. For this it is necessary, further, to introduce universal compulsory polytechnical education to enable the members of society freely to choose a profession and not to be tied down all their lives to any particular profession. To achieve this, it is necessary, further, radically to improve housing conditions and at least double, if not more, real wages and salaries both through direct increases in monetary wages and, especially, through further and systematic reduction of prices for goods of mass consumption." (*Ibid.*)

Only after all these preliminary conditions have been fulfilled, Comrade Stalin teaches us, will it be possible to hope that labor, instead of being the heavy burden it was under capitalism, will be transformed in the eyes of the members of society into a vital necessity, and public property be evaluated by all members of society as the inviolable and sacred foundation of the existence of society. Only after all these preliminary conditions, taken together, have been fulfilled will it be possible to switch from the formula of Socialism—"from each according to his ability, to each according to his labor"—to the formula of Communism—"from each according to his ability, to each according to his needs."

Comrade Stalin insistently warns against frivolous running ahead, against going over to higher economic forms without first creating the prerequisites necessary for that transition.

Comrade Stalin has provided a scientific solution of such great social problems and program questions of Communism as the elimination of the distinction between town and country, between physical and mental labor, and has also elaborated a question that is new in Marxist science—the question of abolishing the essential distinctions between them which still exist in socialist society.

Hence, the Party's plans for the future, defining our perspective and the path of our forward movement, are based on knowledge of economic laws, on the science of the building of Communist society, elaborated by Comrade Stalin.

Comrade Stalin's substantiation of the objective character of economic laws is of the greatest importance from the standpoint of principle. Comrade Stalin teaches us that the laws of economic development, the laws of political economy—irrespective of whether we are examining capitalism or Socialism—are objective laws, reflecting the process of economic development and proceeding independently of man's will. Man can discover these laws, fathom them, utilize them in the interests of society, but he cannot destroy the old or create new economic laws. Economic laws are not created at the will of man: they arise on the basis of new economic conditions.

"Profoundly Erroneous"

Profoundly erroneous are the views of those who believe that the laws of economic development can be created or abolished at will, that in view of the special role which history has conferred on the Soviet state, it can change existing laws of political economy, "mold" new ones or "transform" existing laws. Negation of objective laws in economic life under Socialism would lead to chaos and fortuity. It would lead to the elimination of political economy as a science, for no science can thrive and develop if it does not recognize and study objective laws. Negation of the objective character of economic laws is the ideological basis of adventurism in economic policy, and of utter arbitrariness in the practical direction of the economy.

Comrade Stalin's discovery of the fundamental economic law of contemporary capitalism and of the fundamental economic law of Socialism is a tremendous contribution to Marxian political economy. The fundamental economic law defines the essence of the given mode of production, its main facets and the cardinal processes of its development; it furnishes a key to the understanding and explanation of all the laws of the given economic system.

Comrade Stalin has proved that the principal features and requirements of the basic economic law of contemporary capitalism are "securing of maximum capitalist profit through the exploitation, the ruin, and impoverishment of the majority of the population of a given country, through enslavement and systematic plunder of the peoples of other countries, especially the backward countries, and, lastly, by means of wars and militarization of the national economy which are used to ensure the highest possible profits." (*Ibid.*) This law discloses and explains the crying contradictions of capitalism, and lays bare the causes and roots of the aggressive predatory policies of the capitalist states. The func-

tioning of this law tends to deepen the general crisis of capitalism
and leads to the inevitable maturing and exploding of all the contradictions of capitalist society.

The very opposite of decaying capitalism is the ascending and
flowering system of Socialism. The essential features and requirements of the fundamental economic law of Socialism, discovered
by Comrade Stalin, are: "ensuring the maximum satisfaction of
the constantly growing material and cultural requirements of the
whole of society through the uninterrupted development and perfection of socialist production on the basis of the latest technique."
(*Ibid.*) Comrade Stalin has demonstrated that the aim of the socialist mode of production is not profits, but man and his requirements, the satisfaction of his material and cultural requirements.
Ensuring the maximum satisfaction of the constantly growing material and cultural requirements of the whole of society is the aim
of socialist production, while the uninterrupted growth and perfection of socialist production on the basis of the highest technique
is the means of achieving that aim. The operation of this law leads
to an upsurge of the productive forces of society, to prosperity for
that society, to the steady rise in the material well-being and cultural level of the working people.

Comrade Stalin's discovery of the fundamental economic law of
contemporary capitalism and of the fundamental economic law of
Socialism deals a devastating blow to all apologists of capitalism.
These fundamental economic laws testify that, whereas in capitalist society man is subordinated to the ruthless law of extracting
maximum profit, and for the sake of this profit people are doomed
to fearful suffering, poverty, unemployment, and sanguinary wars,
in socialist society all production is subordinated to man and his
constantly growing requirements. Therein lies the decisive superiority of Communism, the new social system that is vastly superior to capitalism.

Communism arises as the result of the conscious, creative endeavor of the millions of working people. The theory of spontaneity
is profoundly alien to the entire economic system of Socialism.
Capitalist economy, in view of the operation of the law of competition and anarchy in production, is rent with the sharpest con-

tradictions. Comrade Stalin has shown that on the basis of socialization of the means of production, in contrast to the law of competition and anarchy in production, there arose in our country the law of balanced (proportional) development of the national economy.

The law of balanced development of the national economy is not the basic economic law of Socialism, and our practical planning activities cannot in themselves produce the required positive results if they are not guided by the cardinal aim of socialist production and if they do not rely on the fundamental economic law of Socialism. To ensure the steady and uninterrupted growth of social production as a whole, and to create in our country an abundance of products, it is necessary fully to master the art of planned and rational utilization of all material, financial, and labor resources, proceeding in this from the requirements of the law of balanced development of the national economy and adapting all our activities to the requirements of the fundamental economic law of Socialism.

In his works on the economic problems of Socialism in the U.S.S.R. Comrade Stalin has illustrated the entire complexity of the tasks we shall have to solve in the struggle to overcome the difficulties confronting us, and in solving the contradictions arising in the course of building Communism.

"Socialist Contradictions"

Comrade Stalin discovered the objective economic law of the obligatory conformity of the production relations to the character of the productive forces, and substantiated the tremendous cognitive and transforming role of that law. Brilliantly disclosing the processes taking place in our economy, Comrade Stalin showed how deeply erroneous are the views alleging that under Socialism there are no contradictions whatever between the production relations and the productive forces of society. Contradictions unquestionably exist and will exist, inasmuch as the development of the production relations lags behind the development of the productive forces and will continue to lag. It goes without saying that in socialist society things usually do not reach the stage of conflict between the production relations and the productive forces, but it would be dangerous not to notice that contradictions between them can and do exist. We are obliged to note these contradictions in good time, and, by pursuing a correct policy, to overcome them in good time so that the production relations fulfill their role as the main and decisive force determining a powerful development of the productive forces.

The tasks of our forward movement oblige Party workers and workers of the social sciences, and economists in the first place, being guided by Comrade Stalin's program directives, to make an all-round elaboration of problems of Marxist-Leninist theory in their inseparable connection with practical creative work.

Comrade Stalin's works are a vivid indication of the outstanding significance which our Party attaches to theory. Revolutionary theory was, is, and will be an unfading beacon illuminating the pathway of the advance of our Party and our people to the complete triumph of Communism.

Comrade Stalin unceasingly advances Marxist theory. In Comrade Stalin's classical work, *Marxism and Problems of Linguistics,* fundamental propositions of Marxist theory on the laws of social development are raised to a new and higher level, and the questions of the economic basis and the superstructure of society, of the productive forces and production relations, receive all-round elaboration. Dialectical and historical materialism, as the theoretical foundation of Communism, is developed further. Comrade Stalin disclosed the role of language as an instrument for the development of society and pointed to the perspectives of further development of national cultures and languages. In that work Comrade Stalin enriched Marxist-Leninist science with new propositions and opened up new perspectives for progress in all branches of knowledge.

The works of Comrade Stalin on economic problems and on problems of linguistics mark a new stage in the development of Marxism; they are splendid examples of the creative approach to the teachings of Marx, Engels and Lenin. Comrade Stalin teaches us that a dogmatic approach to theory is impermissible and can be highly detrimental to the work of political education of the masses.

Comrade Stalin's theoretical discoveries are of world-historic significance; they equip all peoples with knowledge of the ways of revolutionary reconstruction of society and with the vast wealth of experience accumulated by our Party in the struggle for Communism.

The enormous significance of Comrade Stalin's theoretical works is that they warn us against skimming over the surface, go deep into the heart of phenomena, into the very essence of the processes of the development of society; teach us to see in embryo the phenomena that will determine the course of events, make Marxist prevision possible.

The teachings of Marx, Engels, Lenin, and Stalin impart to our Party invincible force, the ability to blaze new trails in history, clearly to see the goal of our forward movement, quicker and more firmly to win and consolidate victories.

The Lenin-Stalin ideas shed the bright light of revolutionary theory on the tasks and perspectives of the struggle of the masses in all lands against imperialism, for peace, democracy, and Socialism.

"Building a Complete Communist Society"

Comrades!

The Soviet state is now no longer a solitary island surrounded by capitalist countries. We are marching forward together with the great Chinese people, with the millionfold masses of the People's Democracies, and the German Democratic Republic. All progressive mankind sympathizes with us and supports us. Together with all these forces we are upholding the cause of peace and friendship among the nations.

Our mighty homeland is in its prime and is advancing toward new successes. We possess everything that is necessary for building a complete Communist society. The natural wealth of the land of Soviets is inexhaustible. Our state has demonstrated its ability to utilize this tremendous wealth for the benefit of the working people. The Soviet people have demonstrated their ability to build the new society and they look with confidence to the future.

At the head of the peoples of the Soviet Union stands the tried and battle-tested Party, which unswervingly pursues the Lenin-Stalin policy. Under the leadership of the Communist Party the world-historic victory of Socialism in the U.S.S.R. was won and the exploitation of man by man abolished forever. Under the leadership of the Party the peoples of the Soviet Union are successfully working towards realization of the great goal of building Communism in our country.

There are no forces in the world capable of halting the onward movement of Soviet society. Ours is an invincible cause. We must take firm hold of the helm and pursue our course, yielding neither to provocations nor to intimidation.

Under the banner of the immortal Lenin, under the wise leadership of the great Stalin, forward to the victory of Communism!

FUNERAL ORATION FOR STALIN, 1953

At the funeral of Joseph Stalin, in Moscow on March 9, 1953, Georgi M. Malenkov, Lavrenti P. Beria, and Vyacheslav M. Molotov delivered funeral orations. Following is the text of Mr. Malenkov's speech:

Our Party, the Soviet people, all humanity, have suffered a most grievous, irreparable loss. The glorious life-path of our teacher and leader, the greatest genius of humanity, Joseph Vissarionovich Stalin, has ended. In these sorrowful days, the great sorrow of the Soviet people is being shared by all progressive humanity.

Stalin's name is infinitely dear to the Soviet people and the widest peoples' masses in all parts of the globe. Vast are the grandeur and significance of Comrade Stalin's activities for the Soviet people and workers of all lands. His works will live forever, and grateful posterity, in common with us, will praise Stalin's name.

Stalin gave his life in the cause of liberating the working class and all workers from the yoke and bondage of exploiters, in the cause of freeing mankind from exterminating wars, in the cause of the struggle for a free and happy life on earth for toiling man.

Comrade Stalin, the great thinker of our epoch, creatively developed in new historic conditions the teachings of Marxism and Leninism. Stalin's name justly takes its place beside the names of the greatest men in the history of mankind—Marx, Engels, and Lenin.

Our Party adheres to the great teachings of Marxism and Leninism, which furnish the Party and people with the invincible strength and ability to blaze new paths in history.

Lenin and Stalin, in the course of long years, waged under difficult underground conditions a struggle for deliverance of the peoples of Russia from the yoke of autocracy and from the oppression of landowners and capitalists. Headed by Lenin and Stalin, the Soviet people have accomplished the greatest revolution in the history of mankind, have put an end to a regime of capitalism in our country and entered upon a new path, the path of socialism.

Continuing the work of Lenin and steadily developing Lenin's teaching, which illuminates the way ahead for the Party and Soviet state, Comrade Stalin brought our country to a world historic victory of socialism, which ensured for the first time in many thousands of years of existence of human society the abolition of exploitation of man by man. Lenin and Stalin founded the first workers' and peasants' state in the world.

Comrade Stalin worked tirelessly to strengthen the Soviet state. The strength and might of our state are the most important conditions for the successful construction of Communism in our country. It is our sacred duty to continue to strengthen our great Socialist state, the bulwark of peace and security of peoples, tirelessly and in every way.

With the name of Comrade Stalin is connected the solution of one of the most complicated questions in the history of the development of society, namely the question of nationalities.

In the history of the development of human society and the national question, the greatest theoretician of the national question,

Comrade Stalin, secured, for the first time in history within the
frontier of a huge multinational state, the liquidation of national
strife.

Under Comrade Stalin's leadership, our Party has overcome the
economic and cultural backwardness of a people who were formerly oppressed by uniting into one brotherly family all the nationalities of the Soviet Union and forging friendship among nations. Our sacred duty is to strengthen and further the unity and
friendship of the nations of the Soviet Union and to strengthen the
Soviet multinational state and friendship among the peoples of our
country. We are not afraid of any internal or external enemies.
Under the direct leadership of Comrade Stalin, the Soviet Army
was created and strengthened.

Must Keep in Fighting Trim

The strengthening of the defensive power of the country and
the consolidation of the Soviet armed forces were the untiring
concern of Comrade Stalin. Headed by its great military leader,
Generalissimo Stalin, the Soviet Army won a historic victory during the Second World War and delivered the peoples of Europe
and Asia from the threat of fascist slavery. Our sacred duty is to
strengthen by every means the mighty Soviet armed forces. We
must keep them in a state of fighting preparedness for a crushing
rebuff to any attacks of any enemy.

As a result of the ceaseless toil of Comrade Stalin, in accordance
with plans worked out with him, our Party has converted a formerly backward country into a mighty industrial and collective-
farm power and has created a new economic order which knows
no crises nor unemployment. It is our sacred duty to ensure the
further flourishing of our Socialist motherland. We must develop
by every means our Socialist industry, the bulwark of might and
strength of our country. We must develop by every means our
collective farm order and strive for a further upsurge and flourishing of all collective farms of the Soviet country and to strengthen
the union of working class and collective-farm peasantry.

In the internal sphere, our main task is ceaselessly to strive for
further improvement in the material welfare of the workers, the

collective farmers, the intelligentsia, and all the Soviet people. It is a law for our party and government to implement the duty of ceaselessly striving for the good of the people for the maximum satisfaction of its material and cultural needs. Lenin and Stalin created and tempered our Party as a great transforming force of society. Comrade Stalin taught all his life that there is nothing higher than the title of member of the Communist Party.

Calls for Rallying Together

In a stubborn struggle against enemies, Comrade Stalin defended the monolithic unity of the ranks of our Party. It is our sacred duty to preserve this spirit so as to be able further to strengthen the great Communist Party. The strength and invincibility of our Party lies in the unity and close rallying together of its ranks, in the unity of the will and the actions, in the ability of Party members to merge their wills in the will and wishes of the Party. The strength and invincibility of our Party lies in its close ties with the masses of the people. The unity of the Party and the people is based on the Party's constant service to the interests of the people. We must treasure the unity of the Party as the pupil of our eye.

We must strengthen further the unbreakable bonds between the Party and people and train the Communists and all working people in the spirit of high political vigilance, of intolerance and firmness in the struggle against internal, inner, and the foreign enemies.

Under the leadership of the great Stalin, a mighty camp of peace, democracy and socialism has been set up. In that camp, in close fraternal unity with the Soviet people, march the great Chinese people, the fraternal peoples of Poland, Czechoslovakia, Bulgaria, Hungary, Romania, Albania, the German Democratic Republic, and the Mongolian People's Republic.

In a stubborn battle, the heroic Korean people are defending the independence of their motherland. A courageous fight is being waged for freedom and national independence by the people of Vietnam. It is our sacred task to preserve and consolidate the greatest attainment of the people—the camp of peace, democracy, and socialism—to strengthen the ties, friendship, and solidarity of the peoples of the democratic bloc.

We must in every way consolidate the eternal, indestructible and fraternal friendship of the Sovet Union with the great Chinese people and with the workers in all countries of the People's Democracy.

The peoples of all lands know Comrade Stalin as the great ensign of peace. Comrade Stalin directed the supreme force of his genius toward the preservation of peace for the peoples of all countries.

The foreign policy of the Soviet state, a policy of peace and friendship between peoples, forms a shattering barrier to the unleashing of a new war and is in conformity with the vital interests of all people. The Soviet Union has invariably been championing the defense of the cause of peace for its interests are inseparable from the cause of peace the world over.

The Soviet Union has waged and is waging a consistent policy for the preservation and stabilization of peace; a policy of struggle against the preparation and unleashing of a new war policy; a policy of international cooperation and development of business relations with all countries; a policy based on the Lenin-Stalin premise of the possibility of the prolonged coexistence and peaceful competition of two different systems, capitalist and Socialist.

Stalin educated us in the spirit of boundlessly loyal service to the interests of the people. We are the true servants of the people, and the people want peace and hate war. May it come to pass, the wish, sacred to all of us, of people to prevent the spilling of blood of millions of people and to ensure peaceful construction of a happy life.

In the sphere of foreign policy, our main care consists in not permitting a new war and in living in peace with all countries. The Communist Party of the Soviet Union and the Soviet Government consider the most correct, essential, and just foreign policy is the policy of peace among all peoples, based on a mutual trust, operative and supported by facts and confirmed by facts.

The governments must serve their peoples faithfully, and the peoples thirst for peace and curse war. Criminal will be those governments which will want to trick peoples and go against the sacred wish of peoples to maintain peace and prevent a new bloody massacre.

The Communist Party and Soviet Government insist that a policy of peace between nations is the only correct policy which corresponds with the interests of all nations.

Comrades:

The passing of our great leader and teacher, the great Stalin, imposes on all the Soviet people the duty to multiply their efforts to realize the grandiose tasks and increase their Party in the common cause of construction of a Communist society and in the strengthening of the power and defense abilities of our Socialist fatherlands.

Toilers of the Soviet Union, see and know that our powerful fatherland is advancing toward new successes.

We have all that is necessary to build a Communist society. With firm faith in their limitless forces and possibilities, the Soviet people will proceed with the great cause of building Communism. There are no forces in the world which can stop the forward movement of Soviet society toward Communism.

Farewell, our teacher and leader, our dear friend, our Comrade Stalin!

Forward, along the road toward the complete victory of the great cause of Lenin and Stalin!

MALENKOV BEFORE THE
SUPREME SOVIET

On March 15, 1953, Georgi M. Malenkov appeared before the Supreme Soviet, which agreed to his appointment and to the reorganization of the government which he reported. His speech follows:

Comrade Deputies:

You have entrusted me to present for examination by the Supreme Soviet of the U.S.S.R. the composition of the Government—the Council of Ministers of the U.S.S.R. I thank you, Comrade Deputies, for the great confidence and high honor you have shown me.

Comrades, it is already known to you that the Plenum of the Central Committee of the Communist Party of the Soviet Union, the Council of Ministers of the U.S.S.R. and the Presidium of the Supreme Soviet have taken several important decisions directed toward securing without interruption the correct leadership of the country's life. At the present session we should examine these decisions and, in accordance with the Constitution, give the force of law to those measures that the Supreme Soviet of the U.S.S.R., the highest organ of Government authority in our country, finds it possible and necessary to accept and approve.

Started During Stalin Rule

It is necessary to say that measures for the consolidation of presently existing ministries, for uniting in one ministry the leadership of related branches of the public economy, culture and administration, did not ripen only today. For a long time during the life of Comrade Stalin they already were maturing, with his assistance, in our Party and Government. And now, in connection with the heavy loss our country has suffered, we have only speeded up the carrying into life of ripening organizational measures for further development of the leadership of the Government and of economic activity.

Proposing these measures, we proceed from the basis that it is necessary to fight even more actively for the working out of Party and Government plans for further development of the U.S.S.R., and for successively realizing these plans.

We proceed from the basis that the carrying into life of organizational measures in the field of improving Government and economic leadership, which are presented for the examination of the Supreme Soviet of the U.S.S.R., undoubtedly will permit better conditions for the successful achievement of the historical tasks that stand before our country—for the further untiring and all-sided strengthening of our great, multinational Socialist state, and for the strengthening of the powerful Soviet armed forces, ensuring the defense and security of our motherland; further, to develop by all means Socialist industry and to strengthen the collective-farm system, to develop culture and to increase the material well-being of the workers, collective farmers, intelligentsia, all the Soviet people, ensuring more successful progress on the path of building a Communist society in our country.

New Cadres Available

We have the possibility of successfully realizing the organization of consolidated ministries and of realizing all these advantages because we now have at our disposal significantly increased cadres, which have acquired rich experience and which are able to head consolidated ministries.

[*Malenkov then stated the composition of the new government, a full listing which can be found on pages 157–159.*]

Comrade Deputies:

In presenting for examination by the Supreme Soviet the proposals regarding the composition of the Government, the plenum of the Central Committee of the Communist Party, the Council of Ministers of the U.S.S.R., and the Presidium of the Supreme Soviet of the U.S.S.R. proceeded from the basis that the strength of our leadership consists in its collectivity, its solidarity and monolithic nature. We find that the strict observance of this supreme principle is the guarantee of the correctness of the leadership of the country and the most important condition of our further successful movement forward on the path of building Communism in our country.

Foreign-policy Questions

In presenting proposals on the composition of the Government for approval by the Supreme Soviet of the U.S.S.R., I find it essential to announce that the Government, in all its activity, will strictly follow foreign and internal policies elaborated by the Party. We already have announced this position of the Soviet Government. I refer to my own speech, the speech of Comrade Beria and the speech of Comrade Molotov at the funeral meeting of March 9.

In relation to internal policy, our announcement stated with all definiteness that the Soviet Government would in the future strengthen the unbreakable union of the working classes and collective-farm peasants, the brotherly friendship of the peoples of our country; by all means would strengthen the defensive power of the Socialist state; that the law for our Government is the obligation unremittingly to attend to the good of the people for the maximum satisfaction of material and cultural needs, for the further flowering of our Socialist motherland.

With relation to foreign policy, the following fully pertains. The Soviet Government will unchangingly carry out the tested policy of preserving and strengthening peace, ensuring the defense and security of the Soviet Union—a policy of collaboration with all countries and the development of business connections with them on the basis of a mutual observance of interests—and will in the future carry out close political and economic collaboration, strengthening ties of brotherly friendship and solidarity with the great Chinese people and with all the peoples of the countries of the People's Democracy.

Observance of Treaties

The Soviet policy of peace is based on respect for the rights of peoples of other countries, big and small, on observance of established international norms; Soviet foreign policy is based on strict and unflinching observance of all treaties concluded by the Soviet Union with other states.

At the present time there is not one disputed or undecided question that cannot be decided by peaceful means on the basis of the mutual understanding of interested countries. This is our attitude toward all states, among them the United States of America.

States interested in preserving peace may be confident in the present as in the future of the firm peaceful policy of the Soviet.

Comrade Deputies:

The Soviet people have profound confidence in their strength. The power of the Soviet state, the moral and political unity of the Soviet people, are great and invincible as never before. The Soviet Government devotes all its strength to the struggle for the construction of a Communist society in our land, for a free and happy life for the Soviet people.

We go forward along the path of the construction of Communism in the close unity of party, Government, and Soviet people, the friendly, brotherly family of all peoples of the Soviet Union.

INDEX

Index